Religion and Development in Nigeria

Adonis & Abbey Publishers Ltd

St James House
13 Kensington Square,
London, W8 5HD
United Kingdom

Website: http://www.adonis-abbey.com
E-mail Address: editor@adonis-abbey.com

Nigeria:
Suites C4 – C6 J-Plus Plaza
Asokoro, Abuja, Nigeria
Tel: +234 (0) 7058078841/08052035034

Copyright 2018 © Y.A. Quadri, R.W. Omotoye & R.I. Adebayo

British Library Cataloguing-in-Publication Data
A catalogue record for this book is available from the British Library

ISBN: 9781909112995

The moral right of the author has been asserted

All rights reserved. No part of this book may be reproduced, stored in a retrieval system or transmitted at any time or by any means without the prior permission of the publisher

Religion and Development in Nigeria

Edited by

Y.A. Quadri
R.W. Omotoye
R.I. Adebayo

Preface

Religion is being stigmatised and bastardised by different people from different cultures. While Karl Marx sees nothing in religion but mere "opium of the people", Sigmund Freud describes it as "child neurosis" which should not be given any serious recognition. In Nigeria, the numerous challenges bedevilling the nation ranging from political and ethnic crises to socio-economic instability and insecurity have been attributed to religion. These have been amplified and over-publicised that positivity about religion has been downplayed. This prompted the Nobel Laureate, Professor Wole Soyinka to describe religion as an instrument of division and brutality and that unless religion is tamed in Nigeria, religion would kill the Nigerians. He instigated hatred of religion saying: "I do not say kill religion though I wouldn't mind a bit if that mission could be undertaken surgically, painlessly perhaps under anaesthesia effectively sprayed all over the nation or perhaps during an induced pouch of religious ecstasy." This stand and others of such nature are nothing but a clever way of putting religion into disrepute as if religion has not done the nation any worthwhile good.

The fact is that non-recognition of religion as a viable instrument of moral and virtuous development has done the world no good. A society or nation which relegates religion to personal affairs of her citizens witnesses social degeneration, increased murder and crime, euthanasia and other unnatural acts like sodomy, homosexuality and sadomasochism. One therefore needs to acknowledge and appreciate the role of religion in the generation and advancement of selflessness for enhancement of development in the nation. Indeed, hardly can any meaningful development take place in the absence of discipline and God consciousness which all religions teach. In addition, it is difficult to separate religion from man's physical and social environment both at the level of state or social institution where religion influences policies and general societal development; or at the level of individual where the behaviour of individual is not only affected by religion but also confers on him a form of identity. This is corroborated by the submission of Ibn Khaldun that religion provides ethics that the society lives by and guides the society towards development by encouraging cooperation, knowledge and creativity among the people as they begin to found their civilisation. However, when religion is taken with levity, impunity becomes the order of the day.

Numerous pressures mounted on religion to relegate it to the churches, the mosques and the shrines may be an effort in futility in a country like Nigeria where religion is indispensable in the lives of Nigerians and has influenced them in all spheres. Those who kick against religion have failed to recognise the roles religion has played and is still playing in the development of Nigeria, hence the purpose of this book. The book is set to showcase the values of religion in Nigeria and its contributions to the general development of the nation, especially in the areas of education, health, economy and politics. Chapters in the book concentrate on the nexus between religion and development in Nigerian society. This rich compendium contains well-researched articles written by seasoned scholars of religions in the area of African Traditional Religion, Christianity and Islam, to demonstrate that religion is not an antithesis of development.

Y.A. Quadri
R.W. Omotoye
R.I. Adebayo

Table of Contents

Chapter One
Religion and Development: Religiosity and its Effect on
Development in Nigeria 9

Chapter Two
Religious Conflicts, Political Stability and Development in
Nigeria 29

Chapter Three
The Spiritual and Ethical Implications of Oath-Taking in
Nigerian Politics 43

Chapter Four
Religious-Based Dispute Resolution Mechanism of
Independent *Sharī'ah* Panels and their Contributions
to the Development of Judicial System in Nigeria 59

Chapter Five
Religion and Development: A Study of Developmental
Dynamics of *Adamu Orisa* Festival in Lagos 79

Chapter Six
The Role of Muslims in Healthcare Service Delivery
in Nigeria 95

Chapter Seven
Christianity and the Development of Health Care
Services in Okun land, Kogi State, Nigeria Since 1900 119

Chapter Eight
Christianity and Educational Development in
Delta State, Nigeria 143

Chapter Nine
The Impact of Christianity (Sudan Interior Mission)
on Igbomina land, Kwara State, Nigeria 171

Chapter Ten
Islam and the Attainment of the Sustainable
Development Goals (SDGs) in Nigeria 189

Chapter Eleven
The Impact of Sokoto Caliphate on Post-Colonial
Political Development in Nigeria: A Focus on
Selected Personalities 217

Chapter Twelve
The Church and Socio-Economic Development of
Ilorin Metropolis: A Case Study of Anglican
Church in Ilorin, Kwara State, Nigeria 233

Index 249

CHAPTER ONE

Religion and Development: Religiosity and Its Effect on Development in Nigeria

Musa Yusuf Owoyemi
Visiting Senior Lecturer
Department of Civilisation and Philosophy,
School of Languages, Civilisation and Philosophy,
College of Arts and Sciences, University Utara Malaysia,
06010 Sintok, Kedah, Malaysia
owoyemi2@yahoo.com

Introduction

For quite some time, especially from the time of the enlightenment to the modern time, there has been this erroneous belief that religion is an antithesis of development and that for a nation to properly develop, it has to relegate religion to the private realm where it would not play any role in the public affairs of the nation.[1] Better still, others opine that humans have come of age and religion has outlived its usefulness, it should therefore be discarded altogether. However, history has shown that religion is not an antithesis of development. Most of the great civilisations of the world develop as a result of the influence of religion – except the modern western civilisation which developed as a result of the reaction against religion (specifically Christianity). Religions the world over have led to great civilisations. The Egyptian civilisation developed based on the traditional religion of the people and became a great civilisation during the time of the Pharaohs. The Chinese civilisation was based on Taoism (the Chinese traditional religion) and a host of philosophies such as Confucianism and Legalism. The Indian civilisation developed as a result of the influence of Hinduism and later of

Buddhism. In fact, Hinduism and Buddhism have had a lot of influences on many civilisations such as the Malay and Siam in the South East Asia region. In Europe and the Americas, Christianity had a lot of influence on the development of their civilisations. In the Middle East and Central Asia, Judaism, Zoroastrianism and Christianity had major influences on the civilisations that developed in the region until the coming of Islam. With the advent of Islam, the Islamic civilisation developed and spread to all the places mentioned above. Knowledge, science and technology reached a great height during this period and it was this that served as the foundation and an impetus to the development of the modern western civilisation which rejected the teaching of the church after coming in contact with the Islamic civilisation and the Greek philosophies which had been preserved by the Islamic civilisation. The Islamic civilisation had synthesised the Greek philosophy, commented on it and further developed it before it was passed to the modern western world. Likewise, the scientific method had been well developed by Muslim scholars during this period and the modern western world inherited this also from the Islamic civilisation. In fact, for many years in the western universities, the books of Muslim scholars served as major text books in medicine, physics, mathematics, philosophy, and so on.[2]

However, it will be helpful here to give a short insight into why the modern western civilisation developed the way it did. In the modern western world, the unscientific approach of the Church to knowledge in the medieval period led to hypotheses and postulations which were forced on the people as part of their belief. But, when the people had contact with the Islamic civilisation, they started to question some of these beliefs and the fiasco that resulted from this led to the inquisition (the killing of people, especially scholars, who opposed the teachings of the Church on account of new knowledge and insight). Thus, the Church became pitched in battle against philosophers and scientists. The political problem between the Church and the kings at this time made the kings to side with the philosopher-scientists and this resulted in the scholars declaring a rejection of the teachings of the Church and an attack against all traditions (religions) as dogmas which people should not accept at face value but query and subject to empirical findings and rationalism.[3] This, therefore, is how the modern western civilisation developed without religion. Nonetheless, for the sake of argument, one could say that religion also plays a role in this because it (modern western civilisation) developed in spite of it (religion)!

All these show that religion is not a hindrance to development and that religions, in many parts of the world, had been a catalyst for development. Religions have developed civilisations and by civilisation we mean the whole corpus of human culture which covers the entirety of what constitutes human society.

Meanwhile, a question still subsists here how does religiosity affect development if religion is not a problem and an antithesis to development? In order to answer this question, it will be helpful to know what we mean by religiosity and development. It will also be helpful to understand better the kind of relationship that exists between religion and development apart from what has been said above. Likewise, it will be pertinent to see how religiosity affects development in Nigeria as the title of the chapter suggests.

Religiosity and Development: A Definition

Barring the dictionary definition of religiosity as "extreme interest and belief in religion"[4] or the disapproving "state of being religious or too religious"[5] the word (religiosity) is a very difficult term to define because of its usage in varied academic disciplines.[6] It has different meanings depending on the field of research or the academic discipline in which it is being used.[7] While to the theologian, faith is the cardinal importance in religiosity, the psychologists may choose to focus on devotion, piety or holiness as the important thing in religiosity.[8] Still, religious educators may be concerned primarily with belief and orthodoxy whereas a sociologist may focus his attention on religious attendance, doctrinal knowledge, acceptance of belief and life experience of the believer.[9] However, instead of trying to define the term, scholars such as Glock and Stark,[10] Fukuyama,[11] Bergan and McConatha,[12] and Allport and Ross[13] in their works have identified different dimensions of religiosity and how it could relate to different things in human activities. For example, Glock and Stark talked about five dimensions of religiosity which are experiential, ritualistic, ideological, intellectual and consequential all of which, they explained, are connected, respectively, to

(1) the personal faith of the person or his personal experience of the faith, (2) the rites/worship experience of the person in his religion, (3) the beliefs in the doctrines of his religion, (4) knowledge of the tenets of the religion and (5) acceptance of the religion by the person as a result of his knowledge. Fukuyama on his part talked about four dimensions of religiosity which are cognitive, cultic, creedal and devotional which represent (1) knowledge of the religion, (2) the religious practices, (3) personal religious belief and (4) religious feelings and experiences of the person respectively. Likewise, in the book, *Measures of Religiosity* edited by Peter C. Hill and Ralph W. Hood, instead of dwelling on the meaning of the term, religiosity, David G. Benner provides, for researchers, different ways, methods and approaches to measure religiosity in different contexts. This shows that religiosity is better understood in its use than in the way it is defined. However, for our purpose in this chapter, we will concentrate on the idea of Allport and Ross as it is more appropriate to our brief discussion here.

Allport and Ross talked about two dimensions of religiosity – intrinsic and extrinsic religiosity. According to them, people who practise intrinsic religiosity live their religion by internalising totally the creed of their religion, finding their motive for life in their religion and harmonising their other needs in life with their religious beliefs. On the other hand, people who practise extrinsic religiosity use their religion for their selfish ends either by selectively shaping and interpreting their religious creeds to fit their own ends or to enhance their status, sociability and to gain an advantage for their personal ends in the society. It will be helpful here to quote Allport and Ross directly on the meaning of intrinsic and extrinsic religiosity. According to them "the extrinsically motivated person uses his religion whereas the intrinsically motivated person lives his religion."[14] Thus, these two dimensions of religiosity, as propounded by Allport and Ross, are important in our attempt to understand the relationship between religiosity and development.

Now, talking about the meaning of development, like religiosity above, it is a word with many dimensions and it can be used in a varieties of ways either as a prefix or suffice to a lot of terms and concepts. In its dictionary sense, development has been defined in various ways such as "the systematic use of scientific and technical knowledge to meet specific objectives or requirements"[15] or "an extension of the theoretical or practical aspects of a concept, design, discovery or invention."[16] Still more, according to the dictionary, it could mean "the process of economic and social transformation that is based on complex cultural and environmental factors and their interactions."[17] Furthermore, it could stand for "the process of adding improvement to a parcel of land, such as grading, subdivisions, drainage, access, roads, utilities"[18] and others.

As was the case with religiosity, scholars involved in development studies have not agreed on a single definition on the meaning and pattern of development. While there are those who subscribe to structuralism and neo-liberalist views, others hold the interventionist view, alternative/people – centred view and the post development view.

Structuralism is the idea that development is mostly the responsibility of the state. While it aims for a modern industrial society, it nonetheless holds that history is the result of political and economic struggles. For this group of scholars, development comes into being by careful and long-time planning by the state through its historical process.[19]

Neo-liberalism is a capitalist perspective about development. It holds that no development plan or action is needed to be put in place except to have free markets where everyone trades. It believes that the resulting perpetual economic growth will 'trickle down' to everyone in the society and so everyone benefits from the economic growth. Neo-liberalists see history as the result of individual rational actions.[20]

Interventionism recognises that there are losers as well as winners of the neo-liberalists/capitalist progress. Thus, development actions are put in place in order to help the 'losers' to also develop in the society through government intervention in the development process. "More recently, a concern of the negative impacts of capitalist growth on the environment has been considered. In some cases intervention is to remove barriers to modernisation, in others it is to influence the direction of change."[21]

Alternative/People-Centred is based on the idea that, ordinarily, all humans have the ability to reach/achieve their potential. Thus, development simply involves governments and other agencies empowering groups and individuals to make their own choices in order to achieve their potentials. In this sense, individuals and social movements are themselves the agents of change. And development, therefore, is the achievement of individual potentials in the society.[22]

Post development argues that development is not a good thing as it is being thought. This is because, in their view, "development agencies and governments use 'doing good' as an excuse to maintain power and control" over the people and the society.

Thus, from the above, one can see that development has different meanings to different scholars and the thought on what actually development is differs from one scholar to another.

The Relationship between Religion and Development

However, considering our focus in this chapter, if we are to take the holistic approach to development which includes the spiritual and physical aspects of man, then Kadir H. Din's propositions will be very important to mention here.[23] According to Kadir H. Din, development, if it is seen as "de – velope", that is to unwrap something or to expose and open a thing, in contrast to "velope" which means to wrap up, will serve as a "process of unfolding and growth of the spiritual seed of humanity, wrapped within the heart of man, opening and exposing itself to the climate divine, for it to grow gradually fuller and better within the context of the greater universe."[24] In this sense, although development stresses on the metaphysical and the spiritual, Kadir, affirms that it does not negate physical development, "insofar as the physical and the material are necessary and advantageous to the development [of the] spiritual", rather, "this view assumes and accepts material development as 'the significant other' in the process of achieving the spiritual end."[25] Going by what Kadir said above, spiritual development is an important element in material development and vice versa. If this is the case, religiosity, wherever it forms part and parcel of the political culture as is the case in Nigeria, ought to aid and enhance development, not debar it. This is because religiosity ought to be a projection of the spiritual outward into the physical and since the spiritual is not antagonistic to the physical in terms of development, both ought to aid each other in achieving a better society for mankind. This is why it was possible for religions to found great civilisations in the world as explained earlier. However, the defining catalyst for this was what was explained about religiosity by Allport and Ross – the intrinsic and extrinsic dimension of religiosity. Religion was able to achieve what it achieved because the religiosity of its adherents was intrinsic and not extrinsic. The people lived their religions and this metamorphosed into physical development in the form of the civilisations that were mentioned earlier on.

Talking about religions and civilisations (which are akin to development here), Ibn Khaldun in his classical work, *The Muqaddimah*, talks about the cyclical theory of civilisation. That is how civilisations evolved, are destroyed and then re-evolved again to repeat its circle – hence the name cyclical. In this cyclical process, Ibn Khaldun emphasises the important role that religion plays by stating that religion provides ethics that the society lives by and guide the society towards development since it encourages cooperation, knowledge and creativity among the people as they begin to found their civilisation. However, as the civilisation develops, towards the third generation, things begin to take a new turn as religion is taken with levity and impunity becomes the order of the day. Gradually, the civilisation begins to be eroded until it breaks down and another set of people with a strong '*asabiyyah* (social solidarity) take over and start afresh with religion playing its important role. This conclusion was also reached by Arnold Toynbee and Malik Bennabi in their explanation of the important role that religion plays in the founding of civilisations.[26] This shows that religion has a positive relationship with development and it is not, and was never, an antithesis to development as many perceive it to be today. If, therefore, a new dimension is perceived in this relationship, religion is definitely not the problem, hence our focus on the religiosity of the adherents of religions.

Religiosity and its Effect on Development in Nigeria

Since we have shown above that religion is not an antithesis to development but rather aids it and that religiosity of adherents of religions may explain the problem that religion currently has with development, we hasten to justify this claim by looking at the use of religiosity in the political sphere of Nigeria and how this has affected development in the nation.

a. Religiosity in the Political Sphere of Nigeria

Although Nigeria operates a secular constitution, nonetheless, one could describe the nation as a religious nation which is composed of about ninety-seven point two percent (97.2%) Muslim and Christian adherents with the remaining two point eight percent (2.8%) following the Traditional African Religions or unaffiliated to any religion.[27] Thus, with this huge number of Muslim and Christian adherents in Nigeria, one would expect that just as these two religions have played significant roles in the founding of civilisation and act as a catalyst for development, the nation would be on a path of development and advancement in the comity of nations. But, unfortunately, the reverse seems to be the case in Nigeria because the religiosity of the adherents of these two major religions has not yielded the fruit of its glorious past. It seems to be the case that most of the adherents of these religions in Nigeria exhibit what Allport and Ross called the extrinsic aspect of religiosity. In other words, they *use* the religion rather than *live* it. Because of this, religiosity has had a devastating effect on the development of the nation and has not helped the nation in any positive way. The following examples of religiosity in the political sphere of Nigeria will serve to illustrate this assertion.

With the advent of the fourth republic in Nigeria's political dispensation, the issue of religion has taken a new dimension in the nation as politicians have made it a corner stone of their ascension to political office. Immediately the northern politicians and military, who had been ruling the nation for quite a long time to the exclusion of other parts of the nation, agreed to cede power to southern politicians, the issue of religion reverberated in the polity as the southerners felt that the northerners who are mostly Muslims have used the slot of the Muslims and a Christian should be allowed to ascend to the highest office in the land. Based on this, two southern Christians were put forward as candidates for the post with one of them, Chief Olusegun Obasanjo, declaring himself to be a 'born again Christian'. This situation gave birth to the mobilisation of the masses along religious lines with the churches making a prominent political campaign with the slogan 'Jesus Christ has overthrown' the government of the nation.

After the election, which was won by Chief Olusegun Obasanjo the born again Christian, a lot of religious activities were organised to "thank Jesus" for taking over the nation and the president-elect himself was busy paying solidarity visits to churches and meeting men of God for prayers and support for his presidency.

In the northern part of the nation, immediately they realised that the new administration would not dance to their tune and that it has taken steps which they feel are inimical to their interest, politicians started a campaign for the implementation of the *Shari'ah* in the north arguing that this is contained in the constitution of the nation.[28] Although this is true, and there were already *Shari'ah* courts in many of the states, the way this new wave of '*Shari'ah* consciousness' was directed portrayed it as a response to the southern Christian president's 'born again' move and the slogan that Christians are now in control and that the country was going to be the better for it. In other words, the impression was that Muslims, and by extension Islam, has failed the nation and now a Christian, Christianity to be precise, is set to right the wrong(s).

The scenario above resulted in a situation in which many politicians began to see religion as a veritable tool in their quest for political power and a way of reaching out to the masses by appealing to their religious sentiments – since this has become very strong among the masses. Thus, political religiosity became the order of the day as the nation witnessed a situation in which politicians started to display their religiosity in the public sphere.

In the south, politicians frequented the well-known churches and the overseers of these churches became the anointers of politicians. It soon became a frequent phenomenon to open the daily newspaper and see pictures of politicians with these men of God and sometimes kneeling down in front of them for blessings. Even the Muslims among them became frequent visitors to the churches as special guests of honour for final monthly vigil and events.[29]

In the north, *Shari'ah* became a platform of acceptance among the masses. The louder the rhetoric about the implementation of *Shari'ah* by a politician, the more the acceptance of the politician by the masses. Some northern politicians even went as far as entering into agreements with some of the Islamic groups on the implementation of the *Shari'ah* once they are elected into office. This was the case of the Jama'atu Ahlis Sunnah Lidda 'awati Wal-Jihad popularly known as Boko Haram which allegedly supported Governor Ali Modu Sheriff with the agreement that he would implement *Sharī'ah* in the state if he won the election.[30]

However, coming to the concept of religiosity, one would have thought that being a born again, this would translate into a situation in which the nation will be governed in a god-like manner which will aid the development of the nation. But, the reverse was the case. In spite of the fact that the civilian administration since 1999 witnessed a phenomenal rise in income as a result of the increase in the price of petroleum products in the international market, the amount of public funds stolen and squandered in uncompleted projects are monumental! From electrification in which the nation invested a whopping 16 billion dollars without any result, to privatisation in which many of the nations' companies and properties went into private hands at prices that were said to be ridiculous and detrimental to the nation's wealth, gives one an inkling and a contradiction of the public display of religiosity and non-religious governance of the nation.[31]

This attitude of corruption and mismanagement was replicated at the state level where most of the governors also came in as a result of their public show of religiosity.[32] In Zamfara state, which was a pioneer in the implementation of *Sharī'ah*, it was recently revealed by Professor Wole Soyinka in an interview that the then governor, who campaigned with the promise of implementing the *Sharī'ah*, "... when he was asked why he decided to turn Zamfara into a theocratic state in a secular dispensation. He said... that it was the only weapon he had to snatch power. He said the PDP machinery was so strong that he needed something which would appeal to raw emotions, to mobilise and get the governorship."[33] This assertion by Wole Soyinka was corroborated by a research entitled *Controversies about Sharī'ah* carried out by Carefronting-Nigeria, a non-governmental organisation based in Kaduna State Nigeria. According to this research,

> ...it is probably true that Ahmed Sani was not acting on behalf of the Islamic elite, when he began his struggle for Sharia. Most likely he simply wanted to win the gubernatorial elections with the support of local Islamic groups. His contender Aliyu Gusau, the PDP candidate, was a man with excellent political connections....Diplomats who had known Ahmed Sani at earlier stages of his career had the impression that he was not guided by religious motives.[34]

In other words, Ahmed Sani Yerima, used this as an avenue to achieve his political ambition and not because he really loved the religion.[35] To underscore this, he was alleged to be among the most corrupt governors in the nation and his case is still with the Economic and Financial Crimes Commission (EFCC).[36]

The above was not restricted to Zamfara state alone. A host of other northern governors used the same *Shari'ah* issue to either retain their posts or to further their political ambition.[37] But the ironical part of all this is the present fiasco that is going on in the northern part of the nation in form of religious violence where a section of the populace has constituted itself into a religious group, called Boko Haram, which specialises in raiding, maiming and killing innocent citizens.

The above is a summary of the religiosity brought into the political sphere of the nation during the fourth republic and it is not restricted to these few cases mentioned above; it cuts across the whole spectrum of the political landscape and involved the two prominent religions in the nation (that is, Islam and Christianity).

b. The Effect of Religiosity on Development in Nigeria

The effect of this political religiosity on the development of the nation can be seen in three ways which are: (1) the lack of will among the people to ask critical and fundamental questions about the governance of the nation out of religious consideration, (2) lack of will among the people to ask for accountability due to religious consideration and (3) lack of the will to ask for probity as a result of religious loyalty. The show of religiosity by the political class has led to a situation in which each religion and its adherents strives to protect their fellow adherents who are in government by not asking for accountability and probity; and by not speaking out against them even when they know that they are not doing anything to further their interest and the interest of the masses generally in the society. For example, in a recent report on the level of poverty in the nation despite the growth in the economic sector and the increase in the income of the nation during the Jonathan era,[38] people failed to ask critical questions on how the resources of the nation were being utilised by the political class. Instead, what one usually sees and hears among the masses is the taking of sides based on religion and counter claims of Christianisation and Islamisation of the nation. There was no or little demand for accountability and probity by the people as the political elite made a show of religiosity by appearing at religious events and courting religious leaders for support. Likewise, according to the report cited above, the northern part of the nation in which the *Sharī'ah* slogan was at the fore front of the politician campaign recorded the highest level of poverty and this is reflected in the Boko Haram menace that section of the nation is facing.[39] But, instead of the people asking questions, especially considering the fact that there was increase in allocation at that time because of the increase in the price of oil at the international market, what one sees is the continued support of the political class who were championing the *Sharī'ah* implementation programme while social infrastructure and amenities remain unprovided for and unattended to. Also, one of the former governors of Kano State was reported to have spent a whopping N10 Billion naira, (between 2003 and 2011), in sending pilgrims to Makkah while the average northerner on the street could hardly afford a comfortable meal a day.[40] Thus, the show of religiosity by the political class and consideration for religion prevented the people from asking fundamental questions about governance and development because whoever does this will be seen as antagonising the religious programme of the government and some of the political leaders used this sentiment to the fullest in silencing those who dared to query their style of governance and lack of good governance. This, thus, prevented accountability and probity in the polity.

The case is not different in the south. While the Niger Delta area of the south received an unprecedented amount of more than N2.511 trillion of 13% derivation fund alone, excluding federal allocations, between 1999 to 2016, there is little to show that this has trickled down to the poor and downtrodden in that area.[41] Rather, what was witnessed was an alarming looting of the public treasury by governors from that part of the nation.[42]

The case of the Niger Delta is made worse based on the fact that the immediate past president, Goodluck E. Jonathan, is from that part of the nation and under his watch, a whopping amount of five trillion naira was reported stolen between May 2010 and October 2012 of his presidency "through fraud, embezzlement and theft..."[43] There was another revelation by the former Central Bank Governor of Nigeria, now the Emir of Kano, Sanusi Lamido Sanusi, that under the immediate past president's watch, a staggering amount of $20 billion US dollars had not been accounted for by the Nigerian National Petroleum Corporation and despite his reminder and memo to the President on this, nothing was done about it! However, instead of acting on this, President Goodluck E. Jonathan suspended him, until his tenure ran out, when his letter to the President on the issue was leaked to the public! Yet, instead of the people to query this, they see it as a power struggle between the Muslim Hausa-Fulani of the North and a Christian from the Ijaw South. Meanwhile, Niger Delta continues to witness oil spills on a large scale with no visible solution in sight and no tangible provision of social amenities for the people! Finally, in addition, recently, the present administration of President Muhammad Buhari has uncovered massive looting of the treasury during the last days of the previous administration of President Goodluck E. Jonathan which includes the embezzlement of a whopping amount of 2 billion dollars meant for arms purchase to fight the Boko Haram insurgency in the northern part of the nation. Likewise, questionable import waivers running into billions of naira were given to businessmen, companies and religious organisations.[44]

Apart from this, currently, there is a spike of money recoveries by the Economic and Financial Crime Commission (EFCC) from former government officers in the immediate past administration which are believed to be monies embezzled or stolen by these officials in the immediate past administration and one of the reasons why the nation is suffering from economic recession during the new administration as all government savings and reserves have been emptied by the last administration. This revelation explains why there was no infrastructural development in the last administration and the deterioration of basic amenities during the period of the last administration. Apparently, people who were given state responsibilities, both Muslims and Christians, were busy looting and pilfering state's funds to the detriment of the development of the nation and its people – knowing very well that this is against the teachings of their religions! Sadly, instead of the people backing the effort of the current government, what is common among the masses is to see this recovery of public funds from those who just left government as a witch-hunt by the Muslim north against the Christian south without thinking about how these looted funds have affected the development of the nation – and this boils down to the show of religiosity by the political class in the south who appealed to religion in furthering their personal interest at the detriment of the religious opiate masses.

The South-East and South-West of the nation are no exception to the above. In fact, when the People's Democratic Party governors in the South-East and South-West, except Lagos State, were in power, there was no visible development in these parts of the nation. The governors were busy consolidating their powers and spending public funds on irrelevancies while embezzlement, fraud and theft became the order of the day. This explains why many of them, after they were eased out of power, became guests of the Economic and Financial Crimes Commission (EFCC).[45] However, despite the change of party in some of the states of the South-East and South-West, the situation has not changed and instead of uplifting the standard of living of the people, corruption, embezzlement and political concerns continue to be the order of the day while development, provision of social amenities and employment for the millions of jobless educated youths of these regions takes a back seat in the agenda of many of the governors of the states of these regions.[46]

The lack of jobs for the youths and people of these two regions in the south has resulted in a situation in which graduates have become truck drivers, motorcycle (*okada*) riders, armed robbers, fraudsters and recently kidnappers.[47] Yet, due largely to religious consideration, some of these leaders continue to enjoy the support of the people who are not asking critical and fundamental questions especially as it relates to accountability.

All of the above have affected both the human and physical development of the nation in ways that are immeasurable – even expanding to the Diasporas where Nigerians are now mainly identified with drug peddling and internet fraud.[48] While masses based their support for most of these politicians on their perceived religiosity, they hardly question the deeds of these politicians and each time someone is bold enough to query them, religious and tribal sentiments are appealed to and this makes the issue of accountability and probity a problem in the nation. This, in turn, has resulted in impunity and lawlessness which has affected the progress and development of the nation.

Since the issue of political religiosity came to the fore in the fourth republic, one would have thought that this would bring a change in attitude and aid the progress and development of the nation, but, unfortunately, the reverse is the case. And this is due to the fact that people, out of religious and tribal considerations, are not critical of those in power and are not asking for probity and accountability. As a result of this, there has been no meaningful addition to the nation's infrastructure and social amenities while the ones already in existence are continuously becoming decadent by the day. This is despite the fact that funds are budgeted every year for contracts and provision of social amenities. The political class has used the issue of religion to cause division among the people and to divide the nation along religious lines by adding prefixes to the sections of the country describing the north as 'Muslim North' and the south as 'Christian South' which is a fallacy and a deliberate attempt to appeal to religiosity in order to divert attention from the monumental looting of the nation's treasury that is currently ongoing.[49] This description has blurred the real issue that people ought to focus on, especially as it concerns the nation's development, and pitched the people against one another along religious lines. The result is the two fold issue of poverty and religious violence that is currently bedevilling the nation.

Conclusion

From the discussion above in the last section, it is clear that in Nigeria, the use of religion in the political sphere has not yielded the needed result of development and advancement as religion has done before in other parts of the world. The problem, as stated earlier, is that most of the adherents of the two major religions in Nigeria exhibit extrinsic religiosity instead of intrinsic religiosity which is what led other adherents in other places to develop their nations with their religion. In other words, most practitioners of religions in Nigeria *use* their religion through practicing extrinsic religiosity and people who practice extrinsic religiosity use their religion for their selfish ends either by selectively shaping and interpreting their religious creeds to fit their own ends or to enhance their status, sociability and to gain an advantage for their personal ends in the society. This is precisely what many politicians are doing today in Nigeria and this is why religiosity has not led to development in the nation. One can therefore conclude that religion is not the problem in Nigeria, as in other places too, but the adherents of religions who are using it for their selfish interests and thereby making it look as though religion is an enemy of development. The exhibition of extrinsic religiosity by the political class in Nigeria has divided the people along religious lines and has made accountability among leaders in the society to be a difficult subject because of the polarisation that usually develops when such issues are brought up especially if the person who brought it up is of a different faith. Currently, the anti-corruption war by the new administration is being interpreted in certain quarters as a war against the Christians by a Muslim President ignoring the fact that the embezzlement in the last administration is responsible for the current economic problem in the nation and the lack of infrastructural development as monies were brazenly stolen and diverted to private pockets during their period in government. Until Nigerians start to read between the lines and discount the display of religiosity by the political class, it will continue to affect the nation's development and make it difficult to request for accountability from those who are entrusted with position of authority in the nation.

References

1. Jeffrey Haynes, *Religion and Development: Conflict or Cooperation?* (New York: Palgrave Macmillan, 2007), 1-2.
2. Muhammad Abdul Jabbar Beg, *Islamic and Western Concepts of Civilization* (Kuala Lumpur: University of Malaya Press, 1982) and Muhammad Abdul Jabbar Beg, *The Image of Islamic Civilization* (Kuala Lumpur: University of Malaya Press, 1980).
3. William H. Mcneill, *History of Western Civilization: A Handbook* (USA: University of Chicago Press, 2010); Christopher Dawson, *The Making of Europe: An Introduction to the History of European Unity* (USA: The Catholic University of America Press, 2003); Archibald R. Lewis, *Emerging Medieval Europe: A. D. 400 – 1000* (New York: Liebmann 1967); Brian Tierney, *Western Europe in the Middle Ages: 300*

- *1475*, 6th ed., (New York: McGraw-Hill Humanities, 1998) and George Holmes, The Oxford History of Medieval Europe, revised edition, (Oxford: Oxford University Press, 2002).
4. *Macmillan English Dictionary for Advanced Learners*, 2nd ed., (Malaysia: Macmillan Publishers Limited, 2007), 1254.
5. *Oxford Advanced Learner's Dictionary*, 7th ed., (Oxford: Oxford University Press, 2006), 1231.
6. Barbara B. Holdcroft, *What is Religiosity?*, last modified January 1, 2006, accessed May12, 2017, http://files.eric.ed.gov/fulltext/EJ100 6105.pdf
7. Holdcroft, *What is Religiosity?*, 89.
8. Holdcroft, *What is Religiosity?*
9. Holdcroft, *What is Religiosity?*
10. Charles Y. Glock and Rodney Stark, *Religion and Society in Tension* (San Francisco: Rand McNally, 1965).
11. Yoshio Fukuyama,"The Major Dimensions of Church Membership, " *Review of Religious Research*, 2, (1960): 154 – 161.
12. Anne Bergan and Jasmin Tahmeseb McConatha, "Religiosity and Life Satisfaction," *Activities, Adaptation and Aging*, 24 (3), (2000): 23 – 34.
13. Gordon W. Allport and J. Michael Ross, "Personal Religious Orientation and Prejudice," *Journal of Personality and Social Psychology*, no 5, (1967), 432-443.
14. Allport and Ross, "Personal Religious Orientation and Prejudice," 434.
15. *Development*, accessed February 4, 2018, http://www.businessdictionary.com/definition/development.html
16. *Development*, accessed February 4, 2018
17. *Development*, accessed February 4, 2018
18. *Development*, accessed February 4, 2018.
19. Katie Willis, *Theories and Practices of Development* (London: Routledge, 2005).
20. Katie Willis, *Theories and Practices of Development*.
21. Katie Willis, *Theories and Practices of Development*.
22. Katie Willis, *Theories and Practices of Development*

23. Kadir H. Din, ed., *Development and the Muslims* (Bangi: University Kebangsaan Malaysia, 1996).
24. Kadir H. Din, ed., *Development and the Muslims*, 22.
25. Kadir H. Din, ed., *Development and the Muslims*, 23.
26. Ibn Khaldun, *The Muqaddimah: An Introduction to History*, trans. Franz Rosenthal, abridged edition, (London: Princeton University Press, 2015); Arnold J. Toynbee, *A Study of History* (London: Oxford University Press, 1972) and Malik Bennabi, *On the Origins of Human Society*, trans. Tahir El-Mesawi (Kuala Lumpur: Islamic Book Trust, 2002).
27. Pew Forum on Religion and Public Life, *Islam and Christianity in Sub-Saharan Africa*, last modified 2009, accessed August 19, 2017, http://www.pewforum.org/files/2010/04/sub-saharan-africa-appendix-b.pdf
28. Obi Akwani, "The Political Consequences of Sharia," *IMDIVERSITY*, 2014, accessed August 21, 2017, http://www.imdiversity.com/villages/global/news/sharia.asp
29. Abubakar Imam Ali-Agan and Oyeronke Olademo, "The Effect of Religious Pluralism on the 2015 Elections in Nigeria," in *Religious Freedom and Religious Pluralism in Africa: Prospects and Limitations*, eds. Pieter Coertzen, M. Christian Green and Len Hansen (South Africa: SUN MeDIA Stellenbosch, 2016), 193 – 208 and Ebenezer Obadare, "Pastor Adeboye and the Nigerian State: President Jonathan's Kneeling Intervention," *Nigeria village square*, December 30, 2010, accessed August 19, 2017, http://www.nigeriavillagesquare.com/articles/guest-articles/pastor-adeboye-and-the-nigeian-state-president-jonathans-kneeling-intervention.html
30. Obi Ayandike, "What will follow Boko Haram?," *Irinnews*, November 24, 2011, accessed August 16, 2017, http://www.irinnews.org/analysis/2011/11/24/what-will-follow-boko-haram
31. Cosmas Ekpunobi, "Nigeria: Senators Want Obasanjo Punished,". *Allafrica*, December 1, 2011, accessed August 27, 2017, http://allafrica.com/stories/201112010941.html
32. Iheoma Hendy, "List of Ex-Governors whose corruption cases are to be re-opened," *Buzz Nigeria*, n.d. accessed August 27, 2017, https://buzznigeria.com/ex-governors-corruption-reopened/ and

Emmanuel Ogala, "Where are the other Iboris in government?," *Premium Times*, n.d., accessed August 22, 2017, http://premiumtimesng.com/news/4704-Where-are-the-other-Iboris-government.html

33. Saharareporters, "Wole Soyinka: Next Phase Of Boko Haram Terrorism," *Saharareporters*, February 6, 2012, accessed August 16, 2017, http://saharareporters.com/interview/interview-wole-soyinka-next-phase-boko-haram-terrorism-thenews
34. Carefronting, "Controversies about Sharia," *Carefronting*, n.d., accessed August 27, 2017, http://carefronting.org/controversies-about-sharia/
35. Sahara reporters, "Wole Soyinka: Next Phase Of Boko Haram Terrorism," and Carefronting, "Controversies about Sharia".
36. Hendy, "List of Ex-Governors whose corruption cases are to be re-opened"
37. Carefronting, "Controversies about Sharia".
38. A. Ajibola, Nigeria's Poverty Level rises, hits 71.5% - Sokoto, Niger Top List of Poorest States. IFPRI, February 16, 2012, accessed August 20, 2017, http://nssp.ifpri.info/2012/02/16/nigeria-poverty-level-rises/
39. A. Ajibola, Nigeria's Poverty Level rises, hits 71.5% - Sokoto
40. Punch, "Boko Haram: America's Profound Misjudgment," *Punch Newspaper*, April 17, 2012, accessed August 20, 2017, http://punchng.com/editorial/boko-haram-americas-profound-misjudgment/.
41. Nurudeen M. Abdallah, "Derivation Oil States Shared N4.2tr in 15 years," *Daily Trust*, December 22, 2014, accessed August 18, 2017, https://www.dailytrust.com.ng/daily/top-stories/42532-derivation-oil-states-shared-n4-2tr-in-15-years.
42. Isaac Osuoka, "People in the Niger Delta now Recognize that Jonathan is a Waste of Time," *Saharareporters*, January 8, 2012, accessed August 20, 2017 http://saharareporters.com/interview/%E2%80%9Cpeople-niger-delta-now-recognize-jonathan-waste-time%E2%80%9D-%E2%80%93-isaac-osuoka

43. Toyosi Ogunseye, Allwell Okpi and Leke Baiyewu, N5tn Stolen under Jonathan – Investigation. *Punch*, November 25, 2012, accessed August 18, 2017, http://www.punchng.com/news/n5tn-stolen-under-jonathan-investigation/
44. Nigerian Eye, "FG Stops Import Waivers to Dangote, Stallion, Redeemed, Federal Palace Hotel Others," *Nigerian Eye*, February 6, 2012, accessed August 20, 2017, http://www.nigerianeye.com/2012/02/fg-stops-import-waivers-to.html and Bassey Udo and Ini Ekot, "Nigeria Custom Service Indicts Okonjo-Iweala, Says Import Waivers Massively Abused Under Her," *Premium Times*, January 21, 2014, accessed August 18, 2017, http://premiumtimesng.com/news/153709-nigeria-customs-service-indicts-okonjo-iweala-says-import-waivers-massively-abused-under-her.html
45. Hendy, "List of Ex-Governors whose corruption cases are to be re-opened,"
46. Toyosi Ogunseye, "EFCC, ICPC Probe 12 Governors for Massive Fraud," *Punch*, January 6, 2013, accessed August 16, 2017 http://www.punchng.com/news/efcc-icpc-probe-12-governors-for-massive-fraud/
47. Perpetua Onuegbu, Tackling Graduate Unemployment: The Drivers Option. *Vanguard*, December 27, 2012, accessed August 19, 2017, http://www.vanguardngr.com/2012/12/tackling-graduate-unemployment-the-drivers-option/ and Musa Yusuf Owoyemi, Kadir H. Din and Zaharuddin Sani Ahmad Sabri, (2015). "The Diaspora Nigerians' Image Problem of Drug and Fraud: A Case Study of the Malaysian-Indonesian Experience through Newspaper Reports," *Journal of Social Sciences*, 11 (2), 55 – 71.
48. Owoyemi et al., "The Diaspora Nigerians' Image Problem of Drug and Fraud: A Case Study of the Malaysian-Indonesian Experience through Newspaper Reports".
49. Mark Amaza, The North that Southerners don't know. *Tribune*, April 17, 2012, accessed August 20, 2017, http://tribune.com.ng/index.php/politics/39214-the-north-that-southerners-dont-know

CHAPTER TWO

Religious Conflicts, Political Stability and Development in Nigeria

Abdulrasheed Alada Muhammad
Department of Political Science
University of Ilorin
PMB 1515, Ilorin, Nigeria
rashmann1@yahoo.com
+2348065366461

Introduction

Religious conflicts in Nigeria prove to be divisive and pervasive with ominous threats to the country's political stability and entire socio-economic development. Conflict, it should be noted, is an inevitable phenomenon in any human collection and it is the product of disaggregate interests among peoples of diverse backgrounds. Noting the pervasiveness, Aja Apuru-Aja notes that "we affect conflict much as conflict affects us"[1]. His assertion derives from the fact that conflict affects human behaviour and, to this extent, is anti-development. Furthermore, Habibullah Khan and Omar K. M. R. Basharit have argued that it is not possible to separate religion from development because peaceful co-existence of various religious groups within a country especially those with multiple religious affiliations, such as Nigeria, is an essential prerequisite for development in today's highly interconnected world.[2]

Development in this context implies advancement in the entire social, economic and political aspects of a country with the human being as the object and subject of such development. Thus, in spite of government's efforts to attenuate the worst effects of the various competing identities that often result in conflict, it remains a permanent feature of the country's political process. This does not need to be surprising given the fact that the 20th century witnessed the emergence of several modern states as heterogeneous entities defined by one or a combination of ethnic, cultural and religious identities. The competition between them often results in religious conflicts. The insinuation here is that, Nigeria's multi- religious (and multi-ethnic character) was engendered by her colonial experience. Colonialism resulted in the coming together of disparate entities under a single national authority. The implication of this is that different ethno-cultural and religious groups have to co-exist and compete within the same geopolitical entity. While no one is sure of the exact number of Nigeria's religious groups, the duo of Islam and Christianity constitute the dominant groups. Consequently, most discussion of Nigeria's religious multiplicity usually has these two in focus. More important is that relations between the Christian and Islamic groups were characterised more by a race for ascendancy - a situation that has raised religion to the forefront of governance issues. Often, the intense antagonisms between the two produces conflicts with its attendant worrisome consequences for the state. More worrisome is that despite scholars' attempts to explore and explain different strands of the phenomenon, the problem it engenders continues to mar governance in Nigeria.[3] Some recent trends show that religious conflicts are at times a domestic response to external pressures as happenings elsewhere in the world trigger religious violence in the country, thereby constituting a threat to Nigeria's political stability. It is against this background that this study examines the issue of religious conflicts and Nigeria's political stability. The intent is to reveal the character of religious conflicts in Nigeria as well as the inter-connectedness of actions and reactions of groups to various occurrences that are having religious undertone within and outside the country. This is more necessary given the fact that first, such endeavour will deepen our understanding of the seemingly intractable phenomenon of religious conflict and second, it becomes necessary considering the rate at which inter-faith disputes or disagreements, even at supranational level, translate into ferocious religious conflicts within the Nigerian state on the one hand and, on the other hand, how the conflicts further generate external pressures on the country amidst other social, political and economic consequences.

Chapter Two	Abdulrasheed Alada Muhammad, in Y.A. Quadri, Omotoye & R.I. Adebayo(Eds) Religion and Development in Nigeria London, Adonis & Abbey Publishers

Religion and Political Stability: A Theoretical Discourse

The notion of religion suggests an attempt by man to work out a relationship between humans and a super- ordinate or supernatural being. It was borne out of man's endeavours to understand the supernatural in the context of the world he lives in. Thus, religious belief is premised on the assumption that human perceptions of things, whims and caprices require higher powers to help them respond adequately and effectively to all their concerns.[4] Little wonder therefore that it is conceived as a system relating man to an ultimate value epitomised in God or the Supreme Being and embodying a creed, code, cult and a mode of communication.[5] This attempt to capture the essence of religion has given rise to different perspectives from scholars. Dominant among them are the Evolutionary, Marxian and Functional perspectives.[6] The evolutionary perspective not only sees animism as the earliest form of religion but that its understanding is central to understanding the concept of religion and the various evolutionary stages through which it has evolved. The Radical/Marxian perspective on the other hand sees religion as a sigh of the oppressed creature, the sentiment of a heartless world and the soulless condition, the opium of the people. Also, the functional perspective which reflects in the writings of scholars such as Emily Durkheim among others sees religion as performing the functional role of reinforcing the collective conscience of the society – a requisite for social order, stability and development.

A common thread to all the above perspectives, however, is that they all link religion to man's physical and social environment. To this extent, it could be argued that there is largely an interaction between religion and the society within which it functions. First at the level of state or social institutions, religion influences policies and general societal development and second, at the level of the individual, it not only affects behaviour but also confers on the individual a form of identity in the society to the extent that it colours human relationships, struggles and competition. Consequently, because of its tendency to colour relationships, religion has become a major influence in politics and plays significant roles in the entire societal process especially in multi religious societies such as Nigeria. As noted by Muhammad[7], factors that engender stability and/or instability in societies include several cleavage issues that often arise from time to time. If we conceive of political stability as a condition of steadiness and firmness of political institutions and processes within the political system as well as absence of threat to an existing pattern of authority and behaviour, then it could be reasoned that political stability especially in a plural society is a function of several societal factors within the entity. One of such is the role of religion and religious groups especially given its pervasive influence in politics. More so, religion has "the capacity to arouse deep emotions of man and passion towards obedience, commitment and total surrender to the dictates of the religious beliefs".[8] More over in Nigeria, major national development issues are contested for along different lines of cleavages to the point of no convergence and since religion constitutes one of such cleavage issues, it is thus "mobilised and politicised to the point of overt conflict" which is anti-development.[9] To this extent, religion in a society can be an agent of development much as its existence can be anti-development.

Overview of Religion and Religious Conflicts in Nigeria

Broadly categorised, religious groups in Nigeria take either of two forms. First are those religious groups that are indigenous to the entity and they predate the coming of the colonial overlords. These include varieties of African Traditional Religions (ATR) such as *Ogun, Oya and, Amadioha* among others. It is axiomatic to note that in Africa, there are a number of different traditional religions available. They, usually, are specific to the different ethnic groups, and the deities are usually the gods and goddesses that the ethnic group believes in. Each ethnic group also has a shrine which it dedicates to the deities that it believes in. Also, most of these religions do not have written documentation of their beliefs and practices, but they rely on a priest to teach them and to intervene on their behalf.[10] The second category are the foreign inspired religious groups that have come to overshadow existing ATRs. Indeed, the pervasive influence of some of these foreign inspired religions "has drifted some practitioners of A.T.R away from the religion".[11] Among these is Islam which entered Nigeria through contact with the Arabs, Christianity that came with activities of the colonialists, later-day religious

Chapter Two	Abdulrasheed Alada Muhammad, in Y.A. Quadri, Omotoye & R.I. Adebayo(Eds) Religion and Development in Nigeria London, Adonis & Abbey Publishers

groups such as *Hare Krishna, Falumgun and Eckankar* Movement among others. However, as mentioned earlier, Islam and Christianity overshadow other religious groups to the extent that any discourse of religious plurality in Nigeria usually focuses on these two.

Equally to most Nigerians, who usually clad themselves as Christians or Muslims even though they are sentimentally attached to the ATR,[12] religion and faith are important aspects of everyday life as it controls the laws, how people think and act, what one believes, and what one values among others. In fact, religious considerations create a situation of (unnecessary) state's veneration of religious groups especially, Islam and Christianity. Thus it is a potent political force that cannot be ignored in any national issue, be it foreign or domestic. It also continues to be an instrument of manipulation in furtherance of the objectives of politicians. For one, the sowing of the seed of antagonism between Islam and Christianity dates back to pre-independence period when the British colonialists embarked on the policy of protecting the Muslim North from the "destructive influence" of the Christian South[13] but went ahead to amalgamate the two into one political entity. Some are even of the view that the seed of religious conflicts in Nigeria was sown by the colonialists.[14] Added to this is external influence; influence of politics; ignorance and poverty as well as explosive media reports.[15] But the antagonism between Islam and Christianity was latent until the 1977/78 Sharia controversies at the Constituent Assembly (CA) when it came to the fore. Ever since, religion has become an important consideration in Nigeria's domestic politics much as it has become a force to be reckoned with in issues of international relations.

A more worrisome dimension is that while both religions preach peace, the conflicts that often arise from their relations remain a source of sorrow and agony to the citizens and a deep sore to the nation as it regresses development. This is as a result of destruction and catastrophic occurrences that accompany religious crises in the country. For example, between 2001 and 2004 in Plateau state alone, public institutions such as schools and school items worth over 130 million Naira were destroyed in various cases of religious conflicts in addition to loss of thousands of houses and shops.[16] Consequently, this has also placed a question mark on the sincerity and commitment of Nigerians to their religious doctrines.[17] Espousing a global view of the trend of religious conflicts, David Smock noted that religion is a factor in many of the world's most intractable and violent conflicts.[18] Quoting Martins Marty, he went further to note that most of the time, religion as a way to find "communion, consolation and integration into system of meaning and belonging" is not an instrument for killing. But it has revealed itself many times as a suitable weapon for destruction and killing". This to him is true in places such as Kashmir, Sudan and Israel/Palestine.[19]

But while the above examples of countries given by David Smock cannot be compared with that of Nigeria in terms of intensity of the conflicts, there is nothing to suggest that Nigeria may not witness such in the future especially where there is a declining capacity of the state to mediate in conflicts. Equally, geometrical occurrence and intensity of these religious conflicts speak volumes of the likely future implications of this trend.[20] For instance, between year 2000 and 2005, J. Isawa Elaigwu documents about 20 violent conflicts that are religious in nature.[21] Also, Isaac Terwase Sampson documents 30 of such conflict between 1999 and January 2012.[22] Unfortunately till date, this trend has not abated. Although it may not be possible to know the exact number of ethno-religious conflicts that have occurred in Nigeria since independence in 1960 due to lack of adequate statistical data on this issue[23], however, about forty per cent of such conflicts are credited to Nigeria's Fourth Republic[24]. This shows the extent to which religion has become a potent political force in Nigeria. Prior to year 1999, a number of other conflicts have taken place in the country[25].

Character of Religious Conflicts in Nigeria

A deeper reflection on the various conflicts, reveals the character of religious conflicts in Nigeria. First, some conflicts may start initially as religious but eventually produce ethnic outbursts. This is more the case where such conflicts come with some level of political undertone. In other words, the political class often finds in religion, a potent instrument that is used, along with ethnicity, to advance their self-serving political interests. To this extent it could be reasoned that the nature and character of political dynamics in the country usually result in a symbiotic relation between religion and ethnic

---

Chapter Two | Abdulrasheed Alada Muhammad, in
Y.A. Quadri, Omotoye & R.I. Adebayo(Eds)
Religion and Development in Nigeria
London, Adonis & Abbey Publishers

considerations. This is true of most conflicts in the Middle Belt region as well as those producing reprisal effects in other parts of the country. The various conflicts over the Sharia issue in the year 2001 are a particular case in point. As David Smock[26] has pointed out, a conflict identified as religious usually does not (always) stem from disagreements over theological issues. Rather, its impact usually results from the association of religious identity with ethnic division and economic factors. Salawu was thus right when he observes that: over the years the phenomena of ethnicity and religious intolerance have led to incessant recurrence of ethno-religious conflicts, which have given birth to many ethnic militias like the O'dua People Congress (OPC); the Bakassi Boys; the Egbesu Boys; the Ijaw Youth Congress (IYC); and the Igbo People Congress (IPC)[27]

Similarly, the character of the Nigerian state is such that permits to an extent, the interweaving of religious and ethnic issues especially at moments of crises. This is because the different origins of the two predominant religions of Islam and Christianity coupled with their being rooted in separate geographical localities created a situation whereby the resulting religious composition closely follows geographic and ethnic lines. Consequently, while the northern Hausa is predominantly Muslim, the eastern Ibo (including south- south minority groups) is predominantly Christian while western Yoruba are partly Christians and partly Muslims. Little surprise therefore that some religious issues easily wear the garb of ethnicity and vice versa. Equally, it is within this context of ethno-geographical leaning of Islam and Christianity that we can explain the prevalence of religious conflicts in the North and its consequent reprisal attacks in the South-east and South-South whereas the South-West appears less prone to such. In other words, because of its profound religious mix which usually results in kith and kin belonging to different religious faiths, the South West has been experiencing relative peace and harmonious relations between Muslims and Christians than the north and the south eastern regions.

A second discernible character of religious conflicts in Nigeria is that some of these conflicts are purely domestic issues but eventually generate international outcry. The Miss World beauty pageant conflict of November 2002 is an instance of this. Nigeria was to host the 2002 Miss World beauty pageant. Unfortunately, the timing of the event coincided with the period of the Muslim Fast of Ramadan. This made Muslims to be averse to the hosting querying why it has to hold during the holy month. The episode further degenerated into bitter acrimony between Muslims and Christians and eventually climaxed in religious conflicts in some parts of the country. The aftermath was several killings and destruction of properties much as it generated a negative image for the country in the comity of nations. It further led to the transfer of hosting rights of the pageant from Nigeria to Britain.

Yet, a third character of religious conflicts in the country lies is the fact that some conflicts are inspired by happenings within the larger international system. Two peculiar cases are worth mentioning in this regard. The first, which occurred in 2001, was a direct response to the Nigerian government's pronouncement over the US offensive on Osama bin Laden and other terrorist groups in the wake of the September 11 attack on some cities in the U.S. The government had through its then Foreign Affairs minister, Sule Lamido, expressed support for the American offensive. However, riots almost immediately broke out in some parts of the north with Muslims alleging a plan by the government to join hands with the U.S to wage war against Muslims. A second instance was the violence that erupted in parts of the north and Southeast in February 2005 over controversies arising from the 'cartoon caricature' of the holy prophet Muhammad. Twelve cartoons derogating the Prophet Muhammad were published in Denmark's Jyllands- Posten daily in September 2005 and reprinted in some other magazines in Europe. This sparked uproar in the Muslim world where creating images of the prophet is considered blasphemous. According to Islamic tradition any depiction of the prophet, even respectful ones, is banned out of concern that such images could lead to idolatry. Thus, the publication in Denmark attracted ferocious reactions from Muslims worldwide. In this, Nigeria was not an exemption as violence broke out in several states of the north and Southeast with hundreds killed and millions worth of property destroyed. The above description has obvious implications for socio-political and economic stability in the country.

Implications for Political Stability and Development

Development as noted earlier implies growth in the overall social, political and economic fabric of a country. It is a situation where growth is assured and there is no likelihood of reversal. In other words, such growth must be sustainable and reflect in the ability of societal institutions to sustain the momentum of growth. In this case, stability of institutions must be assured. Like any other form of conflict, religious conflicts when they occur leave in their wake, tales of woe, which the country and its citizens have to contend with. In Nigeria, a major consequence and implication of perennial religious conflict is the devastating effect it has on human capital and material resources. With massive loss of lives and property that accompany religious violence, there is no denying the fact that valuable human and material resources would have eluded the country. For instance, in the ethno religious crisis of 1999 between the Hausa community and some traditional worshipers in Ogun State, several items including residential houses and commercial centres were destroyed in addition to loss of tens of lives.[28] The same account but on a higher scale goes for the conflicts that rocked Plateau state between 2001 and 2004 among others in the country.[29] Similar to the above is that pervasive religious conflicts have implications for Nigeria's external image. Indeed, Nigeria's image over the years has been a source of worry to the country owing to many factors. But this has been worsened by perennial religious conflicts or conflicts which are perceived to be religious. The recent call by the United States of America (USA) government to its citizens to avoid going to some states populated mostly by Muslims is a reflection of the kind of image problem which the country faces. More so, investors are discouraged from investing in religious conflict prone areas.

At the social level, there is what may be termed as social cost of religious violence. This manifest in situations where families are displaced, kith and kin separated and ancestral homes are lost on account of religious violence. One plausible effect of this is that individuals seek 'alternative social insurance' in order to survive which they find in activities such as prostitution, banditry, thuggery and other forms of criminality. Such situations aggravate the level of insecurity and therefore stifle developmental goals. Also, individuals tend to flee their ancestral homes to become Internally Displaced Persons (IDP) or refugees in other lands. Related to this is that at moments of conflicts, there is usually free access to sophisticated arms and ammunition by those engaged in violence. Coupled with the fact that there is usually no programme of demobilisation after the conflict is resolved, individuals with arms become a terror to both their immediate communities and the larger society thus constituting security risks.

Beyond the above, religious conflicts also have implications for economic growth and national development. This is because conflicts not only stagnate the economy but also stultify growth much as they scare away foreign investors. Even local entrepreneurs are at the risk of losing their investments thus, reducing the pace of economic activities. Apart from this, the increasing number of internally displaced persons as a result of conflicts aggravates poverty while resources, which could have been channelled to other developmental projects, are diverted by the government to re-settle victims of conflicts.

The first lesson to be derived from our proceeding analysis is that religion has become in the contemporary world, to use the worlds of Ball and Dagger, "a political force pushing in different directions". [30] This implies that nations and indeed Nigeria must wake up to this reality and be more concerned with harnessing the peace-making components and values of its various religious groups. There is no denying the fact that each religion teaches peace and discourages war and conflict. Therefore, religious leaders from different faiths can be mobilised to facilitate peace. This no doubt requires religious leaders from both faiths to teach and practise common virtues such as justice, compassion, kindness and respect for the others' religious tenets.

Second, most of the religious conflicts are products of misconceptions emanating from deep-rooted stereotypes. An example is the erroneous misconception that the *Boko Harram* insurgency in the North-Eastern part of Nigeria was perpetrated by Muslims prompting a former President of the Christian Association of Nigeria (CAN) to call on all Christians in the country to defend themselves against attacks by the Muslims. There is, therefore, the need for the government, religious organisations, groups and other private agencies to join hands in creating an enabling environment that facilitates cross fertilisation of ideas among the different faiths. This on the one hand will bring about greater understanding of each faith and reduce stereotyping and on the other hand, it will reduce to a large extent the tendency of political actors to manipulate religious cleavages in the country.

All the above are essential against the background that religion, especially the Abrahamic faiths of Islam and Christianity, has a transnational existence than ethnic, political and other forms of cultural associations. As such religious disruption or violence in one part of the global system may reincarnate in other parts of the subsystem as witnessed in Nigeria in 2001 with the U.S offensive against Osama Bin Laden after the 9/11 attack on U.S and the global outrage arising from prophet Muhammad's 'cartoon caricature' published in a Swedish newspaper and reproduced in some other European countries.

Conclusion

Religion no doubt is a way of life for so many people across the world. Its cross national existence (especially Islam and Christianity) and sentimental attachment to it by people of different cultures and background makes it a politically active instrument in both national and international politics. Expectedly from its trans-national existence, disruptions at the level of one subsystem produces outburst at another subsystem. Equally, effects of religious conflicts are seen to manifest in the socio-political and economic spheres of life. This is the Nigerian malady where religious conflicts have become a perennial issue the country has to contend with. Indeed, the issue of religion has permeated the country's social, political and economic fabric that no one Nigerian government has ever enjoyed absolute support of both Islam and Christianity faiths at one and the same time. In other words, each successive government has had to battle with containing one religious conflict or the other. This situation obviously poses some threat to social, political and economic development of the country. Although the country may not have been engulfed in a full-blown religious war, nothing seem to suggest that such will not occur given the trend and character of these conflicts. Were these not to be, the issue of religion and inter faith relations deserve utmost attention from both the government and the entire citizens at large.

Chapter Two	Abdulrasheed Alada Muhammad, in Y.A. Quadri, Omotoye & R.I. Adebayo(Eds) Religion and Development in Nigeria London, Adonis & Abbey Publishers

References

1. Aja Akpuru-Aja, *Basic Concepts, Issues and Strategies of Peace and Conflict Resolution: Nigerian and African Case Studies* (Enugu: Kenny and Brothers Nigeria Limited, 2007), 15
2. Habibullah Khan and Omar K. M. R. Bashar , "Religion and Development: Are they Complementary?", *U21 Global Working Paper* (No 006, 2008).
3. Rotgak I. Gofwen, *Religious Conflicts in Northern Nigeria and Nation Building: The Throes of Two Decades, 1980*-2000 (Kaduna: Human Rights Monitor, 2004); Mohammad Gulrez, "Nigeria Muslim Community: Political Connotation". *India Journal of Politics*. xxxvi (3-4), (July-December, 2002), 107-120; Mathew H. Kukah, *Religion, Politics and Power in Northern Nigeria* (UK: Spectrum Books Ltd in Association with Safari Books Export Ltd, 1993);Umar M. Birai, *Domestic Constraints on Foreign Policy: The Role of Religion in Nigeria-Israel Relations, 1960-1996* (Kaduna: Sahab Press, 1993).
4. O. O. Mike, "The Sovereign National Conference, Religion and National Unity: The Paradox and the Solution" in Okpeh O. Okpeh (ed.) *The Sovereign National Conference*, (Aboki Publishers, Makurdi), 2004, 81
5. P. R. A. Adegbesan, "Pragmatic Involvement in Religious Matters: A Case Study of Nigeria" In Stephen O. Olugbemi (ed.), *Alternative Political Futures for Nigeria* (Nigeria Political Science Association, 1987).
6. I. G. Rotgak, I.G., *Religious Conflicts in Northern Nigeria and Nation Building: The throes of two Decades, 1980- 2000,* (Human Rights Monitor, Kaduna, 2006).
7. Abdulrasheed A. Muhammad, "Federalism and Political Stability in Nigeria" *Journal of Sustainable Development in Africa* 9 (4), (2007) 190
8. Gwamna Dogara Je'adayibe "Religion and National Transformation in Nigeria" In Y. A. Quadri, R. W. Omotoye and R. I. Adebayo (eds.) *Religion in Contemporary Nigeria* (London: Adonis and Abbey Publishers Limited, 2016), 9.
9. F. O. Nyemutu, Olakunle Odumosu and Michael Nabofa "Religion and Development in Nigeria: A Preliminary Literature Review" Religions and Development Working Paper 31 (UK: Bingham University, 2009), 7.
10. Rotimi Williams Omotoye "The Study of African Traditional Religion and Its Challenges in Contemporary Times" *Ilorin Journal of Religious Studies*, 1 (2), (2011), 23

11. Arthur E. Davies, 'Secularity and State Practices in Nigeria' in H. O. Danmole et el. (eds.), *Contemporary Issues in Nigerian Affairs*, (Ibadan: SUNAD Publishers Limited, 1995), 80.
12. Eghosa Osaghae, *The Crippled Giant: Nigeria Since Independence*, (London: C. Hurst and Company, 1998), 149
13. Nuzhat Fatima, "Religious Conflicts in Nigeria and their Impacts on Social Life" *Global Journal of Arts, Humanities and Social Sciences*, 2 (4), (June 2014); Bashir Salawu, "Ethno-Religious Conflicts in Nigeria: Causal Analysis and Proposals for New Management Strategies" *European Journal of Social Sciences*, 13, 3 (2010).
14. Bashir Salawu, "Ethno-Religious Conflicts in Nigeria: Causal Analysis and Proposals for New Management Strategies".
15. Olubusola Bosede Akinfenwa "Ethnic and Religious Violence in Nigeria: A proposal for Peaceful Co-Existence" In Y. A. Quadri, et al. (eds) *Religion in Contemporary Nigeria*, (London: Adonis and Abbey Publishers Limited, 2016).
16. Saad Alanamu, Yinusa Muhammed and Muhammed Adeoye, "Religious Violence: Implications and Options for Sustainable Development In Hassan Saliu, Ebele Amali, Josepf Fayeye and Emmanuel Oriola (eds.) *Democracy and Development in Nigeria Vol. 3: Social Issues and External Relations*, (Ilorin: Faculty of Business and Social Sciences, University of Ilorin, 2004), 148
17. Gwamna Dogara Je'adayibe "Religion and National Transformation in Nigeria"; Lydia Bosede Akande "Issues and Challenges of Religion in Nigeria in the 21st Century" In Y. A. Quadri, et. al. (eds.) *Religion in Contemporary Nigeria*, (London: Adonis and Abbey Publishers Limited, 2016), 31-46
18. David, Smock, "Teaching the Religious other", United States Institute for Peace Special Reports No. 143, 2005. Available online at: http: //www.usip.org/pubs/special reports/sr143.html (Accessed on 26th December, 2005).
19. David, Smock, "Teaching about the Religious other".
20. For series of attempts at documenting cases and implications of religious conflicts on Nigeria see, Nuzhat Fatima, "Religious Conflicts In Nigeria And Their Impacts On Social Life" 16; Bashir Salawu, "Ethno-Religious Conflicts in Nigeria: Causal Analysis and Proposals for New Management Strategies" *346;* Ushe Mike Ushe "Religious Conflicts

and Education in Nigeria: Implications for National Security" *Journal of Education and Practice* Vol.6, (2), (2015), 117-129
21. J. Isawa Elaigwu, *"The Politics of Federalism in Nigeria"*, (Jos: Aha Publishing House, 2005), 215-217
22. Isaac Terwase Sampson, "Religious violence in Nigeria", Causal diagnoses and strategic recommendations to the state and religious communities. Available online at: http://www.ajol.info/index.php/ajcr/article/viewFile/78703/69042 (Accessed on 16th January, 2008).
23. Bashir Salawu, "Ethno-Religious Conflicts in Nigeria: Causal Analysis and Proposals for New Management Strategies", 345
24. Bashir Salawu, "Ethno-Religious Conflicts in Nigeria: Causal Analysis and Proposals for New Management Strategies", 345
25. Bashir Salawu, "Ethno-Religious Conflicts in Nigeria: Causal Analysis and Proposals for New Management Strategies" 345; Nuzhat Fatima "Religious Conflicts In Nigeria And Their Impacts On Social Life", 16
26. David, Smock, 'Teaching about the Religious other …
27. Bashir Salawu, 'Ethno-Religious Conflicts in Nigeria: …' 345
28. Saad Alanamu, Yinusa Muhammed and Muhammed Adeoye, "Religious Violence: Implications and Options for Sustainable Development", 148
29. Thisdayonline, Lagos. October 7, 2004.
30. Thomas Ball and Richard Dagger, *Political Ideologies and the Democratic Ideal*, (New York: Haper Collins College Publishers, 1995).

CHAPTER THREE

The Spiritual and Ethical Implications of Oath-Taking in Nigerian Politics

Raymond Ogunade
Department of Religions
University of Ilorin, Ilorin, Nigeria.
raygade@hotmail.com
+2348032569178

&

Awofeko Emmanuel Olusegun
Department of Religious Studies,
McPherson University,
Lagos Ibadan Expressway, Seriki-Sotayo, Nigeria.
emmashalom2004@yahoo.co.uk

Introduction

Oath-taking is not a new thing in Nigerian politics, but it is assuming an alarming dimension in the politics of today because of the horrific behaviours and outcomes of office holders during and after their tenure. Before now, it was scarcely known and discussed. But, this time around, the dimension it is assuming is frightening and highly scandalous. Every new regime in any organisation is expected to commence with political revolution, institutional change, and economic modernisation, and also embark on programmes that will benefit people due to the oath sworn to during its inauguration. However, the reverse is the case today. Oath-taking has become a routine act during the handing-over ceremony to newly elected political officers. Oath-taking in politics today has its origins in religious customs and some forms of binding oaths are found in every culture. Oaths are administered to those entering such institutions as the military, secret societies, religious orders, and marriage.[1]

Oath, sworn statement, vow, assurance, word of honour, affirmation, or pledge as the case maybe is usually based upon religious principles and often used in legal matters. In a court of law, for example, every witness must swear or affirm based on the religion such a person practices that the testimony he or she gives is the truth. Immigrants take an oath of allegiance when they become naturalised citizens. The taking of an oath generally implies some legal or moral sanctions for failing to carry out one's sworn pledge. A trial witness, for instance, may be charged with the crime of perjury for lying while under oath.[2] This has been adopted in politics in general, especially in African countries, which Nigerian politics is not an exemption, for moral justification and service to humanity. Some scholars have written on oath-taking in African culture, the religious perspectives, politics in general, and the consequences of violating it. However, little attention has been paid to oath-taking in Nigerian politics and attitudes of political office holders. This chapter stands to fill that gap. It shall examine critically what oath-taking is all about, especially in Nigerian politics, its importance and spiritual and ethical effects on the people as regards their socio-economic life.

Oath-taking – An Overview

The *Oxford Advanced Learner's Dictionary*[3] defines oath as "a formal promise to do something or a formal statement that something is true". *Encarta English Dictionary*[4] defines it in two ways, first, as "solemn promise", which is, "a formal or legally binding pledge to do something such as telling the truth in a court of law, made formally and often naming God or a loved one as a witness". Second as "words of promise", which is, "the words said when making a formal pledge, especially when reciting a conventional formula such as the ones used in a court of law". From these definitions, an oath of office can simply be said to be a declaration a person makes before undertaking the duties of an office usually a position in a formal organisation or association or in government agencies. Oaths of office in politics are statements of allegiance to the government or people, some of them are affirmations of loyalty to a constitution or other legal scripts, or even to a person. Envoys swear that they will serve the people and work towards the

Chapter Three	Ogunade & Olusegun, in Y.A. Quadri, Omotoye & R.I. Adebayo (Eds) Religion and Development in Nigeria London, Adonis & Abbey Publishers

development of the nation; plaintiffs and defendants swear to tell the truth in court. Even couples swear, be it in court, traditional, church, or *nikkah*, that they will love, care for and be faithful to their partners.[5]

An oath involves calling God and people to witness to the execution of duties, the truth of a statement or the sincerity of a promise, which shall be testified within the period given in a particular situation, post or office. Ayantayo defines it as:

> ...a solemn promise or expression of commitment in which religious words express how a person intends to behave in a given circumstance. ...The introduction or innovation of God's name may be direct as 'God is my witness' or 'I call upon God to be my witness'.[6]

This serves the purpose of ensuring that the person who swears it keeps tenaciously to its terms, which may be done accordingly or otherwise as promised in the oath-taking.

Also, Gbinije sees 'Oath of Office' as "a solemn promise that is legally binding, administered by an officer of law, an approved officer of the profession, club or group, the Head of States, Governors and/or any approved and appointed officer of repute."[7] An oath is a political, social, religious and economic humdinger. The man or woman who takes an oath of office or upon whom an oath of office is administered or devolved is statutorily obligated to carry out his or her functions or duties in the spirit and the letter of the oath of office[8].

An oath is a promise or pledge a person takes before undertaking the duties of an office, usually a position in government or within a religious body. Such oaths are sometimes administered by officers of other organisations, most especially, the judiciaries. Oaths are often required by the laws of the state, religious body, or other organisation before the person may actually exercise the powers of the office or any religious body. It may be administered at an inauguration, coronation, enthronement, or other ceremony connected with the taking up of office itself, or it may be administered privately. This is what people generally referred to as "swearing in". Some oaths of office are a statement of loyalty to a constitution or other legal text or to a person or other office-holders.[9] Meanwhile, under the laws of a state – in a normal circumstance, it is considered treason or a high crime to betray a sworn oath of office.

Oath-taking in African traditional context goes beyond what one can describe or liken to the way it is nowadays. It is done with utmost care. This is because in most cases, its repercussions usually surpass imagination. It is interpreted as a crime against both human and supernatural beings and therefore taken with all sense of gravity and seriousness. Its violation is highly abhorred.[10] A Yoruba common adage on oath or pledge has this to say:

> *Ojo t'omode ba mu'le lo mo*
> *Omode kii m'ojo ti o da'le*
> *Ma se lo'ogun, ma ri*
> *T'omode ba se, dandan ni kori*
> Meaning:
> A child can only know when to make oath or pledge
> He/she does not know when he/she will break it
> 'Don't do it' prevents repercussion
> Once a child does it, he/she must surely face its consequence.

From the above quotation, it becomes evident that it is preferable for one not to engage in oath or pledge in the African traditional settings, rather than breaking or not fulfilling it. Oath-taking is usually applied either whenever there is a secret between two people or parties, which must not be revealed; or when there is an expectation or responsibility from a person or party to discharge. Several tools or religious elements, or deities are used in making an oath or pledge, which indicate the kind of punishment such fellow will serve or repercussion encountered as a result of violation of such oath, hence, this restrains people from either attempting it at all or keep to such oath.

Religiously, scriptures from Christianity and Islam, as well as other world religions go against infringement of an oath or pledge made. They rather suggest or advise people to deviate from taking it no matter what. Christianity teaches that one should rather not vow or make oath than to do so and later fail to fulfil it. It forbids using God to swear or make oath, no matter what. On the other hand, Islam says any vow or oath made with the name of Allah (*Wallahi, Billahi* and *Tallahi*) must be fulfilled.[11] The quotation from the Qur'ān (16:92) "do not make your oaths a means of deceiving one another or your foot will slip after it was firmly placed and you will taste evil for barring access to the Way of Allah and you will have a terrible punishment" suggests the following conditions of making oaths in Islam:

i. The oath has to be taken in Allah's name or his attributes. Any oath in the name of people is not valid.
ii. In Islam, the person taking the oath must be sane and mature. It is not for children.
iii. The oath is not made on something impossible or impracticable. "I swear I will grow wings on my back and fly" as an example is not a valid oath.
iv. *Inshallah* is not used in making an oath in Islam. For instance "*wallahi* I will travel to Syria tomorrow *inshallah*" is not a valid oath if the person who said it failed to travel to Syria the next day.[12]

There are examples of people who involved in oath-taking in these scriptures but failed or violated it and squarely faced the consequences for such debauched attitudes. Similarly, there are punishments meted out for anyone who fails to fulfil his/her oath or pledge in other world religions.

The Nigerian Politics and Oath-taking

Official oath-taking is not strange in Nigerian politics. Before an elected office holder assumes power, he or she is expected to take an Oath of Allegiance and/or Oath of Office, as the case may be. In the advanced democratic countries, being in politics or governance is all about service to the people, operating under the rule of law and with integrity, morality, transparency and good governance as driving points – this is democracy in the real sense – but reverse is the case in Nigerian politics. The core and ethics of oath-taking has suffered a shipwreck in Nigeria and the society is sinking. The whole system has been engulfed by corruption, where selfishness, self-centredness and egoism are almost synonymous with most political office holders.

As it usually happens during oath-taking/swearing-in in Nigeria, the essence and the core value of the exercise come down to the funfair and the wasteful ceremony. As soon as most political office holders get into office, they almost immediately begin to act contrary to the content of their oath of office. Executive and legislative recklessness, high profile corruption, and all sorts of misconducts are not uncommon. Contrary to the content of the Hippocratic Oath, doctors usually abandon their duties to embark on regular strikes. However, without any form of prejudice, some doctors are forced to do so, when certain service conditions become extremely unpalatable. It is also alleged that some policemen, who ought to be friends and guards to the people, now indulge in unscrupulous acts of bribery and corruption that makes one wonder if they are now turned enemies and robbers. Most politicians in the Upper and Lower Houses of Representatives indirectly represent their selfish interests, not for their supposed constituencies. Several examples of these paralysing maladies are "visible to the blind" and "audible to the deaf" in our immediate society, a glance at our dailies will do.[13] It is ironic that some lawyers are now tagged liars; they manipulate the judicial system to favour their friends and the "highest bidders" contrary to the oath they took.[14] It is a truism that many accountants and clerical workers are guilty of pen robbery, discharging their duties for self-aggrandisements, the God-fearing ones are often difficult to find. These attitudes are arguable but they are evident in the undue processes of acquiring power and wealth while attaining offices in the society, giving mediocrity a place of pride against prudence and competence.

Undoubtedly, Nigerian politics is now seen as a 'dirty game' and 'gambling'. It is an activity that makes several people to deny the real person they are if they want to be involved in it. Most public leadership office holders, particularly political office holders in Nigeria do not abide by the constitution but rather obey the 'forces' that brought them to the post. These 'forces' are the godfathers and their political parties. Most of them are reminded of how they either had nothing – money, influence, popularity, and the likes – to contest and gain the post or office, or how they were being brought to the party as 'nobody' to contest. Apart from this fact, most of them think of money spent and debt incurred before they got elected. Most political parties sometimes take advantage of poor economic situations of the grass roots and lure the electorate in this category with money to buy their votes. On the other hand, they also explore the greed for more wealth amongst the elites in the society unfortunately, in order to gain political support from them.

Chapter Three	Ogunade & Olusegun, in
	Y.A. Quadri, Omotoye & R.I. Adebayo (Eds)
	Religion and Development in Nigeria
	London, Adonis & Abbey Publishers

Subsequently, we observe that most political office holders in Nigeria are yet to understand the seriousness and the significance of oath taking. The gravity of integrity that is trivialised when there is non-adherence and non-compliance to the sacred duty of taking an oath of office is yet to sink in when they stand in public-squares to give their allegiances.

Section 7 of the 1999 Constitution of the Federal Republic of Nigeria caters for Public Office Oath-taking using major religious beliefs in Nigeria to protect and uphold the Constitution and the interest of the populace whose resources the office holders are to manage. This constitution contains an oath of office for the president, as well as other officials – senators, representatives in federal and state levels - including members of Congress. The document specifies what each office holder must do and that they "shall be bound by Oath or Affirmation in the Nigerian constitution"[15].

Spiritual and Ethical Implications of Non-adherence and Non-compliance to Oath-Taking

Despite the many changes against the effectiveness of oath-taking in Nigerian politics, the use of an oath is often seen as important to the development of any profession committed to fundamentally noble and moral ideals, which politics should be regarded as one. It guides and guards its partakers to discharge exactly what he/she has bounded himself/herself with – the oath. The survey of the past 17 years of democracy in Nigeria shows that most oath sworn to focused on the commitment politicians make publicly, requiring prospective elected politicians to promise to do their best in caring for the people they represent.[16]

Lovelika Bautista opined that professionalism and core ethical values must be upheld among political office holders rather than the commercialism and materialism most of them are guilty of; that each oath-taker finds fulfilment in his/her indispensable roles as guide and channels to others' needs not only in politics, but also that they should keep in mind the responsibility to follow ethical standard of the oath of office they took.[17] Instead of this, findings show how several politicians – some House of Assembly members known as *Omo'lu* in Ogun State;[18]

Chris Ngige versus Chris Uba in Anambra State; Thoedore Orji versus Orji Uzor Kalu in Abia State, etc. – were drawn into swearing an oath before they can be issued ticket and given support from their parties to contest. This was in order for them not to betray their parties and godfathers, and this affects their allegiance and compliance to fulfilling the required public political oath of office they would compulsorily take.[19] The implication of this is that their commitment is more to their political parties than to the national interest.

In line with this, Joseph Omoregbe concluded that Machiavellianism and the Nigerian politics are the same. He recounted Niccolo Machiavelli's idea as an Italian political thinker, who totally removed morality from politics, with the opinion that any politician who wants to be successful in 'grabbing' power or political offices, need to do that by all means – fair or foul – not taking cognisance of ethical values in display. Once this power is possessed, everything to retain it must be done. To him, political office holders must be shrewd, prudent, practical and swift in all their actions to gain and retain 'power'. Such politicians need not be honest, morally upright, religious, humane or compassionate, but must pretend to be and use such pretence to achieve his/her aim.[20]

Oviasuyi, Ajagun and Isiraoje, postulated from fetish angle of this matter as thus:

> ...there are many secrets surrounding governance and lack of development in this country. The politicians are often in the business of covering themselves because they are on fetish oath, the implications are endless and this has been the major factor that has brought Nigeria to where it is today. Such attitude has encouraged complaints, wickedness, occultism in governance, rigging of election results, do or die politics and disregard for the sufferings of the Nigerian people. Poverty has gone to a very high level, so much so that, it is now a matter of do or die for Nigerians to acquire political power. Politics in Nigeria has become so lucrative that people are ready to do anything to be involved in it, as it is the quickest source of wealth, and this has brought about leadership crisis in the country.[21]

Apparently, the consequences of reneging on the oath taken are grave and enormous. These implications not just pollute the sanctity of office and the personnel, but also the entire country. This is because, there are spiritual entities watching over utterances that were declared during the

---

Chapter Three	Ogunade & Olusegun, in Y.A. Quadri, Omotoye & R.I. Adebayo (Eds) Religion and Development in Nigeria London, Adonis & Abbey Publishers

oath, and the conducts of political public office holders during their tenure of mandate. These spiritual beings will ensure that violations and non-compliance to the oath of office are met with attendant unpalatable outcomes.[22]

Spiritually, oath-taking, particularly with the Holy Scriptures – Bible and/or Qur'ān – has spiritual implications, particularly when such declarations under oath are not upheld. The consequences of non-adherence to oath-taking are listed in the Holy Writs: it brings reproach to the name of God (Lev. 19: 12; Surah An-Nahl, Qur'ān 16:91); it brings one to disrepute (Num. 30:2; Qur'ān 61:2-3); commit atrocities and murders with impunity, disregard for law, order, constituted authority, insensitive to the plight of the masses, and disregard for sanctity of human lives (Hos. 4:2, 10:4); downfall of leaders and by extension the nation (Amos 8:14; Qur'ān 5:91); curses and untimely death over such individuals (Zech. 5:3-4; Qur'ān 58: 16-17); God's anger and judgement (Mal. 3:5; Surah Ali-Imran, Qur'ān 3:77); desecration of the Word of God and God's creatures (Mat. 5:34-36; Surah Al-Munafiqun, Qur'ān 63:2); gross disrespect for God (Mat. 23:16-22).

From the foregoing, these consequences vary depending on how heavy the oath is, and the person in question. However, non-adherence of the oath sworn to by the head of an organisation or a representative, as it is in this study, does not adversely affect only the person, but also the people he/she oversees or governs or represents and the entire nation at large. This has a great effect on the nation in the following aspects:

i. It brings economic woes – affects the economy of the nation since office holders fail to fulfil what they promised in the oath during inauguration, directing national income or resources into their personal purse.
ii. It causes political instabilities – the unstable, erratic, and unpredictable governance in the past to present is as a result of non-fulfilment of political manifestoes and oath of office.
iii. It promotes insecurity – unemployment which has turned many youths to hooligans, thieves, hired assassins, addicts, prostitutes, etc. coupled with insurgencies and different sects disturbing the peace of

the populace is as a result of neglect of political office holders against what they promised and are meant to do.

iv. It encourages corruption – the inordinate ambition by many to gain power or retain (political offices) is to acquire wealth, against their manifesto that captured many people to cast their votes for them and oath-taking during inauguration. Stealing, thuggery, deception, non-accountability and the likes of the political office holders in this nation are a result of misplaced priorities, crime, collapse of educational standard, poor healthcare services, epileptic power supply, scarcity of fuel, decline of interest in agriculture and its products, inadequate water supply, and lots more.

However, at the level of African religion, even though Nigeria is yet to officially adopt indigenous religious symbols/emblems as tools of oath-taking for public offices, does not rule out the fact that violation of the declaration of oaths will not go unpunished.[23] We have seen cases where people reneged on oath sworn to under *Ogun* (Yoruba god of Iron), *Sango* (Yoruba god of Thunder), *Sanponna* (Yoruba god of small pox), and have suffered great calamities.[24] In support of this view, Dopamu has this to say:

> …Thus today, a man may swear rather falsely on the Bible or the Qur'ān with the belief that these do not kill; rather than swear falsely on the emblem of *Ogun*, the god of iron, because he knows that he stands the risk of being hurt by iron implements which are in use in his everyday business[25]

It is a fact in Yoruba and other African religious beliefs that, the active presence of the ancestors (a major element of the structure of African religion) as co-tenants of the African worldview[26] makes it impossible for any political office holder to get away with non-adherence to oath.

The Way Forward

A promise or a vow is something one should not break unless extraordinary circumstances required it, like threat to one's life, or if one were under coercion, but oath of office in politics is seen beyond this, that is, under no condition should anything prevent it from being fulfilled. Why? Because not fulfilling it would be seen as dishonourable by people, for losing honour is quite worse than death. Naturally, the power of an oath comes from the person who is making it; if such person is honourable he or she will follow it to the end, even if it requires death. If not, then, it is just a mere word of deceit. But oath of office is different; it has its power from the constitution that backs it, which is compulsory for as many that want to take up the responsibility that it stands for. A Yoruba adage says *"Mi o le wa ku, ki n j'oye ile baba e"* (a person who is afraid of death, cannot contest or gain power to his/her descendant's post/office). This invariably means that public office holders ought to have considered the implications of violating the oath attached to discharging their duties.

Consequently, the oath of office in Nigerian politics has been rendered impotent, simply because God is 'too patient to act' and 'merciful' to apprehend and severely punish as many that go against the oath they make during their swearing-in into such offices. It is therefore recommended by many[27] that, traditional aspect of oath-taking should be employed in Nigerian politics, where religious cum cultural symbolism or elements are adopted. This is suggested to mount pressure and caution on everyone to strictly adhere to the oath. With this, it is believed that there will be great reduction in the number of people involved in politics, sieve away the chaff from the wheat; and those who eventually participate will surely deliver to a greater extent. Thereafter, the nation will grow faster and develop within a short period of time.

Political office holders in Nigeria must develop the skills to make the appropriate leadership decisions when guidance may be vague on how best to support and defend the Constitution. They must take the time to identify capabilities for addressing the entire spectrum of conflict and wrestle with ways of resolving conflicting priorities. Individuals at all levels must focus on the needs of the nation rather than on personal gains, when serving in public office. Finally, officers must embrace the moral foundation symbolised in the phrase *"so help me God"* since it is the heart and soul of the success of future generations of both born and unborn children.[28]

It is disheartening to have Nigeria in the list of most corrupt countries in the world.[29] This happened as a result of past office holders caught with government assets in different foreign accounts, coupled with many crimes they committed while in office, which are completely against the oath they made. Surprisingly, these people go free most times because they have influential people – godfathers and political caucuses – to bail them out. It is strongly recommended that political office holders should be probed during and after their tenure; and face any punishment for any crime they commit as stated in the constitution. This will serve as a warning to others, and bring about positive change in the future.

Also, it is hoped that leaders – from the President to the least government workers - should focus on how to effectively, efficiently and faithfully discharge the duties of their offices. Moral principles such as discipline, loyalty, tolerance, impartiality, courage, love, honesty, equity and equality where applicable are expected to reflect in the fulfilment of their oaths of office. However, those who fail to do so, should be shown the way out of office and prosecuted. In addition, political parties and god-fatherism, which are the major setbacks to adherence and fulfilment of oath-taking by office holders in Nigerian politics, should be checked. Muhammadu Buhari in his inauguration speech said:

Having just a few minutes ago sworn on the Holy Book, I intend to keep my oath and serve as President to all Nigerians. I belong to everybody and I belong to nobody.[30]

Analysts[31] have interpreted this to mean that he wants to strictly adhere to the oath he made, that is, never to allow his personal interest over his duties; to do the best of his ability to preserve, protect, and defend the constitution of the Federal Republic of Nigeria; to abide by the code of the constitution of the Federal Republic of Nigeria; to do right to all manner of people, according to the law without fear or favour and affection or ill-will as spelt out in the oath. It shows clearly from the statement that both political party and god-fathers will not influence or affect his duty as the president.

Conclusion

Religious beliefs and sayings, as well as moral consciousness and morality that negate the political party objectives and agenda have to be dropped. Morality and sincerity of purpose have been removed from Nigerian politics. Honesty, altruism and accountability were thrown out with it. It saddens one to discover that a richly endowed country with both natural

---

Chapter Three | Ogunade & Olusegun, in
Y.A. Quadri, Omotoye & R.I. Adebayo (Eds)
Religion and Development in Nigeria
London, Adonis & Abbey Publishers

(oil, agriculture, mineral, etc.) and human (intelligence, multi-billionaires, solution-makers, etc.) resources, that help several countries to survive has turned Nigeria into a beggar nation, simply because of national treasury looters, who are primarily involved in politics for their personal or group interests. Emmanuel Ibuot established that this happens because the people are led by "occult-controlled personalities, denizens of the esoteric realm, ritual killers and their sponsors"[32]. He further makes it clear that these reasons are behind the failure of various theories, principles, policies, ideas, scholarly suggestions, and the likes, which have worked in similar situations in other developed and developing nations. This has affected the spiritual, ethical and psychological make-up of Nigerians, resulting into general notion of most people that Nigeria cannot be better again since many are not seeing it being good. Definitely, things would continue to be the same or rather worst except there is moral consciousness and sense of altruism in all, both the people in power or offices and those that are voting them in.

References

1. Peter Duus, *Oath-taking*, (Redmond, WA: Microsoft Corporation, 2008).
2. Steve Sheppard, *What Oaths Meant to the Framers' Generation: A Preliminary Sketch*, (Cardozo L. Rev. De Novo Publications, 2009).
3. Wikipedia. "Oath of Office", Retrieved from www.wikipedia.com on February 22, 2016.
4. Encarta English Dictionary, *Oath* (Redmond, WA: Microsoft Corporation, 2008).
5. H. Obairo, "Pointlessness of Oath-taking In Nigeria", Retrieved from www.news24.com/nigeria/Oath-taking/Pointlessness-of-oath-taking-in-Nigeria-2015-05-19.html. January 23, 2016.
6. J. K. Ayantayo, "Religious Ethical issues in the oath of office in the Nigerian Constitution", *Orita: Ibadan Journal of Religious Studies xxxi*/1 & 2, (1999), 100-101.
7. Bobson Gbinije, "Politicians, Oath of Office and African Deities". Retrieved from www.vanguardngr.com/Oath-taking/Politicians-oath-of-office-and-African-deities/Vanguard News.html February 27, 2016.
8. Gbinije, Bobson. "Politicians, Oath of Office and African Deities"…
9. Wikipedia, "Oath of Office", Retrieved from www.wikipedia.com on April 16, 2016

10. S.A. Adewale, "Crime and African Traditional Religion", *Orita: Ibadan Journal of Religious Studies*, xxvi. (1994), 56.
11. N. Tasan, "The importance of taking oath in daily life", Retrieved from www.thepenmagazine.net/the-importance-of-taking-oath-in-daily-life/html November 18, 2015.
12. Interview, Prof. Z.I Oseni, informant of Islamic Religion, Dept. of Arabic, University of Ilorin, 68 years, 17-01-2017.
13. Nigerian Punch Newspaper, (Tuesday 24th February, 2017), 4.
14. Nigerian Punch Newspaper…
15. H. Obairo, "Insignificance of Oath-taking In Nigeria", (2015). Retrieved from www.naij.com/436699-obaro-comments-on-insignificance-of-oath-taking-in-nigeria.html December 15, 2015.
16. J.K. Ayantayo, "Religious Ethical issues in the oath of office in the Nigerian Constitution"…, 103.
17. Edmund Pellegrino, *"The Medical Journal of Australia", 1993*. Retrieved from www.wol.jw.org/an-Ancient-Oath-With-Modern Significance-Watchtower-online-library.htm January 28, 2016.
18. Lovelika Bautista, "Significance of the Oath-taking Ceremonies", 2013. Retrieved from http:/cuervopropertyadvisory.wordpress.com February 2, 2016.
19. Reuben Abati, "Oath-taking in Nigerian Politics", 2009. Retrieved from https://groups.google.com/forum/#!topic/usaafricadialogue/O97Fg4zyQU8 March 6, 2016.
20. Godwin Ijediogor and Samson Ezea, "Nigeria Politics and Oath Taking", Retrieved from http://www.nigerianbestforum.com/ March 16, 2016.
21. Joseph I. Omoregbe, *Ethics: A systematic and historical study* (Lagos: Joja Educational Research and Publishers Limited, 1989), 56.
22. Interview, Pastor Peter Faleye, informant on Christianity, The Redeemed Christian Church of God, Good news Parish, Off Tanke, Ilorin, 43 years, 16-01-2017; R.I Adebayo, informant on Islamic Religion, Department of Religions, University of Ilorin, 53 years, 24-02-2017; Abdulrasheed Opeyemi Ahamad, informant on Islamic Religion, Student, Department of Religions, University of Ilorin, 28 years, 23-02-2017; Chief Yemi Elebuibon, the *Araba* of *Ifa*, informant on African Religion, 1213 Elsworth Street, Berkeley, California, USA, 76 years, 23-11-2016.
23. Interview, Chief Yemi Elebuibon, the *Araba* of *Ifa*, informant on African Religion…
24. Interview, Chief Yemi Elebuibon, the *Araba* of *Ifa*, informant on African Religion…

25. P.A. Dopamu, "Towards Understanding African Religion", I.A.B. Balogun (ed), *Religious Understanding and Co-operation in Nigeria-reprinted* (University of Ilorin: Department of Religions, 2012), 56.
26. J. Omosade Awolalu and P. Adelumo Dopamu, *West African Traditional Religion* - revised edition (Ibadan: MacMillan Publishers, 2005), 23-25.
27. Interview, Chief Yemi Elebuibon…; Pete Edochie, "Forget Bible, Government Officials Should Be Sworn-In with 'Smaller gods', retrieved from http://www.naijaloaded.com.ng/2017/02/21/forget-bible-govt-officials-sworn-smaller-gods-nollywood-legend-pete-edochie/24-02-2017.
28. P.O. Oviasuyi, S.O. Ajagun and L. Isiraoje, "Fetish Oath Taking in Nigerian Politics and Administration: Bane of Development", *A Journal of Social Sciences*, 27/3 (2011), 193-196.
29. Kenneth Keskel, "The Oath of Office: A Historical Guide to Moral Leadership", 2002. Retrieved from www.barefootsworld.net/the-oath-of-office/htm March 23, 2016.
30. I. Deji, "2016 Top 10 Most Corrupt Country", 2016. Retrieved from www.tv360nigeria.com April 8, 2016.
31. Femi Ajayi, "I belong to Everybody and I belong to Nobody", 2015. Retrieved from http://www.vanguardngr.com/2015/06/i-belong-to-everybody-and-i-belong-to-nobody-2/ April 9, 2016.
32. Emmanuel J. Ibuot, "The Impact of Blood Covenant on Development in Nigeria", *A Journal of African Studies*, Vol. 10 (2013), 24-25.

CHAPTER FOUR

Religious-Based Dispute Resolution Mechanism of Independent *Sharī'ah* Panels and their Contributions to the Development of Judicial System in Nigeria

Abdul-Fatah Kola Makinde
Department of Religious Studies,
Obafemi Awolowo University, Ile-Ife, Nigeria
makindeabdulfatah@yahoo.co.uk or akmakinde@oauife.edu.ng
+2348035065159

Introduction

The Nigerian legal system is based on the English law, *Sharī'ah* and tradition legal systems. This was as a result of colonisation and the attendant incidence of reception of English law through the process of legal transplant. English law has a tremendous influence on the Nigerian legal system, and it forms a substantial part of Nigerian law.[1] However, before the advent of colonial rule and the amalgamation of the protectorates of northern and southern areas to form Nigeria, each of the territories which together constituted Nigeria, had a system of administration of justice; hence, the pre-colonial institutions included courts.[2] The various indigenous people of Nigeria had different methods of dispute resolution mechanism. Among the Yoruba and Igbo, the system revolved around their traditional institutions. It was fashionable among them to refer contentious matters to the head of the family. If he could not settle the dispute, the matter was taken to the head of the compound until a solution could be found at the level of the *Oba* or *Eze* (a traditional head of a town). In the North, there was a bit of formalisation of the legal tradition as founded on the Islamic legal system, the *Sharī'ah*. There was an elaborate court system, the hub of which was the Alkali system. The Emir was the ultimate appellate judge.[3]

Therefore, despite the influence of English law, the Nigerian legal system is not a function of the English law only. It is a function of other laws which make it very complex because of its pluralistic nature. Legal pluralism exists in Nigeria because it is a colony where the law of its former colonial authority exists alongside the *Sharī'ah* and traditional legal systems. The Nigerian constitution, at various stages of its development, recognises alongside the English law, both the *Sharī'ah* and Customary law systems.

The history of judiciary in Nigeria shows that between 1843 and 1973, various courts were established for administration of justice. However, under the Amended Constitution of the Federal Republic of Nigeria, the superior courts recognised as constituting the judiciary are the Supreme Court; the Court of Appeal; the Federal High Court; the High Court of the Federal Capital Territory, Abuja; the Customary Court of Appeal, Abuja; the Sharia Court of Appeal of the States; the State High Courts; and Customary Court of Appeal of States. These Courts are vested with functions or duties of dispensing justice, in accordance with the jurisdiction vested in them.[4]

Aside the above mentioned courts, there are some other alternative means through which disputes are settled. Like in other parts of the world, the Nigerian judicial system also recognises Alternative Dispute Resolution (ADR) having being faced with ever-burgeoning caseloads. Therefore, when parties need to resolve disputes, they may often turn not only to trial before courts but also to alternative methods of dispute resolution.[5] As much as there is ADR recognised by the conventional courts, there are also many organisations related to ADR within and outside the country. In America for example, there are American Arbitration Association (AAA), Better Business Bureau (BBB) – Dispute Resolution Services and Centre for Effective Dispute Resolution (CEDR).[6] Similarly, there are alternative methods that employ *Sharī'ah* law principles for dispute resolution in Nigeria. This seems to be an alternative to *Sharī'ah* courts when there are no opportunities of such courts in southern Nigeria. The methods are employed under Independent *Sharī'ah* Panels (ISP) in south-western Nigeria to allow Muslims in this part of the country to get some of their matters resolved in accordance with *Sharī'ah* law.

This chapter aims at discussing the alternative methods of dispute resolution as undertaken by ISP in south-western Nigeria with a view to

---

Chapter Four	Abdul-Fatah Kola Makinde, in Y.A. Quadri, Omotoye & R.I. Adebayo (Eds) Religion and Development in Nigeria London, Adonis & Abbey Publishers

explicating its contribution to the development of the judicial system in the country. It begins by examining the concepts of ADR and ISP before looking at the rationale for the establishment of ISP. The chapter does not fail to discuss the *modus operandi* of the ISP before making a critical assessment of its contributions to Nigerian judicial system.

Concept of ADR

ADR is a term used to describe several different methods of resolving legal disputes without going to court. It is observed that the rising cost of litigation is making traditional lawsuits impractical for many individuals and businesses. More so, civil courts are noted to face backlogs of dockets, resulting in delays of a year or more for private parties to have their cases heard by a jury. Hence, new types of proceedings have been developed in response to the challenges and they are providing benefits, saving time and money for everyone involved. These include arbitration, mediation, and additional kinds of ADR designed for specific cases and subject matters.[7]

Moreover, ADR is about procedures for settling disputes by means other than litigation; e.g. by arbitration, mediation or mini-trials. Such procedures, which are usually less costly and more expeditious than litigation, are increasingly being used in commercial and labour disputes, divorce actions, in resolving motor vehicle and medical malpractice tort claims, and in other disputes that would likely otherwise involve court litigation.[8] It refers to any means of settling disputes outside of the courtroom. It typically includes early neutral evaluation, negotiation, conciliation, mediation, and arbitration. As burgeoning court queues, rising costs of litigation, and time delays continue to plague litigants, more communities have begun experimenting with ADR programmes. Some of these programmes are voluntary; others are mandatory.[9] The experiment of having more ADR programmes in different communities could have been responsible for the emergence of Independent *Sharī'ah* Panel (ISP).

Establishment of ISP

ISP is an independent panel which serves in an alternative capacity to *Sharī'ah* court. It developed through some Muslim bodies which intended to provide opportunities for Muslims who are not privileged to have Sharia Court of Appeal in their area. It is meant to make arbitration on disputes concerning Muslims and allow them take their civil matters, privately and voluntarily, to ISP for adjudication in accordance with the *Sharī'ah* law. Therefore, like ADR, ISP makes arbitration as one of its cardinal objectives and this indicates why the word 'arbitration' is added to the nomenclature of the ISP in Oyo State.[10] Disputes that are attended to under ISP include marital disputes, monetary disputes, mosque disputes, family disputes as well as disputes among the Muslims either at inter-personal or inter-community level.[11] Other disputes handled by ISP include land matters, elections petitions from Islamic associations, contract and moneylending.[12] Imamship or trade disputes and other personal matters where the parties concerned are Muslims are also taken care of.[13]

The circumstance leading to the establishment of ISP in South Western Nigeria was the non-availability of *Sharī'ah* court in the area. None of the states in the area known as Yoruba land has a judicial system that gives opportunities for Muslims to handle their disputes or adjudicate their matters in accordance with *Sharī'ah*. Makinde and Ostien observe that:

> Over a number of years, Islamic law has effectively been eliminated as a choice of law option in the regular courts. Accordingly, the divorces, inheritance cases, and other civil matters even of Muslims who would choose to go under Islamic law if they could are handled according to Yoruba customary law or 'English' law."[14]

The return to civil rule in 1999 brought about a change in the demand for the establishment of *Sharī'ah* Courts in some states in Yoruba land. The official launching of *Sharī'ah* by the Zamfara State Government on 27th October, 1999 sparked serious demand for *Sharī'ah* in other parts of Nigeria including Yoruba land.[15] The demand was made by making a case for the establishment of Sharia Court of Appeal by presenting a Private Bill to the Houses of Assembly of some states. Three states, Oyo, Lagos and Osun, were particularly noted for the demand and they are the states where ISP is in existence. It becomes pertinent to discuss the establishment of ISP in each of the states.

The first state where ISP was established is Oyo State. Ismaila asserts that "it is the first of its kind to emerge in the South-West Nigeria after the 1999 *Sharī'ah* revolution which was initiated by Zamfara State of Nigeria."[16] Consequent upon the Zamfara State initiative which was followed by many Northern States, Oyo State Muslims under the aegis of Islamic Co-ordination Council started to strategise on how to get *Sharī'ah* Courts established in the State to adjudicate on civil aspect of Islamic law. A Private Bill was presented to the Oyo State House of Assembly in 2001 for this purpose but did not yield fruitful results. When this effort proved abortive, the Muslims of the State opted for a non-governmental option and established Independent *Sharī'ah* Arbitration Panel on Wednesday, 1st of May, 2002 at Ibadan Central Mosque, Ibadan.[17]

The Lagos State followed suit in the same year. A variety of arguments was made for the idea that Lagos State government should establish *Sharī'ah* courts. Like their counterparts in Oyo State, a draft bill was prepared, spelling out the proposal in detail. Muslim members of the House of Assembly were approached and requested to introduce the bill into the House for debate and hopeful enactment. There were also discussions about the bill with some members of the state executive, including the Governor, Bola Tinubu, but they were not favourably disposed to it.[18] As a result of this, Muslims in Lagos State took it upon themselves to set up what amounts to a private arbitration tribunal – the Independent *Sharī'ah* Panel (ISP) of Lagos State – to which Muslims are invited to submit their disputes for adjudication under Islamic law.[19] The Panel was formally inaugurated on 11th of December, 2002 at the Muslim Community Central Mosque in Abesan Housing Estate, Ipaja, Lagos.[20]

Further to the above was the establishment of ISP in Osun State which came later. Like in the earlier two states, Osun State Muslims also felt it necessary to have Sharia Court of Appeal established in their state. The Zamfara State initiative also gingered them into action. There were a lot of strategies which included setting up a committee to look at the modalities for establishing *Sharī'ah* courts, holding of series of lectures, symposia and rallies to express their interest and submission of memorandum by the leadership of League of Imams and Alfas of the State to Osun State House of Assembly in December, 1999 on the need to have *Sharī'ah* courts in the State.[21]

To further press home their demand, the Osun State Muslim Community, an umbrella body of Muslim Associations in the State, submitted a proposal for an amendment of the Law to incorporate the application of *Sharī'ah* or Islamic Law in the proposed District Customary Court and Customary Court Law of Osun State during the consideration of the District Customary and Customary Court Law Bill 2005 by the State House of Assembly.[22]

As it occurred in Oyo and Lagos States where positive results did not come from the government on the demand of Muslims to have *Sharī'ah* Court established, the situation in Osun State was not different. There was no positive response from the government despite all efforts made by the Muslim Community of the State. It was as a result of this that on Sunday 23rd April, 2006 ISP of the State was formally inaugurated at the Oja-Oba Central Mosque, Osogbo. The inauguration was attended by eminent Muslim personalities in the State including legal luminaries.[23]

The ISP established in each of the states mentioned above was constituted to have members who are learned in *Sharī'ah* or Islamic law. Lagos State ISP comprised members with a mixture of those who possess L.L.B. in Islamic Law from the Arab world and L.L.B. in Common Law and Sharia from Nigerian universities[24] and that of Oyo State comprised those with L.L.B. in Islamic Law from the Arab world and those who studied Islamic Law in Nigerian universities.[25] Osun State ISP is a little different in its composition as it is a mixture of the three. It comprised of those with L.L.B. in Islamic Law from the Arab world and those who studied Islamic law in Nigerian universities at the initial stage. Recently, however, a member with L.L.B. in Civil Law and Sharia was appointed to join them.[26] The ISP in each of the respective states started operation since the date of inauguration and continues to operate till date. It is worthwhile to discuss the *modus operandi* of the ISP.

Modus Operandi of ISP

The modes of operation of ISP in the three states are similar but with slight difference in some aspects. It is, therefore, necessary to discuss the modes of operation of ISP in general before discussing the areas of difference in the three states.

The ISP makes use of either a mosque or a secretariat of the Muslim Community in a state for sittings. Cases are, in the first instance, brought to the secretary/clerk of the ISP who stays in office from Monday to Friday. He makes the complainants to put their claims in writing for the purpose of proper documentation. The documents are signed and dated by the complainants who would be asked to produce witnesses to also sign and date the documents. The secretary/clerk then gives date of hearing of the case after submission of the duly signed documents to him while invitation is done through civil summon by letter in which date of appearance would be clearly stated.[27]

Three or four cases are heard at a sitting of ISP depending on the number of cases brought by people, but cases are attended to in the order in which they were filled. The complainant is invited to present his claim while the defendant would be asked to put up a defence. This implies that the claimant is given the opportunity to prove his or her claim while the defendant is allowed to confirm or deny it based on the tradition of Prophet Muhammad that says: "the onus of proof is upon the claimant, and the taking of an oath is upon him who denies."[28] Therefore, the hearing gives room for the parties to make claims and counter-claims and allows the witnesses to make their points as well. More so, the ISP carries out cross-examinations by asking various questions from the parties and the witnesses in order to shed light on the cases and guide in its judgement.[29]

Judgement is usually delivered after satisfactory hearing must have been made. The sources of reference of the panellists are the Qur'ān, Hadīth and the precedents or opinions of the early Islamic scholars and Imams. Although the language of proceedings is Yoruba, the judgement is usually written and typed in English or Arabic after every panellist must have stated his views on the cases and consensus must have been reached. However, whenever a judgement is to be delivered, the Chairman or the Presiding judge does it in the language in which it is written or in Yoruba to the hearing of the audience.[30] Judgement is not enforced on the parties. This is because the ISP has no authority or power to enforce its judgements. However, parties usually abide by the judgements because their appearance before the ISP is voluntary and they are convinced that it is the law of Allah that the ISP uses and whoever comes before the ISP should have decided to follow the injunctions of Allah as stipulated in the Qur'ān.[31]

Once the parties are before the ISP, the proceedings go on in mixture of the Yoruba and English languages and of Islamic and English legal forms. The proceedings are open to the public except, presumably, in very sensitive matters. In some cases, objections, applications, or motions based on Nigerian law may be made and argued and are ruled on in writing. Once the case proceeds to hearing on the merits, Islamic law and procedure take over and all the complex rules of procedure and evidence laid down in the Maliki books of Islamic jurisprudence (*fiqh*) for the disposition of various types of cases are now used.[32] In addition, the ISP adopts the principle of *takhayyur* and *talfiq* by using the views of other schools of thoughts when found necessary and useful.[33] *Takhayyur* is a selection of the relevant parts among the available rulings or opinions of different *madhāhib* (schools of thoughts) and piecing them together (*talfiq*) with a view to harmonising them into coherent and unified formulas for the purpose of legislation and enforcement.[34]

It is, however, necessary to mention at this juncture that the panellists or judges are active participants in the fairly informal hearings, questioning the parties and witnesses to get full views of all versions of facts. There is no court reporter or stenographer – the judges make their own hand-written records as the case unfolds before them. After hearing the case, the judges confer, generally reach agreement on proper disposition of the matter, and one of them is assigned to produce the lead judgement. This is written, formally explained and reasoned, with citations of appropriate authorities, typed up, captioned, signed, certified, and delivered to the parties, just like a judgement of the High Court. The other judges generally concur with the lead judgement.[35]

However, there are some few areas of difference in the modes of operation of the ISP in the three states. While the Oyo ISP sits every Thursday, Lagos ISP sits every fortnight and Osun ISP sits monthly on the first Thursday. Furthermore, Osun ISP seems to be a little different in writing its judgement using both Arabic and English but Lagos and Oyo ISPs make use of English only. One distinctive feature in the modes of operation of Lagos ISP is that it allows lawyers of the parties to appear before it to defend cases. This has not happened to Oyo and Osun ISPs.

The Osun ISP also has a different mode of operation by dividing its sessions into two – one for public enlightenment and the other one for sitting – which does not exist in the other two states. In the first session, lecture is given to the audience about various issues on *Sharī'ah*. This is done by one of the panelists within 40 – 50 minutes. Then that session is closed to allow for the second session which is hearing of cases.[36]

Jurisdiction of the ISP

The jurisdiction of ISP in the three states is restricted to civil matters of marriage, divorce, inheritance, custody of children, monetary disputes, mosque disputes, Imamship disputes, family disputes as well as disputes among Muslims either at inter-personal or inter-community level.[37] However, there were instances when both Lagos and Oyo ISPs were approached with a case of confession of *zina* – fornication which is criminal in nature. While Oyo ISP was tempted to handle the case, Lagos ISP rejected it on the ground that it had no jurisdiction. The two instances are briefly discussed here.

In Oyo State, one Sulaiman Shittu reported himself to the ISP on Thursday, 10th of October, 2002 confessing to have had a pre-marital sexual intercourse with a Muslim sister who was not his legal wife sometime in June, 2002 and requested that he should be punished according to the *Sharī'ah* so as to be saved from the severe punishment on the Day of Judgement. The ISP gave him the opportunity of reconsidering his confession. When on Thursday, 17th of October, and Thursday 24th of October, 2002 Sulaiman Shittu restated his readiness for punishment according to the *Sharī'ah*, the panel asked him to sign an undertaking in order to ratify his wish, and he did. As a result of this, the *hadd* punishment of hundred lashes of cane was given to him on Thursday, 31st of October, 2002 at Oja-Oba Central Mosque, Ibadan where the panel normally sits. The action generated huge hues and cries as well as condemnations by the local and international media.[38] Since that time the Oyo ISP has ceased to entertain any case outside civil matters.

Similarly, one Hamzat Ayeni applied to Lagos ISP to direct that a *hadd* punishment be inflicted upon him, having committed fornication. He emphasised to the panel that he earlier had repented but was of the opinion that until the *hadd* punishment of *zina* was inflicted on him, he would still remain apprehensive of the tormenting punishment of the hereafter. The ISP admonished the culprit but declined jurisdiction.[39] While delivering its judgement, the ISP explained *inter alia* that "… such offences are only punished by an Islamic authority and in Lagos State, the authority is un-Islamic, hence, entertaining criminal matters will only be an exercise in futility."[40]

Contributions of ISP to Judicial Development in Nigeria

With the existence of ISP for more than a decade and half, there is enough evidence to show that the ISP has directly or indirectly assisted both government and people, particularly Muslims, in the administration of justice and resolution of conflicts in the three states where it was established. The ISP has helped in no small measure in mediating on disputed matters among Muslims using alternative dispute resolution mechanism. Findings have shown that some individuals, government officials, judicial workers and legal luminaries who have had one interaction or the other with the ISP had commended its activities and attested to its contributions to the judicial system in Nigeria. In fact, there were instances when the judgements of the ISP were affirmed and held by conventional courts as true judgements. Some of these are explicated here with a view to showcasing the contributions of ISP to the development of judiciary in Nigeria.

According to Uwazie, common ADR project objectives include the decongestion of the court system, the creation of access to justice, promotion of peaceful out of court settlements, conflict prevention or de-escalation, and timely resolution of conflict.[41] The ISP could be said to have displayed these set of objectives in its operations. It has helped in decongestion of the court system and creation of access to justice in some ways. Different cases bordering on divorce, inheritance, custody of children, commercial disputes, disputes on religious matters, family disputes as well as disputes at both inter-personal and inter-community levels had been brought before the ISP and had been successfully administered. Therefore, as people patronise the ISP, it helps in the decongestion of the court system and dispensation of justice. As Adetona asserts, the Lagos ISP recorded an average of fifty cases annually which approximately give a total of seven hundred and fifty since inception.[42] The Oyo ISP recorded a total of eight hundred and sixty two cases[43] while Osun ISP has recorded a total of one hundred and fifty-three cases so far.[44] The table below gives a clear picture of the number of cases the ISP in each of the three states had handled:

S/N	State of ISP	Year of Establishment	Years of Operation	Number of Cases	Average of Cases per Year
1.	Oyo State	2002	15 years	862	57.4
2.	Lagos State	2002	15 years	750	50
3.	Osun State	2006	11 years	153	13.9

Source: The data collected by the researcher

The above table shows that Oyo State has the highest number of cases with an average of 57.4 annually, followed by Lagos State with an average of 50 annually and Osun State has the least with an average of 13.9 annually.

It has also been observed that the project objective of ADR on timely resolution of conflict is noted with ISP. This is in respect to prompt attendance to matters brought before it with a view to achieving justice without delay. Adetona unequivocally points to this fact while remarking on the role played by Lagos ISP on administration of justice thus:

> …the Lagos State Independent *Sharī'ah* Panel has helped tremendously in the administration of justice in Lagos State in a way faster than any of the institutionalised courts in Lagos. It had spent at most, less than three months to dispose of the most difficult case before it, and the minimum of a day in adjudication on matters. This affords those who presented themselves before it, the opportunity to have justice in good time in contrast to the prolonged period of time used in adjudicating of matters in conventional courts.[45]

The ISP has performed mediation roles in settling marital disputes which would have resorted to divorce. There were instances when cases of marriage dissolution brought before the ISP were handled in a manner that eventually led to settlement of the disputes amongst the disputing couples thereby sustaining the homes that would have broken.[46] The motivating factor is the Islamic injunctions discouraging divorce but encouraging reconciliation when dispute is noticed among couples. The Qur'ān proposes arbitration to a breach between couples if reconciliation is discernable[47] while a Hadith of the Prophet clearly points to the fact that the most hateful thing in the sight of Allah is divorce.[48] The ISP therefore explores these Islamic injunctions as a reconciliation mechanism in making disputing couples see reasons in settling for reconciliation rather than divorce. This has yielded results in some instances when marital disputes were amicably settled by the ISP.[49]

Based on the assertion of Uwazie that a well-designed and properly implemented ADR programme in Africa can provide the citizens with concrete and satisfied solutions to their disputes or complaints,[50] it has been noted that some disputants or parties whose cases were handled by the ISP were satisfied with the manner in which their cases were disposed. Ismaila mentions the situation when Oyo ISP received accolades and commendations from the general public, particularly Muslims and those who patronised it. He cites two instances when letters of commendation were written to Oyo ISP. The first was written by one Mr. Abdul-Rasheed Alawusa, the Director of Clean Print Industry, Challenge Area in Ibadan to the Registrar appreciating and commending the role of the ISP in resolving a dispute between him and Elewura-Challenge Muslim Community as a result of the refusal of the latter to observe the terms of a contractual agreement which the Community entered into. The second was from one Mallan Tajudeen Akintayo, the Oyo State Secretary of the National Council of Muslim Youth Organisations (NACOMYO) written to appreciate the manner by which the ISP settled a complaint which Mallam Tirimisiyu Oladipo brought against the leadership of the Ibadan Area Council of the Organisation.[51]

There were also instances when cases of Imamship tussles in some towns or communities were taken to the ISP for arbitration. It is apposite to make reference to the case of Imamship tussle at Ilu-Aro in Egbedore Local Government area of Osun State. It was a case between Oyedeji Subair and Alhaji Kazeem Abioye – Plaintiffs Vs Alhaji Jamiu Faleye – Defendant. The plaintiffs filed an application before Osun ISP claiming that the respondent be restrained from parading himself as Chief Imam of Ilu-Aro because of some atrocities he was alleged to have committed. The ISP took up the matter and while giving its judgement on the case, it analysed the allegations and gave its submission on each of

Chapter Four | Abdul-Fatah Kola Makinde, in
Y.A. Quadri, Omotoye & R.I. Adebayo (Eds)
Religion and Development in Nigeria
London, Adonis & Abbey Publishers

them. It finally submitted that the two disputants or parties should take the cause of reconciliation according to the *Sharī'ah*.[52] This was how the two parties were amicably reconciled and the matter was satisfactorily settled amongst them.

As the case of Imamship tussle reported above was amicably settled by the ISP, there were instances when parties in Imamship tussles did not agree to the judgements of the ISP and as a result proceeded to the conventional courts to seek redress. Our findings show that the courts that heard the cases eventually upheld the judgements earlier given by the ISP. It becomes pertinent to cite two of such cases here. The first case was the Imamship tussle of Obaagun Central Mosque in Ifelodun Local Government of Osun State between Alhaji Abbas Shittu and Alhaji Abdul Azeez Ibiyemi. The Olobaagun of Obaagun, Oba Jimoh Adebisi Okunade II appointed Alhaji Abbas Shittu as the Chief Imam of the town while a group led by Alhaji Raimi Animashaun, the *Mufassir* of the town said that the Oba had no right to appoint an Imam for them and as a result appointed Alhaji Abdul Azeez Ibiyemi as their Imam. Crisis therefore ensured in the town leading to the closure of Obaagun Central Mosque by the Police. The League of Imams and Alfas of Osun State under the leadership of the late Shaykh Mustafa Ajisafe intervened on the matter. The intervention necessitated referring the case to Osun ISP to look at it with a view to resolving it amicably. The ISP invited the two contending parties to present their claims. Four sittings were held by the ISP to listen to both sides before making a submission that Abbas Shittu is more suitable than Abdul Azeez Ibiyemi on the ground of knowledge and recommended the former as the Imam designate for Obaagun Central Mosque.[53]

However, when Animashaun group saw that the report of the ISP was not in their favour, they filed a suit at the High Court of Justice, Ikirun Judicial Division before his lordship, Hon. Justice S. O. Falola to further pursue their intention. Therefore, Olobaagun and Abbas Shittu became 1st and 2nd defendants in the case respectively. Among the claim of Animashaun and 9 others who were plaintiffs against the defendants in the case was that the post of Chief Imam of Obaagun Central Mosque is not part of the traditional chieftaincy titles or honourary chieftaincy titles of Obaagun; hence, they requested the court to give perpetual injunction

restraining the 2nd defendant from parading himself as the Chief Imam of Obaagun. In the cause of proceedings, the court invited the ISP and admitted its report as an exhibit. Thereafter, in the judgement delivered by Justice J. O. Falola on 10th April, 2014, the decision of the ISP was upheld. Delivering the judgement, Justice Falola said *inter alia*:
It is hereby ordered that, based on the exhibits tendered and admitted and the submissions made by learned counsels for the two parties, the court hereby upholds the decision of Sharia Panel on their two conclusions, that is:

a) That Abbas Shittu be and is hereby endorsed as the Chief Imam of Obaagun
b) That the matter is one of Sharia Law in which case this court lacks jurisdiction to entertain.[54]

The second was the case of Imamship tussle of the Central Mosque Isoko in Ejigbo Local Government of Osun State. It was between Jimoh Oyewole Erinkitola – Petitioner Vs Abdul Ghaniy Abdul Hamid – Respondent who were contenders for the Imamship position of the town. The petitioner filed an application at the ISP alleging that the respondent was parading himself as the Chief Imam of Isoko with the help of his collaborators who were joined as co-respondents in the case whereas he (the petitioner) was the appointed Chief Imam by the Muslim leaders and the Oba of the town. The resultant effects of their action led to the closure of the Central Mosque of Isoko by the Police leading to the observance of two parallel Jumu'ah prayers at different places in the town. The ISP did not only hear the case, it went further to conduct interview for both and paid visit to Isoko to listen to the sermons of both contenders in their different mosques with a view to determining the ability of each of them to be an Imam before it eventually gave its judgement. The ISP in its judgement of 2nd April, 2015 upheld the appointment of Jimoh Oyewole Erinkitola (the petitioner) as the Chief Imam of Isoko and ruled that Abdul Ghaniy Abdul Hamid (the respondent) be made the Deputy Imam so as to promote peace and unity in the town.[55]

The ruling of the ISP did not go down well with Abdul Ghaniy Abdul Hamid (the respondent) and his supporters; hence, they filed another application at the High Court of Justice, Ejigbo challenging the appointment of Jimoh Oyewole Erinkitola as the Chief Imam of Isoko. The Olasoko of Isoko, Oba Yinusa Oyebode Oyesala II and two others were defendants in the case. The judgement of Osun ISP was presented at the court and was admitted in evidence as an exhibit. Upon all, the judgement of the ISP was upheld as the judgement of the court. Hon. Justice J. O. Ogunleye who was the Judge of the case stated in his ruling delivered on 12th October, 2015 thus: "The judgement of Sharia Panel of Osun State dated 2/4/2015 is hereby made the judgment of this Court."[56]

It is clearly shown from the foregoing that the ISP helps in the administration of justice in the states where it was established and it is seen by some courts of justice as an alternative outlet that can help in solving problems on some judicial matters with a view to promoting judicial development of the country. In the judgement of a suit between Madam Ayisat Afinni (Applicant) and the President and members of Grade "B" Customary Court, Isolo Lagos State (1st Respondent) and Alhaji Jumat Owolabi (2nd Respondent) before a High Court of Lagos State in Ikeja, Lagos ISP was given due recognition by Hon. Justice O. H. Oshodi. The applicant applied for an Order of Certiorari to remove into the High Court for the purpose of being quashed the entire proceedings and judgement dated 23rd November, 2007 delivered by the Customary Court sitting at Isolo. One of the matters of contention in the suit was whether or not the Customary Court had jurisdiction to dissolve the marriage of the Applicant and the 2nd Respondent. The learned counsel to the 2nd Respondent contended that Islamic Law was part of Customary Law. The position of the Applicant was that her marriage with the 2nd Respondent was solemnised under Islamic Law and contended that the 1st Respondent lacked jurisdiction to have entertained the suit and thus sought an order of Certiorari to quash the entire proceedings and judgement.[57]

The judgement of Hon. Justice O. H. Oshodi of 6th November, 2008 was categorical about the fact that Islamic Law was not the same as Customary Law and recommended that the Lagos ISP was a place that could have been approached on the divorce matter. The judgement reads *inter alia* thus:

Before concluding this judgement, it must be placed on record that there exists in Lagos State Independent Sharia Panels. This fact should answer learned counsel to the 2nd Respondent's 'posers' as contained in clauses 401, 402, 410 and 413 of his submission. The 2nd Respondent should have approached any of these Panels with respect to his desire to dissolve the marriage.[58]

To further explicate on the contributions of ISP to the development of judicial system in Nigeria, it is also apposite to mention at this juncture the book published on selected judgements of Lagos ISP in 2005 by the Lagos State Chapter of Supreme Council for *Sharī'ah* in Nigeria titled: *Selected Judgements of the Lagos State Sharī'ah Panel* which was presented to the public on 5th February, 2005.[59] There is no doubt that such book has become a reference book in the annals of legal history in Nigeria. In fact a legal luminary, Prof. Auwalu H. Yadudu, who wrote the forward to the book, admitted that both students of law and practitioners will find it useful. He acknowledged the contributions of the Lagos ISP through this statement of his:

> What I have found most consoling and re-assuring is that, despite the absence of legal support, lack of official recognition, indeed in the face of official negation even, and the lack of material resources, the *Sharī'ah* Panel, encouraged, one must add, and urged on by the community it serves, has been able to run a judicial system which, in my estimation, be the envy of both Federal and State Governments, judging by the efficiency of its work ethics and processes, the soundness of the decisions reached and the mediation roles it has employed to settle disputes that will, in other official fora, take ages and enormous state resources to resolve, if at all.[60]

Another legal luminary, Justice Habeeb A. O. Abiru of the High Court of Lagos State in his comment under the preface to the book admitted that for the litigants to come voluntarily before the ISP and adhere to its judgements without the need for enforcement machineries underscores the fervent desire of Muslims in the State to guide their activities according to the dictates of *Sharī'ah*. He then noted that: "it is therefore imperative that the *Sharī'ah* Panels be made part of the structures of the system for the administration of justice in Lagos State to cater for this obvious need."[61]

Chapter Four	Abdul-Fatah Kola Makinde, in Y.A. Quadri, Omotoye & R.I. Adebayo (Eds) Religion and Development in Nigeria London, Adonis & Abbey Publishers

Conclusion

Religion, no doubt, plays a significant role in a nation's development not only in the aspect of spirituality but in other aspects of human endeavours. One of such is the role religion has played and is still playing in the legal development of any nation. More so, it is observed that "the nucleus of modernisation, which had helped transform the economies of the world's advanced nations into open and progressive societies, is a well-developed legal and judicial system."[62] Islam, through its law - *Sharī'ah* has contributed in no small way to the development of the legal system in Nigeria. In this chapter, attention was focused on the contributions of ISP to legal development of Nigeria using ADR mechanism. The historical circumstances leading to the establishment of ISP and the modus operandi for its operations were discussed. Going by different civil matters and various disputes at inter-personal and inter-community levels handled by ISP so far, it shows that Islam as a religion has various ways of contributing to the development of a nation. As much as disputes are settled among citizens of a country, there would be peaceful co-existence which would pave the way for development of that country. Hence, administration of justice which is paramount to the development of a nation is being dispensed by Islam through ISP using the mechanism of ADR. The commendations received from some individuals and legal luminaries testify to these contributions. It is therefore recommended that ISP should be made as part of the official structures of the system for the administration of justice in the states where it is established.

References

1. J. Lokulo-Sodipe, O. Akinola, and C. Adebamowo, "Legal Basis for Research Ethics Governance in Nigeria," in Introduction to the Legal System of Nigeria. www.learinng.trree.org/mod/page/view.php accessed April 14, 2017.
2. O. Duru, "The Role and Historical Development of the Judiciary in Nigeria." www.academia.edu/5185440/ accessed April 14, 2017.
3. A. Yusuf, "The Evolution of Ideal Nigerian Judiciary in the New Millennium."

yusufali.net/articles/the_evolution_of_ideal_nigerian_judiciary_in_the-_new_millennium.pdf accessed April 14, 2017.
4. Duru, "The Role and Historical Development…"
5. K. V. W. Stone, "Alternative Dispute Resolution." K. Stan (ed.), *Encyclopedia of Legal History* (Oxford University Press). Available at SSRN: https://ssrn.com 15th April, 2017.
6. HG.org Legal Resources. "Organizations Related to Alternative Dispute Resolution." www.hg.org/adr.html accessed April 13, 2017.
7. HG.org Legal Resources. "Alternative Dispute Resolution (ADR)." www.hg.org/adr.html accessed April 13, 2017.
8. *The Free Dictionary* www.legal-dictionary.thefreedictionary.com accessed April 13, 2017.
9. Cornell University Law School. "Alternative Dispute Resolution." www.law.cornell.edu/wex/ accessed April, 13, 2017.
10. A. K. Makinde, "An Assessment of Independent *Shari'ah* Arbitration Panel in Oyo State." In Y. O. Imam, R. I. Adebayo and A. I. Ali-Agan (eds.), *Dynamics of Revealed Knowledge and Human Sciences*, 1-35. (Ibadan: Spectrum Books Limited, 2016), 1.
11. A. K. Makinde, "An Assessment of Independent…", 15
12. A. K. Makinde and P. Ostien, "The Independent Sharia Panel of Lagos State." *Emory International Law Review*, 22 no. 11 (2011), 936.
13. A. K. Makinde, "The Evolution of the Independent Shari'a Panel in Osun State, South-West Nigeria. In J. A. Chesworth and F. Kogelman (eds.), *Shari'a in Africa Today: Reactions and Responses*, (Leiden: Brill, 2014), 91.
14. Makinde and Ostien, "The Independent Sharia Panel of Lagos State…" 921.
15. Makinde, "An Assessment of Independent *Shari'ah*…" 9.
16. B.R. Ismaila, "A Preliminary Study on Independent *Shari'ah* Arbitration Panel, Ibadan, Oyo State (2002 – 2009)." In M. A. Adesewo, F. O. Falako and R. I. Adebayo (eds.), *Religion and Rule of Law*, (Ilorin: NASRED, 2009), 507.
17. Makinde, "An Assessment of Independent *Shari'ah*…" 9.
18. Makinde and Ostien, "The Independent Sharia Panel of Lagos State…" 925.
19. Makinde and Ostien, "The Independent Sharia…" 921.
20. L. M. Adetona, "The Dynamics of Independent *Shari'ah* Panel in Lagos State, Southwest of Nigeria." *Journal of Nigeria Association of Teachers of Arabic and Islamic Studies*, 8 (2005), 31.
21. Makinde, "The Evolution of the Independent Shari'a Panel in Osun State…" 78-79.

Chapter Four	Abdul-Fatah Kola Makinde, in Y.A. Quadri, Omotoye & R.I. Adebayo (Eds) Religion and Development in Nigeria London, Adonis & Abbey Publishers

22. Makinde, "The Evolution…", 80
23. Makinde, "The Evolution…", 89
24. Makinde and Ostien," The Independent Sharia Panel of Lagos State…" 932-923
25. Makinde, "An Assessment of Independent *Sharī'ah*…" 11
26. Raji, Musa (58). Registrar of Osun State ISP. Personal Interview. 20 April, 2017
27. Makinde, "An Assessment of Independent *Sharī'ah*…"12
28. Imām Yahya An-Nawawī, *Matn al-arba'īn an-nawawiyyah – An-Nawawīs Forty Hadith*, trans. E. Ibrahim and D. Johnson-Davies, (Lebanon: The Holy Koran Publishing House, 1979), 108.
29. Makinde, "An Assessment of Independent *Sharī'ah*…" 13
30. Makinde, "An Assessment of Independent *Sharī'ah*…" 13
31. Makinde, "An Assessment of Independent *Sharī'ah*…" 13
32. Makinde and Ostien, "The Independent Sharia Panel of Lagos State…" 936
33. Adetona, "The Dynamics of Independent *Sharī'ah* Panel in Lagos State…" 32
34. Muhammad H. Kamali, "*Sharī'ah* and Civil Law: Towards a Methodology of Harmonization. *Islamic Law and Society*, 14 no. 3 (2007), www.jstor.org/stable/40377946 accessed October 31, 2016, 391
35. Makinde and Ostien, "The Independent Sharia Panel of Lagos State…" 936
36. Makinde, "The Evolution of the Independent Shari'a Panel in Osun State…" 91.
37. Makinde, "An Assessment of Independent *Sharī'ah*…" 15
38. Makinde, "An Assessment of Independent *Sharī'ah*…" 16
39. Adetona, "The Dynamics of Independent *Sharī'ah* Panel in Lagos State…" 35
40. The Lagos State Chapter of Supreme Council for *Sharī'ah* in Nigeria, *Selected Judgements of the Lagos State Independent Sharī'ah Panel*. (Lagos: Graphix Solution Suite, 2005), 40
41. E. Uwazie, "Introduction: ADR and Peace-building in Africa." In E. Uwazie (ed.), *Alternative Dispute Resolution and Peace-building in Africa*, (UK: Cambridge Scholars Publishing, 2014), 2, docplayer.net/26213003-Alternative-dispute-resolution-and-peace-building-in-africa.html accessed April, 28, 2017.

42. L. M. Adetona, "Dynamics of Islam in Post-colonial Lagos." The 59th Edition Lagos State University Inaugural Lecture Series delivered on 14th March, 2017, 46
43. Data supplied by Saheed Oyeniran, the Clerk of Oyo ISP on 28 April, 2017
44. Data supplied by Raji, Musa, Registrar of Osun ISP during Personal Interview on 20 April, 2017
45. Adetona, "Dynamics of Islam in Post-colonial Lagos…" 49
46. Raji, Musa (58). Registrar of Osun State ISP. Personal Interview. 20 April, 2017
47. Qur'ān 4 verse 34
48. Imām Ib Hajr, *Bulugh al-maram min adillāt al-ahkām*, trans. N. Eweiss (Egypt: Dar Al-Manarah, 2003), 396.
49. Raji, Musa (58). Registrar of Osun State ISP.
50. Uwazie, "Introduction: ADR and Peace-building in Africa", 4
51. Ismaila, A Preliminary Study on Independent *Sharī'ah* Arbitration Panel…518-519
52. Makinde, "The Evolution…" 95-96
53. See the Report of the ISP dated 16th June, 2011 with ref. no. OS/ISP/LP/OS/04/04/11
54. See text of the judgement of the High Court of Justice of Osun State, Ikirun Judicial Division delivered on 10th April, 2014 with Suit No. HIK/13/10.
55. See text of the judgement of Osun ISP delivered on Thursday 2nd April, 2015 with Suit No. OS/ISP/CV/12/090.
56. See text of the judgement of the High Court of Justice of Ejigbo Judicial Division delivered on 12th October, 2015 with Suit No. HEJ/3/2014.
57. See text of the judgement of the High Court of Lagos State, Ikeja Judicial Division delivered on 6th November, 2008 with Suit No. ID/852M/2007
58. The text of the High Court of Lagos State…
59. The Lagos State Chapter of Supreme Council of *Sharī'ah* in Nigeria, *Selected Judgements*…
60. The Lagos State Chapter of Supreme Council for *Sharī'ah* in Nigeria, *Selected Judgements*…i
61. The Lagos State Chapter of Supreme Council for *Sharī'ah* in Nigeria, *Selected Judgements*…iv
62. Banwo & Ighodalo "The Place of Law in National Development." www.banwo-ighodalo.com/asserts/grey-matter accessed April 29th, 2017.

| Chapter Four | Abdul-Fatah Kola Makinde, in Y.A. Quadri, Omotoye & R.I. Adebayo (Eds) Religion and Development in Nigeria London, Adonis & Abbey Publishers |

CHAPTER FIVE

Religion and Development: A Study of Developmental Dynamics of *Adamu Orisa* Festival in Lagos

Danoye Oguntola-Laguda
Department of Religions and Peace Studies
Lagos State University
Ojo, Nigeria.
danoyeoguntola@yahoo.com
+2348028030104

Introduction

The ambivalent nature of religion especially with regard to its political, economic and social values has over time engaged the attention of sociologists as well as scholars of religious studies. It has been established beyond reasonable doubt that religion has both positive and negative influence on its adherents. It can resolve and prevent conflicts just as it can lead to conflicts especially in environments and communities with more than one religious tradition (pluralism). The political and economic potentials of religion is therefore not in doubt. However, it can also retard economic and political development in any society. It is in this regard that J. Milton Yinger[1] and Emile Durkheim[2] established the positive values of religion especially within religious communities and groups. On the other hand, Karl Marx[3] underscores the negative values of religion. To him, religion retards political and economic development of the masses. He posits that political and religious leaders use religious tradition as a tool of oppression to control the mind of the people and force them into compliance.

This chapter's contribution to the book on religion and development is to examine the economic and tourist potentials of religion to the development of the Nigerian nation, especially to Lagos Island local government of Lagos State, one of the 36 federating states in Nigeria;

using the example of a traditional festival; the *Adamu Orisa* in an indigenous community in Lagos (Isale Eko). We shall examine the relationship between religion and development and evaluate the values of *Adamu Orisa* festival in Lagos. We shall conclude by highlighting the economic values of the festival among the people of Isale-Eko in particular and Lagos state in general.

Religion and Development in Scholarship

Ruben[4] established the relationship between academic study of religion and developmental studies using mission studies in Christianity as the basis of his analysis. In this engagement, Ruben was able to establish the underlying motivation for engaging in the interface between religion and development. His argument is argued based on his experience in liberation theology that the basis of development ethics with regard to persistent poverty and marginalisation of the poor and the less privileged. This is the basis of liberation theology which calls for redistributive and participatory development strategies from the perspective of the poor and oppressed. Historically, there has been a paucity in scholarship on the interaction between religion and social and economic development basically because of recent emphasis on secularity and secularism globally. In the opinion of Ruben:

> Gradually both discipline (religion and development) have been growing apart in subsequent periods where secular views of growth based development became dominant discourse and studies on the role(s) of religion in development only received marginal attention in the work of some devoted anthropologists.[5]

However, in recent time the situation has changed for the better. The ethical basis of religion has become the basis of social and economic development of communities, especially in Africa. In Nigeria, religion has become the key driver for socio-economic change. Thus, it becomes imperative in a religious dominated state like Nigeria to re-conceptualise the role of religion in supporting development and the emancipation process. In this regard, Ruben proposes (i) a more mature relationship between religious studies and developmental studies (ii) religion offers important protective devices against investment risk as it provides opportunity to take risks thereby becoming a transformative force. The effort requires a collective action that is usually based on a set of "shared identities" that provide a common sense of belonging.[6]

In Lagos state, faith based organisations play a critical role in providing communities access to basic services. This is common among Christian and Muslim communities. These groups are in abundance in Lagos and they act as efficient development brokers. Such is the case with Redeemed Christian Church of God (RCCG) and Nasrul Lahi-il Fathi Society (NASFAT) in Christianity and Islam respectively. These groups provide basic health care services to their members. They act as agents of human rights and provide platform for reconciliation and reconstruction after civic conflicts and violence. The cases of traditional religious communities and festivals have received less attention by scholars compared to the cases of RCCG and NASFAT.

Scarlett Epstein posits that religion of the people needs to be studied in relation to the development of the society. He cited the example of how Hinduism is shaping the development of India. To him religion should be seen as spiritual capital that has the capacity to mould the social, political and economic development of communities and states. He writes inter-alia:

> The number of micro-level social anthropological studies is continually growing. Many of these (studies) concentrate on what to the economists may appear odd aspect of society such as ritual and religion... and to which he pays little or no attention for instance, and understanding of the complexity of Hindu religious beliefs as they operates at village level... as directly relevant to the problems of developing India's economy. This is but one example that can be quoted to support the claim that development economists work in the dark unless they acquaint themselves with the relevant socio-political literature.[7]

The basic implication of Epstein's submission above is that a good understanding of the dynamics of the economic values of traditional religion is necessary to appreciate the economic and social as well as political development of the communities, states, as well as the nation. This is the case with Yoruba Traditional Religion (YTR) that provides the basis for all engagements of the people. Consequently, the need to evaluate the socio-economic and political values of traditional festivals like *Adamu Orisa* festival in Lagos cannot be over-emphasised.

Several theories have been advanced on the link between religion and development. However, I will mention only two relevant to our discussion in this chapter. There are theories that typify the rational choice approach to religion and development. These theories consider the resilience of religion as a rational economic response to changes in the political, ecological and economic environments where religion operates. Structural theories use family socialisation, social network and a belief in other worldly supernatural elements. These have been the focus of all historical works on the link between religion and economic development. Thomas Aquinas, Joseph Schumpeter, Jacques Le Goff, Marx Weber are notable works in the historical context. Aquinas work in *Summa Theologica* is relevant for poverty alleviation while Schumpeter argue that purgatory was a necessary religious innovation for medieval capitalist development. Marx Weber in his *Protestant Ethics* suggests that development is based on protestant ethics, which is ethics of liberation and freedom to economic development and empowerment based on capitalism.[8]

From the Nigerian perspective, the basis of studies on religion and development have focused on efforts of faith based organisations (FBOs) to respond and appropriate the Nigerian social, economic and health situations by applying the tools of modern economic analysis to formulate programmes for the development of their religious communities and members' empowerment. Such is the case of RCCG's economic empowerment programme for widows, NASFAT's programmes on Human Immunodeficiency Virus Infection and Acquired Immune Deficiency Syndrome (HIV/AIDS), and Catholic Church of Nigeria's programme on HIV/AIDS that provide retroviral drugs for members who test positive to HIV/AIDS. My investigation has revealed (based on my studies of various traditional religious groups in Lagos) that traditional religious groups have no defined programmes for development of their communities as well as members. However, during notable traditional religious festivals like the Osun Osogbo festival and Adamu Orisa in Osogbo and Lagos respectively, the communities are enveloped by serious economic engagements that have

Chapter Five	Danoye Oguntola-Laguda, in
	Y.A. Quadri, Omotoye & R.I. Adebayo (Eds)
	Religion and Development in Nigeria
	London, Adonis & Abbey Publishers

led to development of the immediate communities where the festivals take place as well as, the Nigerian nation as a whole.

The Adamu Orisa Festival

What is often seen and known about the Adamu Orisa festival are the white robed masquerades that parade Lagos on the festival day. The religious rituals are often known only to the initiates. The sociology of this festival has generated various political and economic implications for the traditional politics, economy, and tourism in Lagos. Lagos State Government has at various occasions underscored the tourist potentials of the Adamu Orisa festival and has invested heavily on it. During the festival, socio-economic activities in Lagos are always at a climax. Lagosians get temporary employment (trading, crafting and weaving) as additional sources of income thereby making the festival a source of social and economic capital, contributing to the development of the state and that of the indigenous settlement known as Isale- Eko.

We shall raise issues for the politics and economics of Lagos with the thesis that traditional festivals have the potentials to generate social and economic capital for the people and the state while not neglecting the spirituality of such festivals.

Adamu Orisa Traditions

The Adamu Orisa is a deity or divinity in the sparsely populated Lagos pantheon. The origin of the deity is shrouded in obscurity. The general belief among the people is that it was brought into Lagos pantheon from the ancient Benin Kingdom (this was the subject of a survey I conducted among the people in 2013 with the use of questionnaires, more than 75% of the respondents agreed with this position). All attempts to corroborate this claim have so far proved abortive. There is no trace of any deity or masquerade that possesses liturgy, traditions and patrons like the Adamu Orisa in Benin presently. According to the late custodian of the deity, Taorid Ibikunle (Akinsiku of Lagos), the deity was brought into Lagos by Apena Ajasa. Its first stop was at Oke Ipa. Apena Ajasa brought *Adimu* and *Awo Opa* (a secret society) to Lagos. The former was located at Ita

Ado while the latter was at Irele (the meeting place of the group near Erelu square Isale Eko). Adamu is worshipped every fifteenth day- *Itadogun*.[9]

There are two types of Adamu Orisa. The Adimu is the female while Ogunron is the male. These two deities were worshipped in conjunction with other deities at OkeIpa before they were brought to Lagos. One of the others is *Erikina* (a deity akin to Èṣù also known as elégbá in some Yoruba communities) This deity is synonymous with evil. This will explain why its worship has today receded into the background, but has not been completely forgotten. Ogunron is still being worshipped but is more expensive to propiate and appease. Elements of worship include; Ẹlẹ́dẹ̀ (pig), Ògógóró (local rum); pẹ́pẹ́yẹ (duck); adìẹ (cock); àgbò (ram); epo (palm oil); omi (water); obì (kolanut); efun (local chalk); atare (alligator pepper), among things. In the 18th century, the Adamu Orisa became a socio-cultural festival in Lagos.[10]

This play, which derives its name from the deity, is often performed in honour of dead prominent Lagosians. It must be announced by the reigning monarch (Eleko, the king of Lagos) who, through his lieutenants, will contact the custodian at Ita Ado in the Ologun Agan's compound. He sends gifts to the cult known as *Ikaro*. It often includes all elements of worship of the deity and money to assist the *aborè (Akinsiku)* to prepare for the festival.

The parade of the deity is now attached to the Eyo masquerades. These masquerades are clad in white apparels (*agbádá, àrópaḷe* and *ibòjú*). With a designed brown staff known as *Opànbata*. Tradition of the origin of the Eyo differs from that generally held about Adimu Orisa. Eyo is said to be from Ibefun, a town in Ogun State, southwest Nigeria.[11]

However, the masquerade has undergone some modification both in its apparels and paraphernalia. The Eyo at Ibefun does not have *aropale* (wrapper) neither does it use *Ape* (otherwise known as *keremesi*, the royal cap used for the coronation of title chiefs and king of Lagos) and *Opanbata*. They instead use *Irukere* (horsetail) and ordinary cap of wool material. According to Taliat Akinlaja (Ologun Atebo of Lagos), the change is based on the belief of the founding fathers that it is more honorable to greet with the *Opanbata* than *Irukere*, and the *aropale* is imperative to preserve the myth of the masquerade as *araorun*[12] whose body must not be exposed. The *Ape* is to underline its affiliation to the royal cult of the king of Lagos.

The Eyo are to provide protection for the Adamu Orisa during the festival. Therefore, all Eyo must take cue from the cult of Adamu at Ita Ado. There are many Eyo groups. They are differentiated by the colours and adornment on their *ape*. As at 2012, when the last festival was held, there were about 56 Eyo groups. Out of this number, five are considered to be the paramount groups. These are: Eyo Adimu (attached to Orisa Adimu), Eyo Okanlaba (also known as *Alakete pupa*), Eyo Oniko (attached to *Orisa Oniko* a masquerade that is claimed to have its origin among the Ijebu in Ogun State), Eyo Ologede (attached to *Orisa Ologede* also a deity worshipped like Adimu at the Olugbani cult in Lagos very close to Ologun Agan at Ita Ado) with Eyo Agere making up the number. All these groups have specific duties to perform with regard to the festival. Orisa Oniko is to ward off all impending evils before the festival; *Orisa Ologede* is to pray for peace and progress of the land. *Orisa Agere* is to pray for material blessings and fertility of women in the land. *Alakete pupa* has no Orisa, but play the role of police during the festival. They are to report any dissident groups to the Adimu cult for proper sanctions.

The Adamu Orisa must visit all sacred groves in Lagos for ritual purposes. The *Abore* must also carry out some functions at specific groves in the course of the festival. He leads the cult party to *Agodo* to carry out the early morning ritual known as *Ikido*. The deity dances to *Arigo* drum sets at Agodo, from here he proceeds to *Imoku* where the *Igbe* drum set are on display (The *Igbe* drum is accompanied with a dirge during the Eyo Festival, but it sometimes could be used as praise song for prominent Lagosians. It is predominantly played by women who have reached menopause).

At Enu Owa, Adamu Orisa pays obeisance to *Erikina* and also greets Orisa Oniko at Alagbeji. It is compulsory that the deity makes a stop at the Oba's palace at Idugaran, after which he can then proceed to visit all other prominent Lagosians. In the morning, Adamu Orisa must visit Oju Olokun and Abegede for ritual purposes before all other ritual sites mentioned above.

The importance of Adamu Orisa festival in Lagos cannot be over-emphasised. In fact some indigenes of Isale Eko, make it a duty to partake in the festival. It is a male cult but women, wives and daughters of the family of Eyo groups, often escort the masquerades with praise songs and cognomen. It also forms part of the coronation process that must be done for a deceased king by the incumbent king. The festival is used as purification for the land. This demonstrates its social-economic dimensions. During the course of the festival, prayers are offered for peace, progress and prosperity of the town.

Traditions of Origin of Adamu Orisa in Lagos History

There are various traditions on the origin of Adamu Orisa into Lagos pantheon. These traditions had generated a lot of political conflicts, sometimes with fatal consequences. It has also affected the political structure of Lagos viz-a-viz, economic empowerment of some families in Lagos. In this regard, there are two major traditions and another two which could be subsumed under the broad categories. We shall now examine these traditions:

Ologun Agan Tradition

The Ologun Agan is the present custodian of the deity. They claim that the deity belongs to them. In fact, it was brought to Lagos by Apena Ajasa from Benin. It made its first stop at Oke Ipa, a town at Ikoyi, on the outskirts of Lagos. Ajasa being the Apena of Osugbo and leader of the Awo Opa fraternity in Lagos brought the deity to Ita Ado (as an acquired divinity from the Benin pantheon) where it is presently domiciled. It was brought alongside other deities like Erikina, Ogunran and Esu among other deities. These deities are worshipped at Oke Ipa every fifteenth day (Itadogun). At Ita Ado, Adamu Orisa is presently in the custody of Ologun Agan family under the leadership of Akinsiku who is the *Abore* and Ologun Atebo, the white cap chief in the family. In recent time Ologun Agan has also been made a chief in this regard. It is interesting to note that it is from the compound of Ologun Agan that Adimu Orisa makes its appearance. According to Chief Taliat Akinlaja, the Ologun Atebo of Lagos, Adamu Orisa had from inception in Lagos being in the custody of his family under the control of its priests *Abore*, known as Akinsuku[13] This claim was denied by the Ogunmade tradition on the origin of Adimu Orisa in Lagos.

Chapter Five | Danoye Oguntola-Laguda, in
Y.A. Quadri, Omotoye & R.I. Adebayo (Eds)
Religion and Development in Nigeria
London, Adonis & Abbey Publishers

The Ogunmade Tradition

One of the families in the struggle for the *"custodianship"* of Adimu Orisa is the Ogunmade family. They trace their origin to Benin. They claim it was their fore bearers that introduced Adimu Orisa to Lagos. The tradition is that, Ejilu and Malaki came to Lagos from Benin on commercial ventures. These brothers are hunters and fishermen. They came with their younger sister Olugbani during the reign of King Ado in Lagos. They settled at Iduntafa. Olugbani then a maiden, married king Ado with her brothers' consent. However, for a long time, she could not procreate. The King consulted Ifa, and was directed to appease and propitiate the deities of Olugbani family in Benin. On the directive of the king, Ejilu and Malaki travelled to Benin and brought back four deities. These are Adimu, Ogunran, Oniko and Ologede. They were all stationed at Oke Ipa (This story was corroborated by Chief A.B. Akinlagun[14] as published in *Lagos Weekend*, of 12th December 1986, but Benin was substituted for Ibefun in Ogun State of Nigeria).

After the appeasement and propitiation of the deities, Olugbani conceived and gave birth to Erelu Kuti (a female). Erelu gave birth to two children, Ologunkutere and Sokun. Ologunkutere later became a king in Lagos in the mid 18th century while his brother Sokun was made Ogboni Iduntafa, now known as Onilegbale of Lagos. Hitherto, king Ado had made Ejilu the first Onilegbale of Lagos. He was succeeded by his brother Malaki on the stool. Malaki had no children, but Ejilu had three children, i.e. Kulugbe, Olasoro and Ibiye Oroye. Ibiye Oroye, a lady, married the king of Ibefun and gave birth to Ogunmade. Ogunmade later became the Ogboni Iduntafa. It was Ogunmade that brought Eyo to Lagos from Ibefun (his patrilineal home) to celebrate the funeral of his maternal uncle Sokun. From then till date, Adamu Orisa, Oniko, Ologede and Ogunron were merged with Eyo as a socio-cultural festival in honour of kings, royal personae and prominent indigene of Lagos at funeral.

With the demise of Ejilu the four deities were distributed among his three children, as follows:

Oniko - Kulugbe
Ologede - Olugbani/Olasoro
Adimu and Ogunran - Ogunmade (the son of Ibiye Oroye)

It was Ogunmade that gave Adimu and Ogunron to ApenaAjasa family at Ita Ado for custody due to the influence of Islam and Christianity that had entered Lagos. The former was prominent in the Ogunmade family.

The two traditions cited above are the major oral history surrounding the origin of Adimu Orisa deities in Lagos pantheon in league with other deities earlier cited. It points to the origin of Eyo and how it became a socio-cultural festival in Lagos. The Ogunmade tradition put the political stool of Onilegbale of Lagos (also known as Ogboni Iduntafa) into contention. According to them, their maternal ancestor, Ejilu, was the first Ogboni Iduntafa, a title given to him by King Ado in appreciation of his role as his in-law and the part he played during the attempts to make Olugbani procreate (This was the story of the Ogunmade family in their attempt to claim the custody of the chieftaincy of Onilegbale in Lagos.[15]

This story was refuted by Chief Akinlagun, the Onilegbale of Lagos who reigned till 1987. Thus we have the *"Akinlagun tradition"*. This tradition in an attempt to explain why Ogunmade was never Ogboni Iduntafa, and the origin of Adimu Orisa and other deities mentioned above as well as the Eyo masquerade in Lagos.

The Akinlagun Tradition

King Ado had three children, Gabaro, Akinsemoyin and Kuti (the last being daughter of Olugbani). The two sons had at various times succeeded their father on the throne of Lagos, while Kuti was the first Erelu of Lagos. She had two male children; Ologunkutere and Sokun Ologunkutere succeeded Oba Akinsemoyin while Sokun was installed as Ogboni Iduntafa. Thus, Sokun was the first Ogboni Iduntafa (not Ejilu as claimed by Ogunmade tradition). It was Ejilu and Malaki that brought Eyo to Lagos from Ijebu Ibefun, their homeland (this also is against the position of the Ogunmade that they are from Benin). The Eyo masquerade was brought to Lagos to perform the final funeral rites of Olori Olugbani. The Eyo was stationed at a village at Oke Ipa under the supervision of the Ogboni Iduntafa and his attendants. Eyo usually travelled from Oke Ipa to Lagos for funeral ceremonies (a claim refuted and rejected by Chief Taliat Akinlaja, the Ologun Atebo of Lagos, that Eyo had never been to Oke Ipa because, it is a taboo for Eyo to cross any river).

The other deities associated with the Adamu Orisa play in Lagos were brought into Lagos from different places but not from Benin (as claimed by the Ologun Agan and Ogunmade traditions). The Adimu and Ogunran were brought to Lagos by Ejilu and Malaki from one of their visits to Oyo Ajaka (old Oyo Empire). The Oniko was introduced to the Lagos pantheon by Sogbo from Ajase in Badagry area of Lagos. It explains its resemblance to Sangbeto. Ologede was brought by Lawani a son of one of Olugbani's slave from Iloro, a village on the outskirts of Lagos in present day Victoria Island. Laba (Okolaba) was brought to Lagos from Ijede as a gift to Sokun by his friend. The Agere was introduced to Eyo play by one Bante Sheda, who resided beside Oju Olobun, on Dosumu Street in Lagos. He denied the indigeneship of the Ogunmade and preferred them to be identified as Ijebu Ibefun people. Thus they have no claim to any stool in Lagos political history and structure. (This may not be correct as maternal lineage is often used in Lagos traditional politics to determine the right to the throne and stool of the ancestors).

The summary of Akinlagun tradition with regards to Adimu Orisa is that while Eyo is from Ibefun, Adimu was from Oyo Ajaka, but was brought to Lagos pantheon by Ejilu and Malaki. This goes to support the Ogunmade tradition as to the ownership and source of both *"Adimu pantheon"* and Eyo masquerade in Lagos. This will confirm that Akinlagun tradition only seeks to demonstrate that the Ogunmade has no claim to the stool of Ogboni Iduntafa (Onilegbale of Lagos).

The three traditions so far mentioned are the contending traditions on the attempt to reconstruct the oral history of the Adamu Orisa play in Lagos traditional culture and religion. Although there are other traditions, like the Igbesodi and Olugbani traditions, their claims are akin to those of the Ogunmade and Ologun Agan's traditions. While Igbesodi toe the line of Ologun Agan, Olugbani support the Ogunmade tradition.

Adamu Orisa Festival and Development in Lagos

With the date of the festival announced, all indigenous people of Isale-Eko take advantage of the festival to engage in economic and social activities that often bring income to the people. Such activities include weaving of the *Iboju* (veil) for the masquerades. This requires a special skill at weaving of Yoruba traditional cloths known as *aso-oke*. This is made from heavy yarns that are imported from Northern Oyo towns of Iseyin, Igboho and Okeiho. The *iboju* weaving creates immediate employment for the female folk. Youth and the young at heart go to the forests to cut the staff of the Eyo masquerades. These staffs are known as *Opambata*. They require a special skill for them to be crafted into beautiful staffs. Adults give such training to the youth who then make income from the sales of the staffs after beautifying them with designs. The average income from the sale of staff is above 5million Naira as at the last festival in 2012. The white robes used by the Eyo groups are also business for local market women who are into the business of clothing. As mentioned above, the rituals for the festival take days to come to maturation. During this period ritual elements such as goats, pigs, dogs, cow, local rum, palm oil, kola nuts, and bitter kola among other items always have their best sales.

The Adamu Orisa festival also comes with its unifying value. All members of ruling house where Eyo comes out for parade are united in the efforts to ensure a successful outing for their Eyo groups, although, it can be argued that they do this for financial benefits that comes with the staging of the festival. The Lagos state government invests heavily in the Eyo festival anytime it is performed. All Eyo groups are funded by the state through the Eleko. Such funds are often shared out among members of the family after the festival. In spite of this observation, the unifying value of the festival cannot be over emphasised. The Chief Mustapha Bajulu, a member of the Onigemo family, said that over 200 members of the family scattered all over the Country and the Diaspora, return home for the festival.[16] According to Wasiu Junaid[17] a member of the Olorogun Adodo family, Eyo festival is a good time to meet members of the extended family who are not resident in Lagos. They come in good number to be part of the festival. It is a period when some Lagos indigenous families fix meetings of unification.

Chapter Five	Danoye Oguntola-Laguda, in
	Y.A. Quadri, Omotoye & R.I. Adebayo (Eds)
	Religion and Development in Nigeria
	London, Adonis & Abbey Publishers

The most important development value of the Eyo festival is in its tourism and cultural values. The tourist potentials of the festival have also been identified by the Lagos state government. Since 2009, the festival has been re-organised to include a parade by all Eyo groups at a designated space to showcase the beauty of the Festival to non-Lagosians and tourists from outside Nigeria who are interested in Festivals. An official number of how many tourists visited Lagos during the festival is not readily available at the Lagos state secretariat but unconfirmed reports suggest that over 10,000 tourists from Nigeria and beyond witnessed the Eyo festival in 2009 as spectators at the parade group of all Eyo groups at Tafawa Balewa complex in Lagos. The culture of the indigenes of Lagos Island of the state also comes to play. In this regard various sets of drums are brought to the fore. These include the *Arigo, igbe, gbedu* drum sets. These drums play various roles during the festival as earlier mentioned above. The gbedu drum sets are specially for the Eleko and his royal family. But visitors to the Kings palace are also welcomed with it. It should be noted however that other modern drum sets have been introduced into the musical mix of the festival. These include the *Dundun, Bembe* and *Gangan* drums, *Sekere* as well as trumpets of various kinds and shapes. Jazz drums are also on display. Various Eyo groups deploy these drums during their parades all around Lagos and during the formal display at the parade ground for all Eyo groups. Various dances are attached to the various drum sets. The dance *to arigo* drums at *the Agodo* is not the same with the dance at *Imoku* where the igbe drums are played.

The period of the festival also increases the business of hotels around Lagos Island. During my count, over 50 hotels are on Lagos Island. All are often booked to capacity during the festival. In fact, during the 2012 festival the Manager of Hotel Lawa on Igbosere street, claimed that the hotel was fully booked a week before the festival.[18] Local food vendors are also in business. Sea foods, which are the focus of traditional Lagos food, are very much on sale. Crab, prawn, fish, among other sea foods are prominent. Alcoholic beverages are also sold in large quantities.

For the festival, Lagos state government has had reasons to embark on road construction as part of the preparation for Adamu Orisa festival. Such roads have opened up links to the community and have increased economic and social activities. Health service delivery by the state government also goes on the increase during the festival. This is to cater for the health needs of both the masquerades and the spectators. It should be noted that some of these developmental projects do not stand the test of time, but some have remained part of the community development projects even till now.

From the above discourse on the developmental values of Adamu Orisa festival, it is obvious that the festival is an identity for indigenes of Isale Eko as it provides for them a common sense of belonging as Ruben suggested.[19] It further strengthens the submission of Epstein when he posits that religion provides a form of "spiritual capital" that moulds sociology, politics and economic development of a nation.[20] In the case of Adamu Orisa, the festival has over time become an avenue for cultural, economic, political and tourism development of Lagos state. It should be mentioned however that Faith based Organisations (FBOs) are not common in African Traditional Religious groups but the available festivals can provide opportunities for the people to be economically engaged as discussed above. The Lagos State government has often used the festival to promote the tourism potentials of the state and its cultural values. While it could be argued that the festival is limited to the people of Lagos Island, its unifying value for all "Lagosians" in the Diaspora cannot be over emphasised.

Conclusion

In this chapter we have demonstrated how the Adamu Orisa festival has brought development to Lagos state in the area of tourism, small scale businesses, and the show case of culture of the people. We have also shown how the festival has impugned on the businesses of Lagos indigenes. Although, we observed that in as much as tourists want to see the Eyo festival for its fun fare and cultural values, there are some aspects of the festival that are against the spirit of the cosmopolitan nature of Lagos. Isale Eko which is the epicentre of the Eyo festival is home to one of the biggest pharmaceutical markets in Nigeria (Idumota medicine market). During the festival, pharmacists are forced to lock up their shops. Further, Non-Yoruba elements in Lagos Island often vacate the area for fear of violence that often occurs from rivalry among Eyo groups.

Chapter Five	Danoye Oguntola-Laguda, in Y.A. Quadri, Omotoye & R.I. Adebayo (Eds) Religion and Development in Nigeria London, Adonis & Abbey Publishers

References

1. Emile Durkheim, *Elementary Forms of Religious Life* (London: George Allen and Unwin, 1912), 201.
2. J.M, Yinger, *Religion in Struggle for Power* (Durham: Duke Press, 1946), 212
3. Karl Marx, A Contribution to the Critique of Political Economy, in *Collected Works of Karl Marx and Frederick Engels*, 29, (1984), 233
4. Ruerd Ruben, Can Religion Contribute to Developments? The Road from Truth to Trust" in *Exchange*, 40 (London: Brill Press, 2011), 225.
5. Ruerd Ruben, Can Religion Contribute to Developments? The Road from Truth to Trust, in *Exchange*, 40 (London: Brill Press, 2011), 226.
6. Ruerd Ruben, "Can Religion Contribute to Developments? The Road from Truth to Trust" in *Exchange*, 40 (London: Brill Press, 2011), 230.
7. S.T. Epstein, *South India: Yesterday, Today and Today*. (London: Macmillan, 1973), 6.
8. M. Weber, *The Protestant Ethics and the Spirit of Capitalism* (London: George Allen and Unwin, 1904), 148
9. Oral Interview with Taorid Ibikunle (Akinsiku of Lagos) Age: years, at Ifa Ado Isale-Eko, Lagos.
10. *Lagos News newspaper*, (Lagos: June 30th 1988), 13
11. *Lagos Weekend Newspaper*, (Lagos; December 12th 1986), 18
12. Interview with Chief Akinlaja Taliat, Olorun Atebo, (Age 78, at Ita Ado, Isale-Eko 2005).
13. Interview with Chief Akinlaja Taliat
14. R.A. Ogunmade, and Yole Dabiri, The Ogunmade Brought Eyo to Lagos, in Lagos Weekend, (February 13th, 1987), 8
15. Interview with Adio Ogunmade (65 years, Lagos: Amuwo Odofin, 2005).
16. Interview with Mustapha Bajulu (54 years, Bajulu of Lagos, 2014).
17. Interview with Wasiu Junaid Eko, an Indigene of Isale-Eko (2014).
18. Interview with Hakeem Onilegbale (65 years, Isale Offin, Lagos Island, 2014).
19. Ruerd Ruben, Can Religion Contribute to Developments? The Road from Truth to Trust" in *Exchange*, 40, (London: Brill Press, 2011), 230.
20. S.T. Epstein, *South India: Yesterday, Today and Today*, (London: Macmillan, 1973), 6.

ORAL INTERVIEW

NAMES	VOCATION	AGE	LOCATION
Akinsiku, Isiaka	The Abore (Priest) of Adamu Orisa	89	IsaleEko
Akinlaja, Taliat	White Cap Chief, Lagos.	75	IsaleEko
Late Ogunmade, Adio	A member of Ogunmade Family	78	IsaleEko
Akinlagun Family	Anonymous	74	IsaleEko
Sanni, Habeeb	Academic	52	Ojo, Lagos
Jinadu, Musliu	Chief Onilagbale of Lagos	78	IsaleEko
Mustapha Bajulu,	Chief Bajulu of Lagos	54	Isale Eko
Wasiu Junaid-Eko	Indigene of Lagos	50	Isale Eko
Hakeem Onilegbale	Indigene of Lagos	65	Isale Eko

Chapter Five | Danoye Oguntola-Laguda, in
Y.A. Quadri, Omotoye & R.I. Adebayo (Eds)
Religion and Development in Nigeria
London, Adonis & Abbey Publishers

CHAPTER SIX

The Role of Muslims in Healthcare Service Delivery in Nigeria

Rafiu Ibrahim Adebayo
Department of Religions,
University of Ilorin,
P.M.B. 1515,
Ilorin, Nigeria.
adrafhope@yahoo.com or rafiu@unilorin.edu.ng
+2347035467292

Introduction

Knowledge of medicine seems natural to all cultures and civilisations, as it is natural to seek treatment for any ailment. However, a cross-fertilisation of medical knowledge was facilitated through interaction between people of different cultural and civilisational background. It is not therefore a surprise that when the Muslims came in contact with the ancient Greeks, they drew heavily on the medical heritage of the Greeks, as they translated their works into Arabic. They were motivated into taking this step through some medical-related Qur'ānic verses that speak on health, food, milk, honey, plants, physical and spiritual cleanliness, and standing on the fact that all that are in heavens and the earth are made subservient to man to discover and made beneficial for their wellbeing (Q. 22:65; 31:20; 45:13). The exploration of the Qur'ān and ahadith of the Prophet became useful data for the Muslims to embark on medication using different products and plants for the welfare of human beings.

The spread of Islam to what now constitutes Nigeria made what can be called Islamic mode of healing became introduced to the area. Indeed, wherever Islam went then, it went with its healing method which was used to heal many people and also rescue many communities which were facing communal feuds and raids then. One area where religion has influenced Nigeria generally is in the area of health care services. Ever before the advent of colonial masters and before the establishment of conventional hospitals in Nigeria, Nigerians had traditional means of healing themselves. This they did through different means one of which was taking lives of innocent animals and that of human beings in the name of sacrifice to appease gods to ward off the spirit of certain ailments like small pox. With the introduction of Islam, the early Muslim clerics performed wonderfully well in curing different ailments believed to have been magically inflicted by witches and other unholy spirits. Indeed, some towns in Yoruba land embraced the new religion by virtue of the efficacy of the prayers and spiritual assistance rendered by Muslim clerics not only to individuals but also to towns like Osogbo, Ede, Ikire and Ede in Osun State.[1] It is on this basis that this chapter intends to assess the role of Islam in the development of health-care services in Nigeria with a view to appreciating the extent of Muslims' involvement in the sector.

Muslims in the development of Healthcare centres in Nigeria

The role of Muslims in the establishment of hospitals in Nigeria cannot be underestimated. Their nasty experience in the hand of those who use their hospitals for evangelical purposes forced many of them to wake up from their slumber and rise to the task of establishing their own hospitals. The Ahmadiyyah[2] Muslim group established Muslim hospitals in different states of the federation. For instance, there is the Ahmadiyya Muslim Hospital in Ifako-Ijaye Lagos, the Ahmadiyya Muslim Hospital in Ijebu-Ode, the Ahmadiyya Muslim Hospital in Apapa, Lagos State, the Ahmadiyya Muslim Hospital in New Bussa and the Ahmadiyya Muslim Hospital in Kano. In 2016 alone, over 200 patients were said to have got free eye treatment in the Kano branch of the Ahmadiyya Hospital. Other Muslim organisations in the country have also shown concern for the good health of Nigerians. For example the Ansar-Ud-Deen Society has one clinic in Lagos and one hospital in Oyo. Also in Lagos, the Madaniyyah Women Muslim Hospital was recently opened on 28th February 2016. It is an all-female Muslim hospital established to check the degrading and inhuman treatment meted out to Muslim women in

Chapter Six	Rafiu Ibrahim Adebayo, in Y.A. Quadri, Omotoye & R.I. Adebayo (Eds) Religion and Development in Nigeria London, Adonis & Abbey Publishers

public hospitals.³ There is also the Solace Hospital in Lagos established by The Muslim Congress.⁴ In Oyo State, there are KLM Muslim Hospital, Agodi, Ibadan; the Muslim Hospital in Ogbomoso and Saki Muslim Hospital in Oke-Ogun area of Oyo State. In the northern part of the country, there are the Muslim Specialist Hospital, Zaria; the Jama'atu Nasril Islam (JNI) Muslim Hospital, Kaduna; Kubwa Muslim Community Hospital; As-Sunni Hospital in Maiduguri; FOMWAN Hospital, Kaduna; TATBIQ Hospital in Kinkinun, Kaduna; ITAM Hospital of the International Islamic Relief Organisation, and the Islamic National Hospital for Women and Children, Garki, Abuja[5] to mention but a few.

It needs to be mentioned that Muslims have been taking a drastic measure to address cases of insanity resulting from demonic possession. Some psychiatric hospitals and centres are being managed by Muslims using different forms of *ruqya*.[6] Dagimum identifies some centres established by Muslims in Kebbi and Sokoto states. They include Rahmaniyya Islamic Medical Center in Kebbi State with branches in the nooks and crannies of the state, Al-Huda Nasara Islamic Herbal Center, and other Muslim individual *Ruqya* practitioners like Malam Lauwali Gidan Jodi and Malam Yahaya, Ibn Sina, and Malam Shehu in Sokoto.[7] Jimoh also identifies such hospitals in the South-western part of Nigeria. They include the *Ihya'u Sunnah* World-wide Nigeria Limited Agege, Lagos and the Heritage Islamic Hospital, Ibadan under the directorship of Alebiosu and Ismail respectively.[8] This effort of Muslim exorcists has greatly influenced treatment of mental illness and it has complemented the efforts of the few existing psychiatric hospitals which are sparsely located in Yaba, Lagos; Aro in Abeokuta; Enugu, Kaduna, Sokoto, Maiduguri, Calabar and Oselu in Benin City and other few psychiatric departments in Teaching hospitals in Nigeria.[9]

Apart from establishing hospitals, Muslims have taken it upon themselves to organise different health-related programmes to sensitise the people of the need to be conscious of their health. This takes the form of organizing health talks, conferences on health and visitation to hospitals. For instance, more than 800 indigents were said to have benefitted from the NASFAT Agency for Zakat and Sadaqat (NAZAS)'s healthcare programme which was organised in collaboration with the

Nigeria Islamic Medical Association of Nigeria (IMAN) to give free medical service to the less privileged in the society in February 2017.[10] The beneficiaries of the programme were provided with screening treatment, health education and distribution of drugs administered by experts including pharmacists, physiotherapists, radiotherapists, medical laboratory scientists, nurses, midwives, gynaecologists, paediatricians and opticians. The motive for organising such a programme is succinctly mentioned by the organisers of the programme in the following sentences:

> We realise that in our society it is not everybody that would be able to afford medical care in private hospitals or can go through the rigours of our health care institutions. The purpose is to bring it to the doorsteps of the people living in rural areas so that they can benefit. Not only that, but for them to know and understand their health status and, in case we discover some health issues that we won't be able to handle here, we give them referrals to the doctors (some of them are here). Again, as an organisation, we will foot the medical bills of those that are beyond the reach.[11]

Corroborating the above motive, one of the conveners of the programme, Dr. Mustapha Alimi, opines that the essence of the programme is to combine prayer with creating enlightenment programmes to people on how to take care of their health and to propagate Islam through health programmes. He concludes:
Let Muslims know that there are medical doctors in Islam and also to encourage our members to aspire to be medical doctors. We give them talk on health and social, educate, enlighten and provide free health services to people. The whole idea is that if we have people who need help we refer them because it is an outreach programme. For me, it has been wonderful touching lives.[12]

Additionally, scholars in Nigeria have influenced the health sector through their writings. Among those identified by Elisha Renne are Abdullahi Dan Fodio, Muhammad Bello and Muhammad Tukur. While Muhammad Tukur emphasised prayer as the primary source of prevention and cure, Abdullahi Dan Fodio maintained that the health of the body itself was akin to a form of prayer, as well as the need to consult physicians who were knowledgeable about medical treatments and professed Islam as their religion. The condition of religion as a condition for visiting a physician is against the submission of Tukur who believed that some useful medical information from a non-Muslim practitioner was allowed.[13] Apart from various medical debates on healing, there are many prayer books written by some scholars on different ailments and the appropriate prayers to combat them. Among such prayer books in Yoruba land are *Iwe Adura Iwosan to Daju* which contains the *Hirsu a-Rih al-Ahmar al-Kubrah* which the author claimed is meant for curing stroke and such ailments which can lead to dumbness and deafness, for poverty alleviation and opening of good fortunes.[14] There is also another prayer book titled *Adua Ajebi-ina – Lakun Dinukun* which contains prayers on various ailments – mental, physical and psychological medication.[15] The *Du'ah al-Ghayat al-Maqsudat al-Kubrah* authored by Alhaji Abdul-Azeez Ahmad Balogun al-Ilawy al-Adabiyy, also contains the usage of some Qur'ānic chapters for healing purposes.[16]

Methods adopted by Muslims in the healthcare delivery

To get sick is natural in the perspective of Islam and this is why palliative measures are put in place for Muslims who are ill in the discharge of their religious rituals. Such a Muslim is allowed to observe his prayers in postures convenient for him, and he is not expected to observe the obligatory Ramadan fast as well.[17] Health in the record of Islam goes beyond absence of disease or infirmity; rather, it encompasses complete physical, mental and social well-being. It therefore puts in place some preventive measures for mankind to remain healthy. The Qur'ān in the first instance warns man to abstain totally from anything that can lead to his destruction among which self-medication, drug abuse and indiscriminate sexual affairs fall. The Qur'ān describes adultery as abomination and an evil way (Q17:32) and so outlawed it not only to avoid sexually transmitted diseases and AIDS, but also to sanitise man biologically and psychologically.[18] It also enjoins moderation in the consumption of food and drinks (Q7:31). Islam further enjoins adequate rest after stressful daily works (Q28: 71-73). In addition, it enjoins total abstinence from unlawful things like consumption of pork and intoxicant liquors. The prohibition of consumption of pork is an effective antidote against some diseases as confirmed by Glen Shepherd cited by Sadiq and Dikko who write:

One in six people in the USA and Canada has germ in their muscles – trichinosis from eating pork infected with trichina worms. Many people so infected have no symptoms. Most of those who do have, recover slowly. Some die. Some are reduced to permanent invalids. All were careless pork eaters…. No one is immune from this disease and there is no cure. Neither antibiotics or drugs or vaccines affect these tiny deadly worms. Preventing infection is the real answer.[19]

In the same vein, whoever is accustomed to taking alcohol stands the risk of being infected with liver cirrhosis, peptic ulceration, oesophageal varices, acute panereatitis, peripheral neuropathy, heart problem and damage to the fetal in addition to other socio-physical and physical problems like marital tension, sexual offences, road accidents and insecurity of the offspring of the drunkards.[20]

In addition to the above, Muslims generally keep to the ethics of sanitation and hygiene most especially before observing *ṣalat*; they perform ablution which involves washing of hands, face, feet and other parts of the body. Muslims are also expected to observe their prayers in clean and hygienic environment in addition to cleaning their body and cloth. They are also cautioned against urinating in standing or stagnant water to avoid contaminating or polluting water and so guard against water borne diseases like guinea worm, schistosomiasis, urinary bladder infections and diseases of the liver among others.[21]

However, taking preventive measures does not imply that one would never fall sick. When sickness comes, Muslims are expected to seek treatment and take medication. The Prophet of Islam is reported to have said: "Take medication, for Allah never creates a disease except that He creates its cure."[22] He further warned against using medicine prepared from *haram* source, as Allah will not make *haram* substance a cure.[23] As such, Muslims have delved into some medicinal herbs recommended by the Prophet; some of which are lemons and antimony. The sour citrus from which lemon juice is produced is good for the treatment of diarrhoea and it expels all bilious diarrhoea and palpitations, while antimony is recommended by the Prophet as the best eye medicine which glorifies the sight and makes the eyelashes grow.[24] In addition, Adesina gives an elaborate explanation of the use of honey as taught in the Qur'ān 16:69 and some traditions of the Prophet. Such include the use of honey for treatment of painful menstruation, sore throats, fever, blockages of the liver bladder and kidney, hair care, cough, lice and small pox, dental care and gum protection.[25]

The Prophet's declaration that there is no disease that Allah has sent down except that He has also sent down its treatment,[26] prompted some Muslims to delve into some medicine prescribed by the Prophet to heal some diseases and illness and some mentioned to be efficacious in the Qur'ān. Some of the medicinal plants mentioned in the Qur'ān are *safarjal* (Quince), *basal* (Onion), *tin* (figs), *zanjabil* (ginger), *kafur* (camphor tree), and *laymun* (lime). In Nigeria, some Muslim clerics are noted to be specialists in the field of Prophetic medicine. Some of the products used by these people are *habbatus-sauda* (black seeds) used for treatment of genito-urinary infections, infertility, and hypertension; garlic used for lowering of blood pressure and cholesterol, fighting infections and preventing cancer; *miswak* which is meant for checking mouth diseases, aids the process of digestive function and serves as remedy for headaches. The efficacy of the prophetic medicine has been confirmed by those who are acquainted with its use.

Islam realises the fact that some illness could be averted and healed using prayers and supplication. There are instances of this in the Qur'ān where some prophets were afflicted with certain health challenges and with fervent prayers, such challenges were overcome using the spiritual means of supplication. It suffices to cite the following Qur'ānic passages in respect of Prophets Ayyub and Zakariyā:

> And Ayyub (Job), when he cried to his Lord: "Verily distress has seized me, and You are the Most Merciful of those who show mercy." So We answered his call, and We removed the distress that was on him, and We restored his family to him (that he had lost) and the like thereof along with them as a mercy from Ourselves and a Reminder for all those who worship Us… And Zakariyā when he cried to his Lord: "O My Lord! Leave me not single (childless), though, You are the Best of the inheritors." So We answered his call, and We bestowed upon him Yahya (John), and cured his wife (to bear a child) for him. Verily, they used to hasten on to do good deeds, and they used to call on Us with hope and fear, and used to humble themselves before Us (Q. 21: 83-90).

The above quotation is an indication that some health challenges could be solved or checked spiritually. The case of Ayyub is an indication that with divine intervention through supplication, one's health could be restored while lost estate could be regained.[27] From personal experience, this author witnessed the case of a woman who was in the labour room for many hours. When her husband was informed that the woman would be delivered of the baby through caesarean operation, he quickly rushed to members of his religious organisation for spiritual assistance. These people withdrew to a temporary mosque in the hospital premise and during the process of the prayer; the woman successfully delivered the baby without any operation.

However, some scholars have come up with prayer books in different languages and on different ailments with various prayers prescribed to face them. It is however observed that some of these prayer books contain various un-Islamic invocations like calling the names of jinn and other prescriptions that are alien to Islam.

Another means of solving health problem through prayer is exorcism *(ruqya)*. This is performed by the experts in the field to deliver victims of spiritual attacks through the use of some verses of the Qur'ān and other substances prescribed by the Prophet. Apart from using *ruqyah* to treat those who are possessed by jinn, it is also used to treat snake or scorpion bites. Different methods are adopted by exorcists in carrying out the *ruqyah* Islamically. These include removing the charm or untieing the knots, commanding the jinn to leave in case of demonic possession, cursing the jinn if he refuses to leave the patient, reciting some Qur'ānic chapters and verses, using some medicinal fruits and the taking of a bath for the possessor of evil spirit.[28] Other orthodox means adopted is placing the right palm directly on the head of the victim before reciting some Qur'ānic chapters and verses into the right ear of the patient. Additionally, different other methods are adopted by Muslim exorcists to carry out their professional duty. Jimoh, who has written extensively on exorcism, explains some of the methods thus:

> In addition, ingredients such as the black seed *(Habbatu 's-Sawda')* and *Al-titi* may be ground together in powdered form and burnt as incense in the presence of the possessed who is covered with a thick cloth so that he really inhales the fragrance of the incense. With this, the demon may be chased away. The sick may also be given to drink

undiluted fresh cow milk for upward of twenty-one days while the verses of exorcism are read inside (sic) water. Twenty-one fresh lotus leaves *(Sidr)* are ground together and poured in the water before the recitation. The sick takes three sips of the water and bath with the remaining. This process continues for a period of twenty-one days. Other ingredients that this category of Muslim exorcists use include; *Zaytun, Turabi 'l-Misk, 'Anbar, Siwak Madinah, Tamar Ajwat, Safran, Zamzam Water, Khali Tufa', Sha' 'Sh-Shayatin, Dukhan 'sh-Shayatin*, honey, *Bukharu 'l-Jinn*, etc.[29]

Apart from the above, Jimoh further identifies some practices of the exorcists in Yoruba land, such as asking the patient to sit on a mortar and carry a copy of the Qur'ān on his head while some Qur'ānic chapters are read on him for a prescribed number of time; squeezing fresh *odundun* leaves, and applying the juice and *zaytun* (olive oil) on the fontanelle of the sick. Others include writing some Qur'ānic chapters and verses on wooden slate and washing such in form of *hantu*, with fresh *ajeobale* leaves squeezed in a bowl and then asking the patient to drink it.[30] Exorcists in the northern part of Nigeria equally use some methods peculiar to them. Such include use of certain herb or substance for the patient to inhale, which they believe are harmful to the jinn, and playing *ayāt* of the Qur'ān and other supplications on an audio recorder among others.[31] Whatever the case may be, it is crystal clear that Muslim exorcists have contributed immensely to healthcare delivery in Nigeria. Many stubborn diseases and ailments which could not ordinarily be treated by orthodox medicine practitioners have been addressed and healed by the exorcists.

Another means of healing among the Muslims in Nigeria is the art of writing on wooden or iron slate using a kind of ink called *tadaa*, and washing such writing for the patient to drink or to rub on his body. This is popularly called *hantu*. In most cases, the writing on the slate involves drawing what is called *Khatimi* or *waqf* which is making of the required invoked selected prayers into a summarised diagram form (see fig. 1). It is *khatim* when the contents written inside the table are in letters while it is *waqf* when such letters are translated to figures (See fig. 2).[32] *Khatim* or *waqf* takes different shapes and forms some of which are as indicated below.

ه	ل	ل	ا	م	س	ب
م	ه	ل	ل	ا	م	س
د	م	ه	ل	ل	ا	م
د	د	م	ه	ل	ل	ا
ن	د	د	م	ه	ل	ل
ا	ن	د	د	م	ه	ل
ب	ا	ن	د	د	م	ه
س	ب	ا	ن	د	د	م
م	س	ب	ا	ن	د	د

Fig. 1 An example of *Khatimi*

Source: Culled from *Kitab Ismullah al-A'tham liltukhi fi Muntada as-Sarh ar-Ruhani* retrieved from asarah.arab.st/t105-topic on 15/4/2017.

١٤٣٦	١٤٩٢	١٤٩٨	١٤٧٥	١٤٣٩
١٥٢	١٤٥	١٤١٩١	١٤٤٥	١٤٤١
١٤٩٤	١٤٥٧	١٤٢٩	١٤٥١	١٤٢٩١
١٤٤٧	١٤٩٥	١٤٥٣	١٤٥٥	١٤٩١
١٤٨٤	١٤٤٩	١٤٥٨	١٤٥٩	١٤٩٧

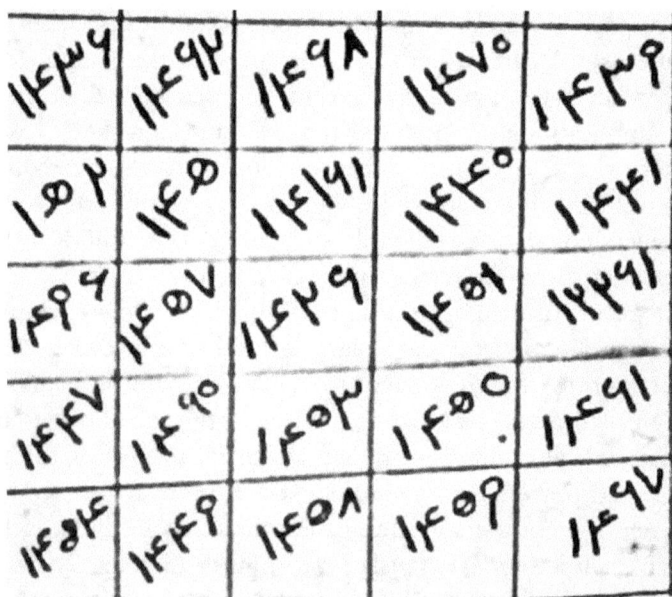

Fig. 2: A Sample *waqf* culled from bodediop.wordpress.com/geomancie-africaine-3/comment-page-4/ accessed on 15/4/2017.

At times, ingredients such as honey, salt, are added to the washed liquid to enhance the efficacy of the *hantu*. Although, the use of *hantu* for healing purposes has been condemned by some scholars, those who adopt this method of healing rely on some sayings of great Muslim theologians for practising it. For instance, Ibn Taymiyyah submitted that it is permissible to write something from the Qur'ān with ink made from allowable substances for the afflicted or sick and that the writing may also be washed and drunk.[33] In our own view however, what is written, how such is written, and the ingredients added to the *hantu* will determine the permissibility or otherwise of this practice. For instance, writing a name other than that of Allah, like names of jinn, or adulterating verses of the Qur'ān for the purpose; use of ink prepared from forbidden source, and adding substances which are not Islamically permissible, make *hantu* unlawful. This submission is made in conformity with the tradition of the Prophet which says that Allah will not make haram substance a cure.[34]

The Motivating Factors for the Muslims' involvement in healthcare services

Historically, Africa is a land where superstitious beliefs reign and where witches and other spirits are believed to be controlling many lives. Africans therefore constantly patronise and consult herbalists and oracle diviners to get their problems solved and to peep into what the future has in stock for them.[35] Awolalu and Dopamu admit that Africans used magic negatively to cause the death of their assumed enemies using invocations and incantations. Poisonous things like snakes or scorpions could be sent by sorcerers to attack their victims and that sorcerers could use the practice of bad magic called *'èpè'* – curse, to cause their target to become insane or even commit suicide and could also use their evil power to attack their enemies with thunder. Refuge therefore needed to be sought in those whom they believed possessed spiritual powers so as not to be victims of the sorcerers and witches.[36] With their acceptance of Islam, they shifted to Muslim clerics *(alufa or aafa)* whom they believed possessed spiritual powers to heal their ailments and prepare for them charms against the attack of evil spirits. A Muslim cleric was therefore a herbalist in the garb of an Islamic scholar. He thus used this power to attract people to the new religion. Closely related to this is the acceptance of Islam by some people who had the knowledge of traditional healing before their acceptance of Islam. Such people used their previous knowledge of traditional healing to treat their patients under the pretext of Islam. They could not be totally exonerated of syncretism as they mix traditional healing system with that of Islam. That notwithstanding, some factors could be responsible for the Muslims' involvement in healing either in the traditional Islamic ways or the conventional orthodox method.

One of the motivating factors for the Muslims' involvement in healing services is the Qur'ān which is considered the source of healing in Islam. The Qur'ān for instance describes itself as a source of healing and mercy to believers (Q17: 82) and as healing for the diseases of the heart (Q.10:57). Not this alone, some verses of the Qur'ān mention the use of some substances as containing curative power and efficient in healing some ailments. Particular reference could be made to honey which the Qur'ān describes as a healing for mankind (Q16: 68-69). Indeed, the Qur'ān allows chemotherapy in form of experimentation with herbs and other plant and animal products. It also allows psychotherapy in form of stabilising one's mind so that belief and acceptance of the curative methods are concretely established; and surgical therapy which is a healing system in form of cutting or dissecting a section of the body. These instances in the Qur'ān are considered a source of inspiration for healing of different methods adopted by Muslims in the field.

Closely related to the above is that the Prophet in many of his sayings enjoined Muslims to look for the cure of any form of ailment bedevilling them. He was said to have prescribed honey for a patient suffering from irregular bowel movement and he got cured after administering it repeatedly.[37] In *Ṣaḥīḥ Bukhārī*, it was reported that 'Ā'isha, a wife of the Prophet recommended *At-talbina* (a kind of porridge prepared from honey, milk and white barley flour) for curing certain ailment.[38] The *hadith* also gives the efficacious use of some Qur'ānic verses to heal certain illness. It cites an instance where *Sūratul-fātihah* was used as *ruqya* for treatment of snake bite.[39]

Furthermore, the past records of Muslims' achievements in the field of medicine and health care generally served as a motivator for Muslims to be involved actively in healing services. In the history of Islam,

Muslim scientists and physicians had played significant role in developing healthcare practices, tools and ethics, all which are still relevant to this day. The Umayyad Caliph Al-Walid (705-715CE) was said to have established institutions for lepers and the blind in Damascus while the Abbasid Caliphs ventured into establishing hospitals in the caliphate and First Aid stations were established near mosques. There were military hospitals, city hospitals, mental hospitals, jail hospitals and female hospitals.[40] Prominent among such hospitals cited by Adebayo were the Nuri Hospital in Baghdad (1154C.E), Monsuri Hospital in Cairo (1279C.E), Adudi Hospital in Baghdad (981 C.E) and Marakiah Hospital in North Africa (1200C.E).[41] In view of the numerous contributions of Muslims to medical discoveries, it is written:

> The field of medicine would not have gone far in the Islamic world without the dedication of Muslim scholars who made numerous advances and discoveries that have enhanced our understanding of healthcare. Muslim physicians, for example, were among the first to differentiate between smallpox and measles, as well as diagnose the plague, diphtheria, leprosy, rabies, baker's cyst, diabetes, gout and haemophilia. While Europe still believed that epilepsy was caused by demonic possession, Muslim doctors had already found a scientific explanation for it. Muslim surgeons were also pioneers in performing amputations and cauterisations. They also discovered the circulation of blood, the use of animal gut for sutures and the use of alcohol as an antiseptic. Other Muslim innovations include surgical instruments and glass retorts, as well as the use of corrosive sublimate, arsenic, copper sulphate, iron sulphate, saltpetre and borax in the treatment of diseases.[42]

Despite the above remarkable contributions of the Muslims to the health sector, the Muslims, influenced by some internal problems amongst them coupled with other external challenges went into a state of slumber and so relented in their struggle to make positive impacts in the medical line. They therefore relinquished their medical achievements to Europeans who also tried to erase the Muslims' impacts in the field to give false impression that they were the harbingers of modern medicine. They transmitted the knowledge acquired from the Muslims to many parts of the world. In Nigeria, the Christians were noted to be in the forefront in establishing hospitals. As far back as 1705, the RCM had established a 60-bed hospital in the kingdom of Kororofa, while the CMS Hospital was established in 1905 at Iyi-Enu near Onitsha.[43] This step taken by them was aimed at using healing for evangelisation and Christianisation purposes. The Muslims therefore have no option than to come up with their own medical options or else they stand the chance of sacrificing their faith in the name of healing and medication.

In addition to the above, the Muslims were motivated to make their impacts felt in the field of medicine and the establishment of health centres because of the hard and bitter experience they suffered in the hands of Christian medical personnel. In other words, series of exposure of Muslim patients in the hospitals owned by the Christians and even public hospitals mainly dominated by Christian personnel in terms of embarrassment and harassment ranging from asking pregnant or nursing Muslim women to sing and pray in the Christian ways, to asking them to remove their hijab, forced the Muslims in Oke Ogun side of Oyo State to establish the Muslim Hospital in Shaki in 1974.[44] It has to be noted that Muslims have greatly suffered some sort of discrimination in public hospitals dominated by Christian personnel and those privately owned by them. Such hospitals were used as a ground for conversion of Muslims through sermon and gospel preaching to Muslim patients while those who resisted the preaching received low attention from the veteran evangelical nurses. It was also observed that Muslims' bills were higher than those of Christians while caesarean births were much more common with Muslim women than with Christians.[45] Buttressing the last point with personal experience, Olayiwola narrated how his wife was admitted to a state-owned hospital in Iseyin, Oyo State and the nurses, all Christians, told her that she required prayer to deliver safely. With the refusal of the husband to grant the prayer, he was told that his wife would be delivered of the baby through a Caesarean section which could only be done at a Catholic hospital – Our Lady Hospital. Surprisingly however, the wife shortly gave birth to a baby girl. He therefore concluded:

> If I had allowed them to pray, that birth would have been a miraculous feat resulting from their prayer. If I had surrendered and taken her to the suggested hospital my innocent wife would have had to undergo

unnecessary sufferings spend some time nursing unnecessary wound and spend the remaining part of her life carrying unnecessary scar that could be a harbinger to one or two more of its kind – courtesy of EXTREME RELIGIOUS MALICE.[46]

The above is another instance of abusing religion and how it is being used to create unnecessary vendetta. Should the blame be on religion or its practitioners who refused to take to the teaching of that religion?

Another notable factor for Muslims' active involvement in healthcare services is the high rate of health challenges facing people many of which could not be healed in the hospital but through spiritual means. In a public lecture delivered by the Chief Imam of the University of Ibadan, Professor Abdurrahman Oloyede, he narrated the experience of a boy who used to fall sick during examinations and who dreamt one day that a heavy load was put on his head. The boy was said to have been taken to a *Mallam* who wrote some verses of the Qur'ān on a wooden slate *(Hantu)*, and gave it to the boy to drink for some days and since then he did not have such a dream again and did not fall sick during examinations any longer.[47] According to Jimoh, economic recession, marital disappointment, frustration, and loss of job have forced some youths into engaging in criminal acts, such that they become addicted to drugs and resort to demonic rituals which eventually culminate in psychiatric disorder for many of them. They thus become mentally deranged, emotionally imbalanced and behaviourally irrational. Such demonic possessions are mostly being taken to psychiatric hospitals, and for scarcity of such hospitals, some Muslims who have knowledge of *ruqya* for healing established their own hospitals using different forms of *ruqya*.[48]

Apart from the above, the Nigeria health delivery system is facing a lot of problems. The problems could be smelled from three different sectors that have to do with the personnel in the field, namely the qualified, the semi-qualified or quarks, and the traditional healers. Nigeria is no doubt in short supply of qualified medical personnel. This explains why unprofessional and quack people parade themselves as professionals dabbling into various health issues that do not fall within the scope of their shallow medical knowledge. Dwellers of the rural areas have nasty experience of the operation of these quacks who apart from prescribing fake, contaminated and expired drugs, also engage in abortion and illegal operations. Apart from fake and unqualified doctors, there is the problem of the professionals in the health sector. These are medical personnel who do not believe in any other means of healing than the orthodox medicine and so look at other means of healing with contempt.

The problem of the traditional healers is their prescription of sacrifices which in many cases lead to *shirk*. The perception of the orthodox medical personnel and the idolatrous prescriptions of traditional healers have been proved wrong by the Islamic healing methods. Many Qur'ānic and Prophetic medical prescriptions have been proved potent and are so practised by Muslims in the field. The patronage of the Prophetic medicine practitioners by people of different faiths therefore motivate them to enquire further on this type of healing and to probe further into means of integrating this into conventional medicine using various diagnosis instruments.

Challenges Facing Muslim Practitioners in the Health Sector

Hiding under the pretext of healing, some Muslim practitioners have consciously and unconsciously fallen into *kufr* through the method adopted by them which are mostly syncretic. Balogun observes that some *Aafa* in Yoruba land are fond of adulterating Qur'ānic verses, writing names of jinn, using blood or urine as ink; combining Qur'ānic texts with traditional medicine; using intoxicants, blood, urine, dead animals or part of human body as *gaari tira*.[49] Jimoh and Opeloye also cite an instance where faeces of sheep is dried up, ground and used as ingredient for a patient to drink.[50] In addition, some go to the extent of invoking spirits chanting incantations, preparing black soap mixed with some ingredients like alligator pepper, leaves and tuber of different plants; preparing pomade using live tortoise and live hen burnt together to ashes and then mixed with shear butter *(ori)* or palm-tree oil *(adin)*. Some are so syncretic that they take their clients to a stream or a crossroad for bathing exorcism believing that the spirit in the stream or at the crossroad will heal the sick.[51] Such a practice is no doubt against the teaching of Islam on healing, as it has been clearly mentioned by the Prophet that no treatment is inherent in unlawful means. It also amounts to desecrating the Glorious Qur'ān. As if this practice is not restricted to the Yoruba

Muslim clerics, Balogun further cites the submission of Shaykh Uthman ibn Fodio on the practice of those he referred to as apostates in the following words:

> Among them (i.e. apostate) is one who claims that he is a Muslim performs acts of Islām and yet, he writes the Qur'ān and the names of Almighty Allah on filthy objects such as dead people's bones or the head of a dog (or its bone, live or hunting one) or he writes the Qur'ān or the Names of Almighty Allah with blood spilled during slaughter or he writes the Qur'ān or Allah's name and then washes it with water, then shreds a snake's slough and mixes it with the water (the water may be sewn into an amulet).This one too is an unbeliever who is not subject to the rules of Islām.[52]

The above is an indication that some Muslim clerics who take to healing may end up becoming syncretic and may even lead their clients to *kufr* through their prescriptions and practice. In such a case, some un-Islamic practices creep into Islam, giving Islamic colouration, and whereas they are anti-Islam and unorthodox.

Another serious challenge is the general belief that Prophetic medicine is all-effective, efficacious and so has no side effect. What is certain is that what is effective for a person may not be so for another person. This is however not noted by some Prophetic medicine practitioners who prescribe the same medicine for different ailment and without taking note of the side effects of such medicine. For instance, garlic is known to be effective in lowering blood pressure and cholesterol, fighting infections and preventing cancer;[53] yet it can prolong bleeding and can cause bad breath, body odour, diarrhoea and burning sensation in the mouth or stomach. Raw garlic might also cause skin damage.[54]

Closely related to the above is that many of the practitioners do not actually diagnose the body system of their clients. They only listen to their complaints and prescribe drugs they feel could cure the ailment. Those practitioners do not also take precautionary measures in handling some cases. They do not know the health implication of what they are prescribing not only on their clients but also on the practitioners themselves. For instance, it is observed that those who work with garlic are susceptible to asthma and other allergic reactions.[55] It therefore becomes imperative for practitioners of Prophetic medicine to be acquainted with modern healing system for them to give correct diagnosis, precise dosage and become familiar with means of avoiding contagious diseases so that in their bid to treat patients they do not become infected with such diseases.

One other challenge of Muslims' involvement in healing is that many of them do not follow Islamic etiquettes while carrying out their healing activities. Some do not observe the Islamic teaching of isolation when treating people of the opposite sex. Such people are prone to sexual intimacy which is against the spirit of Islam. Some do not also abide by the standard set for hygiene, as their consultation rooms are mostly dirty, untidy and unkempt.

On the part of the existing Muslim hospitals in Nigeria, it has been observed that a major problem facing them is dearth of medical personnel. Some Muslim hospitals are on the verge of closing down due to lack of adequate personnel to manage them. It got to a stage that a Christian was appointed as the Medical Director of the Muslim Hospital in Shaki. In a situation like this, hardly can a hospital function in line with the teaching of Islam when the head himself is a novice in that direction.

Conclusion

So far, we have attempted to study the roles played by Muslim organisations and individuals in the development of the health sector in Nigeria. Apart from the efforts made along the development of the orthodox medicine and healing, they have been influenced by Islam to come up with alternative Islamic therapy which has proved potent and effective and through which many have become relieved and totally healed of their ailments. It is our hope that Muslims would continue to strive in the direction of healing through pure Islamic manner and would shun those practices which have no root in Islam in their practice. They are equally expected to improve on the quality of their medical services by applying some conventional methods of diagnosing their clients, so that appropriate prescription would be made. Finally, Muslim schools and universities need to rise to the task of encouraging more Muslim children to study medicine and related disciplines, so that the gap between Muslim patients and medical personnel could be bridged.

Chapter Six	Rafiu Ibrahim Adebayo, in
	Y.A. Quadri, Omotoye & R.I. Adebayo (Eds)
	Religion and Development in Nigeria
	London, Adonis & Abbey Publishers

References

1. R.I. Adebayo, "Islam in the Contemporary African Society" in I.S. Aderibigbe and C.M. Jones Medine (eds) *Contemporary Perspectives on Religions in Africa and the African Diaspora*, (New York: Palgrave Macmillan, 2015), 101-118.
2. The Ahmadiyya Muslim Jama'at was formally established in Nigeria in 1916, twenty-seven years after its inauguration by Mirza Ghulam Ahmad popularly called Imam Mahdi. For more information about this group in Nigeria, see Taoheed Ola Shoboyede, "100 Years of Ahmadiyya in Nigeria: A Brief Appraisal" on www.championnews.com.ng accessed on 15/4/2017. See also I.O. Oloyede, "Islam in Nigeria: A Century of National Islamic Societies." Keynote Address presented at the International Conference on Islam in Nigeria delivered on safar 1, 1436H (November 24, 2014) at the University of Ilorin. See also Olayiwola Abdul Fattah, *Islam in Nigeria: One Crescent Many Focuses*, (Lagos: Sakirabe Publishers, 2007), 142-158. See also Cyril Glasse, *The Concise Encyclopaedia of Islam*, (Ghana: EPP Books Services, 2002), 33.
3. www.iwitness.com.ng/female-muslim-hospital-opens-lagos, accessed on 23/2/2017.
4. A. Tajudeen, "Potential Islamic-oriented Medical Schools: A Study of Some Selected Muslim Hospitals in Nigeria" in A. Kamal, A.G. Habib, I. Bala and U.J. Gwandu (eds), *Islamic Universities: Philosophy and Practice (Proceedings of the Second International Conference on Islamic Universities)*, (Kano, International Institute of Islamic Thought, 2015), 134-138.
5. www.islamicmovement.org/index.php , accessed on 23/2/2017.
6. *Ruqya* literally means incantation which is said purposely to ward off evil or harm. It involves the recitation of prescribed chapters and verses of the Qur'ān for healing purposes
7. M. Umar Dagimun, "Exorcism *(Ruqyah)* in Islamic Medicine: A Study of Some Tibbi Practitioners in Kebbi and Sokoto States", *NATAIS Journal of the Nigeria Association of Teachers of Arabic and Islamic Studies*, vol. 19, (2016) 19-34.
8. S.L. Jimoh, "Psychiatrist Doctors and Muslim Exorcists in South-west Nigeria: Need for Collaboration" *Ife Journal of Religions*, vol. 9, (2013), 63.
9. Jimoh, "Psychiatrist Doctors and Muslim Exorcists…" 64.
10. *The Guardian*, Saturday 11 February 2017 in https://guardian.ng/news/800-indigents-benefit-from-nazas-healthcare-programme/ accessed on 9/4/2017.

11. *The Guardian,* Saturday 11 February 2017 in https://guardian.ng/news/800-indigents-benefit-from-nazas-healthcare-programme/
12. *The Guardian,* Saturday 11 February 2017 in https://guardian.ng/news/800-indigents-benefit-from-nazas-healthcare-programme/
13. E. P. Renne, "Islam and Immunization in Northern Nigeria" in http://www.ascleiden.nl/Pdf/paperrenne.pdf accessed on 25/2/2017.
14. Alhaji I.A. O. Bello, *Iwe Adura Iwosan to daju: Hatha Hirsu ar-Rih al-Ahmar al-Kubrah ma'a Khatimihi)* 18th Edition, (Osogbo, n.p. n.d) 1-27.
15. Alhaji I.A. O. Bello, *Adua Ajebi-Ina – Lakun Dinukun,* (Osogbo: n.p, n.d) 4.
16. Alhaji Abdul-Azeez Ahmad Balogun al-Ilawy al-Adabiyy, *Ducah al-Ghayat al-Maqsudat al-Kubrah* (Cairo: 'Isa al-Baby al-Haylabi wa-shirkāt, 1978).
17. Qur'ān 2: 184 exempts the sick ones from fasting.
18. L.A. Jimoh, "The Dangerous Stride of *Az-Zina* and Sustenance of the Social and Public Health" in M.A. Folorunsho, I.O. Oyeneye and R.I. Adebayo (eds) *Religion and Modernity* (National Association for the Study of Religions and Education, 2007), 257 -262.
19. S. Alkali Abba & D. Barau, "Muslims' Abstinence From Pork – Medical Highlights"; *Al-Ilm, Magazine of the Islamic Medical Association;* vol. 4, No. 1, (Zaria: Ahmadu Bello University Teaching Hospital. 1989), 55
20. G. A. Mohammed & B. Farouk. Alcoholism: The Medico-Islamic Perspective"; *Al-Ilm, Magazine of the Islamic Medical Association,* vol. 4, No. 1, (Zaria: Ahmadu Bello University Teaching Hospital. 1989), 41-44
21. U. Jimoh Muhammad, "Preventive Practices in the Health Care System: A Reflection from Islamic Ethics" *Al-Ijtihad: The Journal of Islamization of Knowledge and Contemporary Issues,* vol. 8, No. 1. (2010), 196-209.
22. M.M. Khan, *The Translation of the Meanings of Sahih Bukhari,* (The Book of Medicine, vol. 7, Hadith 582), (Beirut: Dar al-Arabia, undated), 338.
23. M.M. Khan, *The Translation of the Meanings of Sahih Bukhari.*
24. J. Abdur-Rahman As-Suyuti, *Medicine of the Prophet,* (London: Ta Ha Publishers Ltd, 1997), 34-35.
25. A. B. Adesina, "Therapeutic Uses of Medicine in the Context of Islamic Teaching, *The FAIS Journal of the Humanities,* vol. 4, No. 2, 2010, 131-144.
26. M.M. Khan, *The Translation of the Meanings of Sahih Bukhari,* 338.
27. Muhammed S. Akanbi, "Supplication as an Alternative Medicine and Theraupetic Device: A Case Study of Prophet Ayyub's Experience" in M.A. Folorunsho, I.O. Oyeneye and R.I. Adebayo (eds) *Religion and National Security,* (National Association for the Study of Religions and Education (NASRED), 2006), 257-264.
28. M. Umar Dagimun, "Exorcism *(Ruqyah)* in Islamic Medicine, 25-27.

29. S. L. Jimoh, "Exorcism Practices in South-West Nigeria: A Comparative Analysis", *Journal of Islamic Studies and Culture*, Vol. 2, No. 3, (September, 2014), 47-61. Other works of Jimoh relevant to this discourse are: S.L. Jimoh, "Demonic Possession Exorcism by Yoruba Muslim *Aafas* in Osun State of Nigeria: A Critical Examination." Unpublished Ph.D. Thesis submitted to the Department of Religions, Lagos State University, Ojo, 2007; S.L. Jimoh, *Demonic Possession: An Islamic Antidote*. (Lagos: Jamciyyat Junud Dini 'l- Islamiyyah, 2012); and S. Luqman Jimoh, "The practice of written and bathing exorcism among Yoruba Muslim *Aafas* in Nigeria: A Theological Appraisal," *The Islamic Quarterly*, vol. 53 Number 2, (2009) 154-160.
30. S.L. Jimoh, "The Reality of Sorcery *(Sihr)* as a Force of Evil: Roles and Tasks of Yoruba Muslim Clerics in South-West Nigeria" in www.inter-disciplinary.net/at-the-interface/wp-content/uploads/.../jimohperpaper.pdf accessed on 2/3/2017.
31. M. Umar Dagimun, "Exorcism *(Ruqyah)* in Islamic Medicine, 29-30.
32. H.A. Arazi, "The Place, Usage and Significance of Numbers in the Islamic Healing System" in G. Aderibigbe & Deji Ayegboyin (eds) *Religion, Medicine and Healing*, (Nigerian Association for the Study of Religions and Education, 1995) 83-88.
33. Ibn Taymiyyah, *Majmū' Fatāwā*, (vols.1-2), (Madīnah: King Fahd Publishing House, 1995), 64
34. M.M. Khan, *The Translation of the Meanings of Sahih Bukhari*, 339-340
35. Ade. P. Dopamu, "African Religion (AFREL) and National Security: The Yoruba Perspective" in M.A. Folorunsho, I.O. Oyeneye and R.I. Adebayo (eds) *Religion and National Security* (National Association for the Study of Religions and Education, 2006), 2-13.
36. Ade. P. Dopamu, "African Religion (AFREL) and National Security.
37. M.M. Khan, *The Translation of the Meanings of Sahih Bukhari*, 339-340.
38. M.M. Khan, *The Translation of the Meanings of Sahih Bukhari*, 342.
39. The hadith reads: Narrated by Abu Sa'id Al-Khudri, "Some of the companions of the Prophet came across a tribe amongst the tribes of the Arabs and that tribe did not entertain them. While they were in that state, the chief of the tribe was bitten by a snake (or stung by a scorpion), they said to the companions of the Prophet: "Have you got any medicine with you or anybody who can treat with *Ruqya*?" The Prophet's companions said: "You refuse to entertain us, so we will not treat (your chief) unless you pay us for it." So they agreed to pay them a flock of sheep. One of them (the Prophet's companions) started reciting *Sūratul-Fātihah* gathering

his saliva and spitting it (at the snake bite)). The patient got cured and his people presented the sheep to them, but they said: "We will not take it unless we ask the Prophet whether it is lawful. When they asked him, he smiled and said: "How do you know that *Suratul-Fatihah* is *Ruqya*? Take it (flock of sheep) and assign a share for me." See Khan, 360-361.

40. A.R. Nowsheravi, "Muslim Hospitals in the Medieval Periods" *Islamic Studies*, Vol. XXII, No. 2. Summer 1983, 53-54.
41. R. I. Adebayo "Integrating Religiosity into the Health Sector: The Relevance of Islamic Values to Medical Ethics" in Y.O. Imam (ed) *Religion and Health Sciences*, (Maiduguri: Association for the Study of the Interplay between Religion and Science (ASIRS), 2009), 109- 124.
42. Tbaba "The Contribution of Muslims to Medicine" in http://www.nairaland.com/1885137/contributions-muslims-medicine, accessed on 23/2/2017.
43. S.N. Adiele, "The Place of Religion in the Development of Nigeria: Christianity and Medical Services is Southern Igboland" in I.A. B. Balogun, P. Ade Dopamu, R.A. Akanmidu and I.O. Oloyede (eds) *The Place of Religion in the Development of Nigeria*, (Ilorin: Department of Religions, University of Ilorin, 1988), 280-298.
44. S. L. Jimoh, "Health Care services and Hospital Management in Islam: Policies and Distinct Features" *Al-Ijtihad: The Journal of Islamization of Knowledge and Contemporary Issues*, vol. 5, No. 1. (2004), 38-54.
45. A. Olayiwola, *Islam in Nigeria: One Crescent Many Focuses*, (Lagos: Sakirabe Publishers, 2007) 235-236.
46. A. Olayiwola, *Islam in Nigeria: One Crescent Many Focuses*, 236.
47. The lecture was delivered in Ikirun by Professor Abdulrahman Oloyede, the Chief Imam of the University of Ibadan at the *Fidau* programme of Late Alhaji Alimi Aremu Agbetu, the Seriki Adinni of Oke-Obaagun Mosque, Ikirun, on 19th February 2017.
48. Jimoh, "Psychiatrist Doctors and Muslim Exorcists…" 64.
49. Muhsin Adekunle Balogun, "Syncretic Beliefs and Practices amongst Muslims in Lagos State Nigeria; with Special Reference to the Yoruba Speaking People of Epe." Unpublished Ph. D Thesis of Department of Theology and Religion, University of Birmingham, Edgbaston, (2011), 277-289.
50. M.O. Opeloye & S.L. Jimoh, "The Yoruba Muslims of Nigeria and the Glorious Qur'ān", *NATAIS Journal of the Nigeria Association of Teachers of Arabic and Islamic Studies*, Vol.7, (2004) 79.
51. Jimoh, "The Reality of Sorcery *(Sihr)*
52. Alhaji Abdul-Azeez Ahmad Balogun al-Ilawy al-Adabiyy, *Ducah al-Ghayat al-Maqsudat al-Kubrah*, 283.

53. V.P. Londhe, A.T. Gavasana, S.S. Nipate, D.D. Bandawane and P.D. Chaudhari, "Role of Garlic (Allium Sativum) in various Diseases: An Overview"; *Journal of Pharmaceutical Research and Opinion,* vol. 1. No. 4 (2011), 129-134.
54. www.m.webmd.com/vitamins/ai/ingredientmono-300/garlic accessed on 3/3/2017.
55. www.m.webmd.com/vitamins/ai/ingredientmono-300/garlic accessed on 3/3/2017.

CHAPTER SEVEN

Christianity and the Development of Health Care Services in Okunland, Kogi State, Nigeria Since 1900

Lewu, M. A. Y.
Department of History and International Studies,
University of Ilorin, Ilorin, Nigeria.
iyemoso@gmail.com
+2348033573113

Jide Ige
Department of History and International Studies,
University of Ilorin, Ilorin, Nigeria.
jide_ige@yahoo.com
+2348036065687

Afolabi, A. S.
Department of History and International Studies,
University of Ilorin, Ilorin, Nigeria.
abeafolabi@yahoo.com
+2348030438315

Introduction

Okun land is located in the north-east of Yoruba land, just below the confluence of rivers Niger and Benue, within latitude 7.30^0 N and 8.35^0 and longitude 5.20^0 E and 5.30^0 E.[1] The people found in Okun land known as Okun-Yoruba, (simply referred to here as Okun) include the Bunu, Ijumu, Owe, Oworo and Yagba who speak a variant and mutually intelligible dialect of Yoruba.[2] Majority of Okun people are Christians while a small minority is Muslim leaving still a smaller fraction as Tradition practitioners.[3]

According to Ayandele,[4] health care became an integral part of missions' agenda in order to attain their objective of evanglisation. Consequently, the Sudan Interior Mission (SIM) and the Roman Catholic Mission (RCM) were actively involved in providing health care services to Okun people from the beginning of their sojourn in Okunland. They were able to impact positively on the lives of Okun people through the establishment of schools and hospitals. The SIM built hospitals in Egbe, Isanlu, Mopa, Koro and Ponyan while the RCM built health care facilities in Kabba, Isanlu and Ponyan but could not build one in Egbe as planned because of financial constraint.[5] This study focuses on the SIM Hospital, Egbe and St John's Catholic Hospital, Kabba.

Okun World View of Medical Care

Okun people perceived healthy wellbeing in physical and spiritual dimensions. The physical man is believed to encompass the visible aspect, which can be touched and controlled by man, while the spiritual man is made up of soul, spirit and body, which can only be controlled and regulated by a Supreme Being. Hence, for a perfect health, these three aspects must be complementary and be perfectly free from any problems, aches and distortions. Consequently, they believed that any dysfunction and problematic aspect of man must be connected to one of the components.[6] Taylor[7] opined that "illness and sickness arise when there is a breakdown in the harmony between man and the elemental forces in the world." This could be metaphysical, moral, spiritual or ontological. This is further buttressed by Smith[8] who argued that African's belief system is predicated on physical and metaphysical indices. According to Paul,[9] the metaphysical index of Okun culture weighs rather more heavily on their world view on health than the physical; therefore, the popular belief that nothing happens to man without the knowledge of the Supreme Being holds sway among Okun people.

Ailments such as malaria, fever and headaches were categorised as physical problem as they could emerge due to factors that could be controlled by man, like stress, unhygienic environment as well as contaminated food and unclean water. On the other hand, paralysis, mental illness and bareness were categorised as spiritual problems, because the causes were unknown. Consequently, physical ailments required physical elements to cure while spiritual ailments required spiritual cure.[10]

On the other hand, Western medical care is predicated on scientific factors as the causes of sicknesses or ailments, generally referred to as the 'germ theory' and malfunction of body mechanisms. To the Okun people however, sicknesses or ailments are caused by various factors; which include witchcraft, sorcery, hypnotism, heredity and marital infidelity among others.[11] Morley's etiological categorisation and explanation of diseases into supernatural or ultimate and non- supernatural or immediate causes seem to be similar to the Okun's perception of causes of ailments. By supernatural, he means diseases traceable to supra-sensible forces, malevolent agents or acts which are not directly observable, such as witchcraft, spirit, demon or evil eye. While non-supernatural diseases are caused by perceived pathogenic agents.[12]

Also, the Okun people perceived witches as personifying evil, innately wicked and causing harm on other people through the possession of mysterious powers hidden to ordinary people, Idowu, described them as:

> Human beings of very strong determined wills with diabolical bent; (they) are the veritable wicked ones who derive sadistic satisfaction from bringing misfortunes upon other people......[13]

Despite the difference in the above perception, a detailed study of both ideologies revealed a commonality in the psychological cause of psychotic ailments. The Okun believed that mental disorder could arise from a distressed or unstable mind even when physical appearance seems normal. Lambo's study on the European ideology revealed that some people born under Virgo zodiac sign are said to be prone to certain diseases.[14] An example is that the radiation from the cosmic agents like the moon, sun and planets exerts a kind of influence on man, either for good or evil. It has been generally observed that the moon has an influence on the brain; hence, lunatics or the mentally ill usually become wild and behave more abnormally when a new moon appears.[15] This observation is in tandem with Okun belief that lunatics become more violent and wild at the appearance of a new moon.

According to Paul[16] and Olaoye,[17] sicknesses could also be inflicted on an individual who might have deliberately or inadvertently offended persons with spiritual or diabolical powers; meaning that by nature, man dwells in dual worlds, physical and spiritual. They explained further that physical human beings operate in the spirit realm far beyond the imagination of ordinary mortals where they could influence the spiritual being of an individual for good or evil through diabolical means. That is why one hears of arrow shooting, *ta l' ofa or so l' ata*.[18]

Health Care in Pre- Christian Okun

Without any doubt, traditional medicine is the oldest method of healing in Africa as obtained among other peoples such as the ancient Greeks, Babylonians, Jews, Chinese and Indians, among others.[19] Therefore, in pre-Christian Okun societies, traditional medicine provided healing and cures for people. Paul[20] noted that traditional health practice in Okun land at this time was such that everybody was responsible for himself and others; with the example that if any member of a family was indisposed, all members rose up to bring respite to the member. This, he likened to modern day first aid given to patients before proper medical care is provided. He noted further that this was possible because health education was not limited to any group but most family heads often carried everybody along. Consequently, minor ailments such as malaria and body aches were usually treated by the individual or families with the use of herbal remedies, while those that persisted were referred to traditional health practitioners. One would then not be wrong to describe Okun traditional health care as communal or family based. This situation therefore buttresses Maclean's description of traditional medicine thus;

Medical treatment starts at the household level. Practically everyone can cite recipes for the relief of common symptoms by the use of herbs and materials close to hand. Every household has its own favourite prescription which has been proven over time and many plants growing wild on patches of waste land between the compounds are recognised for their specific therapeutic properties. Infusion for headaches, fever and jaundice, stomach aches, purges, inhalation, imbrications and ointments can be recommended by people of all ages.[21]

Just like in other parts of Yoruba land,[22] there were two categories of traditional medical practitioners in *Okunland*, the *Babalawo* and *Ologun; Onisegun* or *Elegbogi*, who had many similarities but had distinct differences in practice and methods of diagnosing and treatment. In fact, their functions overlap, hence the same name may apply to them in the local dialect. The *Babalawo* or medicine man engaged in the science of understanding, preventing and treating of diseases using his knowledge of plant and animal substances, as well as supernatural forces. He tried to understand the nature and etiology of disease or illness through divination before embarking on treatment. The treatment could be therapeutic or prophylactic.[23] On the other hand, magic is not therapeutic in nature rather; it caters for human .concerns that are not associated with disease or illness. Magic is used to produce, procure, enhance or induce non-therapeutic needs of people such as the desire for victory, success, luck, protection from danger, good harvest, and successful businesses or evil forces, rain for crops, followers, for others to love them, employment and a host of other needs. These concerns are different from pathological or therapeutic conditions of human beings and are dealt with by the use of magic. Yet, the Yoruba classified magic as *oogun*. However, there are cases where magic could be used to complement medicine in the treatment of people. The procedure has magical as well as physiological effects and could be referred to as magical-medicine with both magical and therapeutic elements. Thus, showing the interplay of magic and medicine where man used available resources of nature for his own benefit.[24]

Despite the distinctions in their functions, it is important to note that an individual often combined he different professions. It is hard to get a medicine man that is not knowledgeable in herbal properties, or some form of magic. Consequently, many medicine men can also be called magicians or herbalists and *vice versa*, although, their knowledge in one art may not be as wide as in the other. For the avoidance of any doubt, we shall refer to the professionals as "men of hidden supernatural power".[25]

In Yoruba land, the *Babalawo* is a diviner who has verse esoteric knowledge and secrets, which he uses to pry into human problems, events, future and causes of sicknesses through divination. He uses the *Ifa* oracle to consult the Supreme Being to know the causes of ailments and remedy for cure, especially when the problem appears spiritual. They often rely on sacrifices as remedies for ailments,[26] while the *Ologun; Onisegun* or *Elegbogi* is an expert in herbal formulae with verse knowledge or herbal preparations to cure ailments. They also fall into two categories;

one specialises in herbal preparations to treat adults, the other focuses on treating children and is referred to as *Eleghe Omo* or *Al'agbo*, while some combine the two.[27] In this regard, Maclean commended that;

> Although the later are primarily concerned with treating bodily symptoms through the use of herbal remedies, while the former specialises in a form of psychotherapy for mental troubles and in diseases due to supernatural influence or malevolence, in fact, they have much in common. Thus, a herbalist whose management of a case after prescribing several medicines has been unsuccessful, may resort to some simple divination procedures to clarify his diagnosis. On the other hand, a diviner is generally familiar with a large number of medicines of his own speciality.[28]

There were traditional midwives, usually elderly women, who had the dual roles as *Eleghe Omo*, herbalist, as well as *Agbegi*, birth attendant. They took care of the ante-natal, delivery and post-natal needs of women in the community using herbs and sometimes offering some sacrifices as prescribed by *Ifa* oracle.[29]

As noted above, health care was provided mainly by traditional medicine men and women using herbs; however, during the colonial period, a decision was taken at the 1929 Conference of Residents to ratify the recommendation of Ormby Gore and Stan on health care. Thereafter, the colonial government decided to expand health care services to rural areas by building Dispensaries, train Dispensers and other health workers. Subsequently, Native Authority (NA) Dispensaries were launched in 1930 in Kabba, Ikare, Okene and Koton Karfi, among others, (these towns were all in Kabba Province then).[30] By 1931, the building of the NA Maternity was completed, although there were no buildings in the out stations, mobile clinics were put in place in Kabba District. Each community had a specific day when the NA Medical team paid a monthly visit. Serious cases were referred to Kabba, while complicated ones were referred to the government hospital in Lokoja.[31]

Christian Missions and Health Care in Okunland

Our attention is focused on the SIM Hospital, Egbe and the RCM Hospital, Kabba, as discussed below.

(a) The Sudan Interior Mission (SIM) Hospital, Egbe

The founder of SIM hospital, Tommy Titcombe, anchored his missionary vocation on three major principles, namely, evangelism, education and health; using the latter two principles as means to achieve the first. During his evangelism journeys around Yagba land with his companion, Daniel Adeniyi, the diverse health challenges he saw among the people prompted him to fashion out a way to help them.[32] He started with treating their sores, *ooju*, the common prevailing ailment that afflicted the people, by dressing the wounds after applying medicines, which he probably brought from Canada for his own personal use.[33] Titcombe took this step to prevent them from patronising the herbalists and contradicting the belief in their new Christian faith, which frowned at any dealing with traditional medicine practitioners rather than put their faith in God for healing.[34] Titcombe further condemned sacrifices to appease the metaphysical forces; female circumcision, traditional immunisation against poisons and evil forces as well as all kinds of magic, invocation and incantations.[35] Despite the fact that some people did not appreciate his free treatment and continued to patronise herbalists, he decided to treat them at home instead of them going to the clinic and also induced them with gifts of fruits, milk, and mirror, among others.[36] This marked the beginning of SIM health care services in Yagbaland, an integral part of Okunland.

As his patients increased, Titcombe introduced the shifting method of treating them morning, afternoon and evening. Paul,[37] noted that Egbe people were not impressed by Titcombe's efforts and their attitude remained cold initially but many patients patronised him from the surrounding villages of Koro, Odo-Eri, Okeri Ofirin (now Iyamerin), Ejiba, among others. Titcombe's marriage to Ethel McIntosh in 1915 marked a turning point in the history of SIM health care services in Okunland. Their combined efforts led to stopping the practice of killing twins, who were deemed to be evil. Hitherto, the twins were killed and their mother sent on exile. The first twins saved by the Titcombes were named Reuben and Ruth. The birth of twins by Tommy and Ethel Titcombe and their successful upbringing finally convinced the Egbe people that there was nothing evil about twins and their killing was stopped.[38] In 1916, Tommy saved the life of a baby boy whose mother had died giving birth to him. By tradition, the boy would have been buried with his mother but his father smuggled him to the Titcombes who adopted and named him Mackenzie after Ethel's pastor, who led her to the Lord. Subsequently, Ethel Titcombe started a small maternity home in her house, probably to continue to save the lives of twins and orphans. The success in their endeavours encouraged the couple to build a maternity clinic in 1925.[39]

The clinic was erected on a piece of land donated by the reigning traditional ruler, Olu of Egbe, Oba Owojaiye. Through their hard work, the support of Oba Owojaiye and converts, the forty (40) bed spaced maternity clinic was completed in 1926 by direct labour. Thus, the genesis of what metamorphosed into the SIM hospital, in Egbe.[40] Tommy and Ethel Titcombe, who had no medical qualifications, managed the maternity until 1927 when the first medical doctor, Dr. Harry Peaston came from Canada. Unfortunately, Dr. Peaston, had to return to Canada shortly because of ill health.[41] A trained nurse, Margaret Lang, popularly referred to as *Olutonju* (care giver) was also on the staff list and worked for many years. Other members of staff included indigenous people such as Messes Seth Ige and Odutola, who assisted in caring for in-patients, laundry as well as administering drugs. Thus, a mini hospital with maternity, clinic and dispensary began in Egbe in 1926 mainly for evangelism since people were treated free. Their success in Egbe encouraged the Titcombes to establish dispensaries or out-patient clinics attached to SIM mission stations.[42]

In 1927, the SIM opened a dispensary in Mopa followed by another in Isanlu in 1951. Despite the availability of healthcare services in these dispensaries, the generality of women in Egbe and Yagba land still preferred the traditional herbalists to take their deliveries. With the higher success rate of hitch-free deliveries and preservation of lives in the dispensaries as compared to the traditional herbal homes, the women soon embraced the Titcomb's maternity.[43] This however generated serious problems and resentment between the herbalists and owners of the dispensary. After delivery in the dispensaries, the women still preferred to use the traditional herbal preparations, *agbo,* for their post-natal care to the chagrin of Ethel Titcombe.

The women were often taunted for their preference to avail themselves of the western orthodox method of delivery by the traditional medicine men, who claimed that their babies' bones would not be strong enough to cope with the geographical and topographical conditions needed as Africans living in Africa; noting that orthodox medicine was meant for white people. One may dismiss this as superstitious but it could be interpreted as a sign of the high esteem in which the Okun people held their tradition and culture.[44] Aside persecution by the herbalists, finance and difficulty in acquiring drugs also constituted problems to the Titcombes' effort in providing orthodox health care to Okun people. Drugs were procured from the mission in USA and Canada; transporting the drugs often took several months to arrive at Egbe. The fact that fees were not charged for their services made it financially difficult for them as they relied on donors from their home Missions.[45] In addition, the outbreak of World War 1 of 1914-1918 seriously affected the transportation of materials by sea, the most reliable form of transportation then hence, the Titcombes were unable to access the dugs needed for their patients.[46] Furthermore, the negative economic consequences of the war, which led to the economic depression of 1929 meant that aids were drastically reduced.[47] In order to overcome the financial constraints, the Titcomebs embarked on trading in European cloth and second hand clothes, *bosikoro*; the clothes ordered from Lagos were sold very cheaply to the people and sometimes on credit. Apart from raising funds to buy drugs for the maternity through this trade,[48] the Titcombes were also able to reduce the exploitation of traders from South-east Yoruba land, referred to in the local parlance as the *osomalo*, who used to sell cloth to people in Egbe and its environ at outrageously expensive price.[49] In 1929, Ethel Titcombe had to return to Canada as a result of illness and never came back but her husband returned to continue his missionary work until August 1930 when he too left for health reasons.[50]

Despite Titcombe's departure from Egbe, he continued to follow the trend of events in the maternity as well as muster financial and manpower supports from Europe and America.[51] Through his effort, the missions in Canada and USA sent delegations from time to time to monitor the progress and assess the needs and problems of the maternity. Another positive impact of Titcombe's effort is the arrival of an additional expatriate missionary nurse from Canada in 1935; a qualified nurse, Miss Ansla Thompson, popularly called *Ayo* (meaning happiness in the local dialect) to complement Miss Lang's effort in the maternity.[52] Assisted by Mrs. Deborah Ajayi, popularly called *Mamma Ile Ogun*, (mother of the maternity) a ward attendant; they all worked hard to keep the maternity active for several years until they retired in 1952.

The Transformation of Egbe Maternity into a Full-fledged ECWA Hospital

Without resident medical doctors to attend to serious illnesses that required surgery, the maternity was run by European and indigenous missionaries including trained nurses. Complicated cases were referred to the Baptist Hospital Ogbomoso and Ilorin General Hospital. Often times, such patients died in transit as the hospitals were located about 188 and 138 kilometres respectively.[53]

During another visit by Rev. Tommy Titcombe in 1942, he realised the urgent need for a full-fledged hospital to meet the needs of the people, especially because of the high mortality rate of patients during transits to bigger hospitals outside Egbe.[54] A leprosarium was also established in the same year. Egbe people objected to this move because of the belief that leprosy was contagious hence, social interaction was prevented.[55] They feared that the settlement would lead to the contamination of *Wele* stream, their major source of water. Economic interactions with the lepers were also seen as possible means of infecting members of the community, hence the objection.[56] Objection to the settlement near the new hospital in Egbe led to its relocation to Ejiba, about twenty (20) kilometres away in 1945. There, lepers from all over Nigeria were treated. Orphanages were established in Mopa and Oro-Ago.

Contributions of ECWA Hospital, Egbe

The hospital rendered medical, surgical and maternity services under five clinics, antenatal, maternal, child health care, immunisation and family planning. There was also a well-equipped laboratory with a capacity to carry out wide range of laboratory investigations for diagnostic purposes, such as X-ray, ultrasound, electrocardiogram and intensive care. Other services included mortuary and eye care. Eye care services personnel visited the villagers to provide services monthly, serious cases that required surgery were referred to the hospital's eye centre.[57]

The ECWA hospital was accredited by the National Postgraduate Medical College of Nigeria to train Resident Doctors in General Medical Practice since 1982 where highly skilled General Practice Consultants have been trained. Such professionals include Drs. Tayo Ojo, Ayo Fagbemi, Michael Obadofin, Odeigah and Dr.(Mrs) Ehalaiye, who have become useful citizens in different parts of Nigeria. The hospital is also a major training centre where many Nurses and Midwives have been trained and are working inside and outside Nigeria.[58]

HIV/AIDS Centre

The hospital is one of the approved sites by the National Agency for Control of Aids for Antiretroviral therapy and is actively involved in the HIV/AIDS prevention and management, providing screening for blood donors, pregnant women risk groups, pre-testing, and post-testing. Community training and counselling of youths are also undertaken.[59]

Making Pregnancy Safe

This is a World Health Organisation (WHO) initiative. Under the programme, the hospital is a secondary referral facility for World Health Organisation for pregnancy and delivery services in West Yagba. The hospital is also designated as a Centre of Cervical Cancer Screening by the World Health Organisation.[60]

Trainings

The hospital provides training for students of Community Health from the Schools of Health Technology, Idah, Kogi State and Kagoro in Kaduna State. Furthermore, the ECWA Hospital, Egbe offers a Family Medicine Residency Programme and multi-service care facility. In addition, through outreach programmes, the hospital is involved in community education from which many people have benefited. The internet café in the hospital has enabled members of staff stay connected to the world and update their knowledge as well as keep abreast of global issues. The ECWA Schools of Nursing and Midwifery are located on the hospital compound, along with the Chapel of Blessing.[61]

Other ECWA Medical Institutions in Egbe

There are two medical institutions in Egbe. They are ECWA School of Nursing and ECWA School of Midwifery. In 1955, Dr. and Mrs. George Campion, SIM Missionaries established the ECWA School of Nursing making it one of the earliest Nursing schools in former Northern Nigeria. In fact, it was the only School of Nursing in the former Kabba and Ilorin Provinces established to train young men and women as Christian nurses to provide the much needed staff for Christian health institutions, such as, Egbe Hospital, SIM and other hospitals in Nigeria. The SIM Nursing Training School, Egbe, as it was called then graduated the first set of Nurses in 1959. Many of them are found working not only in mission hospitals but also government hospitals while the privileged ones are working outside Nigeria.[62]

The school had been adjudged one of the best schools of Nursing in Nigeria because of the high academic and moral standards evident in the way graduates of the school are rated in the society. However, the school was not allowed to admit students for twenty years, between 1972 and 1992, because it had failed accreditation; arising from operational difficulties such as inadequate finance, shortage of staff, essential hospital departments and infrastructure. After failure to be accredited for the second time, provisional approval to start readmitting students into the school was granted by the Nursing and Midwifery Council of Nigeria and it was re-opened in 1992 under the leadership of Dr. S.B. Agaja as the Medical Director. It was re-named Evangelical Church of West Africa (ECWA) School of Nursing, Egbe.[63]

ECWA School of Midwifery

This is the second ECWA medical institution. The Midwifery Training School (MTS) as it was known was established by the Sudan Interior Mission (SIM) in 1971 to train Community Midwives. The programme transited from training Community Midwives to the training of Basic Midwives, graduating the first set in March 1980.[64] Direct Entry student

Midwives were trained up to March 1988 when it admitted the first set of Post Basic Nurses as Student Midwives and has since admitted both Basic and Post Basic students into the school. In 1992, the Nursing and Midwifery Council of Nigeria inspected the school and ordered the proprietor to choose between Basic and Post Basic Training programme.[65] Subsequently, the school was fully registered with the Nursing and Midwifery Council and licensed to train Post Basic Midwifery students who had successfully completed and passed the final qualifying examination for General Nursing to practise as Nurses.[66]

The school's excellent performance has earned it commendation several times from the Nursing and Midwifery Council of Nigeria. About 1,566 midwives produced between 1977 and 2008 are doing excellently well within and outside Nigeria.[67] The ECWA School of Midwifery trained disciplined and dedicated Midwives to cater for the health needs of individuals, families and community as well as witnessing to patients in words and in deeds through quality and compassionate healthcare[68]

ECWA Health Centres in Isanlu, Mopa, Koro and Ponyan

The Evangelical Church Winning All (ECWA) in Yagba land today, can boast of four health centres, namely in Isanlu, in Yagba East Local Government, Isanlu, Mopa, in Mopamuro Local Government Area, Koro in Yagba West Local Government Area, and Ponyan in Yagba East Local Government Area. Some of the ECWA health centre buildings or structures had been constructed since the early 1930s when the early Missionaries came to Yagba land for evangelism, for instance, the ECWA health centre buildings in Isanlu and Mopa. It is important to note that, the health centres were revived again in 2008 and have since been functioning prominently and attending to the community with quality health care services and evangelism.[69]

Most of the villagers where these ECWA health facilities existed patronised them because of their quality and affordable health care services. None ECWA member also enjoyed the facilities just as obtained in Egbe hospital, the mother hospital. Some drugs are produced and labeled by ECWA. These include, ECWA Cough syrup (for children and adults), ECWA Mol syrup (for children), Piriton, syrup, and some eye drops like Gantanmycin, Chloraphinicol, Predisolone, Zink Suiphate, Timilol, Polyvidon, Amethocain, Fluorenscein, Dexamethasone and Sodium Chromoglycate. These drugs are available in ECHP Drug store, ECWA Central Pharmacy Ltd in Jos, Plateau State Nigeria and CHAN Pharmacy.[70]

(b)   The Roman Catholic Mission

The Roman Catholic Church (RCM) saw the provision of medical care of the people as a means of evangelisation, hence the establishment of medical centres in Kabba, Isanlu and Ponyan between 1960 and 1995. These clinics were operated by Catholic Priests, Reverend Sisters and Local Catholic Faithful until they were taken over by the military government in 1976. Some were returned while others were never returned to the Catholic Mission. In fact only St John's Hospital in Kabba was returned after the commissioning of the Kabba Specialist Hospital; Isanlu and Ponyan are still being managed by the government.[71]

In the 1960s, Catholic Mission operated some mobile clinics in Okunland, one of such was the Saint Vincent Mobile Clinic, managed by the Eucharistic Heart of Jesus (EHJ) Sisters. The mobile clinic travelled around in a van to provide health care services to communities and dispensing drugs to the sick daily. Complicated cases were referred to St. John's Hospital Kabba, for treatment. This continued until the late 1970s when it collapsed after the departure of the white Missionaries because of the old age. Furthermore, the lack of financial and human resources prevented the continued running of the mobile clinic by the Okun people.[72] However, while it lasted; Okun people derived a lot of health benefits as well as conversion to Christianity. Details of the activities of St John's Hospital are discussed below.

St. John Catholic Hospital

The hospital was established in 1956 by the Holy Ghost Priest (Spiritans) from Canada for the purpose of evangelisation.[73] It started operating as a maternity/dispensary in a small two room building within the premises of the Roman Catholic Mission (RCM). It was run by a British Missionary, Dr Joan Clathworth at the invitation of the Catholic Bishop of Lokoja Diocese, Dr. Augustine Delise who had jurisdiction over

Kabba and all of Okunland. The Bishop saw the provision of health care as a powerful tool to evangelism.[74] Assisted by two ward attendants in the maternity, Dr. Clathworth ran the out-patients clinic so efficiently that she was fondly referred to as *Iye,* Mother. Thus, the maternity was popularly called, *Asibito Iye,* Mother's Hospital rather than its original name, St Vincent Clinic, which rendered highly subsidised free services. Some Midwives were also trained.[75]

As their services expanded, there was the need for larger accommodation, therefore the RCM, with voluntary labour by the Catholic community in Kabba built a new and larger hospital on its present location at St. Monica's college Road. Asante, Kabba, in 1960.[76] there were initially, two main wards, male and female, with three departments, Surgery, Maternity, and Outpatients. Dr. Joan Clathworth was the first resident Doctor, assisted by some Okun people, Joseph Obada (a nurse), Peter Ibiejemite (Theatre Department) and Joseph Baiyegunhi (Laboratory Assistant). Although these people never became doctors, they were regarded as fore-runners of the Catholic faith in Kabba as they combined their medical duties with evangelism as Sunday School Teachers or better still Catechiests.[77] Dr. Joan Clathworth continued the good work of evangelism through the provision of excellent medical care to Okun people in Kabba and its environ until she left for England. Subsequently, Dr. Matel and Gagnon from Canada, assisted by some Grey Nun Reverend Sisters namely Alice, Annette, Teresa, Gloria and Matron managed the hospital until it was taken over by the Military government in 1976.[78]

However, when the Kabba Specialist Hospital was commissioned in 1983, St. John's Hospital was abandoned and left to decay. During this period, it was left unattended to, the structures became dilapidated and some of the facilities were stolen.[79] Thirteen years later in 1996, Kabba Deanery in Lokoja Diocese or the Catholic Mission took charge of the hospital again under the watchful eyes of Bishop Ajomo, the Bishop of Lokoja. The Bishop brought Reverend Sister Julie Duran from Jos to re-activate the hospital, which has since been run as a General Hospital rendering medical services required of a Secondary Health Care Provider without specific specialisation. New members of staff were recruited for effective operation, a Management Board was instituted which was chaired by a Catholic Priest for the day to day operation of the hospital. Aside the Resident Doctors, Missionary Doctors, occasionally visited from Canada and the USA to offer free assistance to patients of St, John's Hospital. Medicines were also donated by Canada, the USA and Germany.[80]

Current Trend in St. John Hospital

St. John hospital located on St, Monica's College Road in Asanta is currently being managed by a seven-man management team. It is chaired by Reverend Father Joseph Tolorunshagba under the proprietorship of Bishop Martin Olorunmolu, Bishop of Lokoja Catholic Diocese. Members of the Board include:

1. Reverend Fr. Joseph Tolorunshagba- Chairman
2. Dr. Barnabas Isa- Member
3. Mr. Peter Ibiejemite– Member
4. Mrs. Stella Obayotan – Member
5. Mrs. Amodu – Member
6. Mr. Paul Ojo
7. Dr. Peter Abejide Eyanro – Member (Late and yet to be replaced).[81]

There are usually resident Doctors but no resident Consultants. However, whenever the need arises, arrangements are made for Consultants from Kogi State Medical Centre in Lokoja to visit the hospital once or twice a week or monthly. Although there are trained Auxiliary Nurses attending to patients with eye complaints, a specialist eye doctor also visits the hospital once a month from Lokoja Medical Centre to see patients with eye problems. Patients from the hospital are often referred for X-ray services to the Government General Hospital, Kabba. However, St, John's Hospital offers high quality mortuary services, consequently, other hospitals in its environ with less efficient facilities deposit corpses there pending burial in the surrounding towns and villages. Corpses are even brought from outside the state to be nearer home until burials take place.[82]

There are four main wards, male and female, made up of surgery and medical for each gender. There is also a labour room, a well-equipped and standard operating theatre as well as a Doctors' room; four amenity (special) rooms, two each for male and female patients who can afford the two hundred Naira fee per night. Those who cannot afford it pay a hundred Naira daily in the main ward. Four isolation rooms for male and female patients with infectious diseases such as Human Immunodeficiency Virus\Acquired Immunodeficiency Syndrome (HIV/AIDS) and Tuberculosis, (TB) among others are also available in the hospital as the General Hospital has no facilities to treat patients for such diseases. A free Aids Reliefs Clinic holds every Tuesday and Thursday. All patients are treated, without ethnic or religious bias, sometimes medical outreach is conducted at Fulani settlements around Kabba.[83]

Members of staff include the Matron; two Nurses, two Auxiliary Nurses, one Senior Community Health worker, two Extension workers and one Junior Community Health Officer. One Principal Nursing Officer (PNO) is seconded by the government to St. John's Hospital. Some of these personally go for medical outreach to surrounding villages, sometimes accompanied by a Doctor. They also supervised the Catholic Dispensary at Ogidi, which has been taken over by the government. Accommodation is provided for essential staff such as Doctors, Theatre Nurses, Pharmacists and some Nurses or members of staff who so desire.[84]

According to the Hospital Administrator, Reverend Father Joseph Olorunshagba, foreign assistance came from Canada, America and Germany, particularly from *Kinder Mission Werk Die Sternsinger*, a German children's NGO, *Mesere*. The NGO is run by a German Catholic children choir which raises funds to help other children. Money raised is sent directly to a drug company which sends drugs and other medical supplies already requested to St. John's Hospital at intervals for the past eight years. The Bishop pays to collect the drugs from the Post office.[85] Another NGO, the Catholic Caritas of the Federation of Nigeria (CCFN), also gives assistance to the hospital. Generally, over five thousand out-patients are attended to per annum, treating illnesses such as malaria, diabetes, hypertension, T.B, among others.[86]

Some Challenges of the Hospital

The major challenge is finance. As a self-sustaining institution, patronage is low despite the very low fees charged for their services. Apart from that, the T.B unit built in 2014 by the Kogi State Government, which should have been generating some revenue is poorly equipped; no beds and limited equipment. The thirty-two (32) available bed spaces are hardly fully occupied unless the Kabba General Hospital is on strike or during outbreaks of any diseases. Consequently, many of their facilities are underutilised resulting in low revenue. Besides, the hospital is poorly staffed, only one Resident Doctor and a Corper Doctor, usually posted there for their one year mandatory service.[87]

Conclusion

We have traced health care services in Okun land since the pre-colonial and pre – Christian Mission periods looking at the Okun people's world view of health care. We noted that they perceived healthy well-being in physical and spiritual dimensions involving the body, soul and spirit, which must be complementary for a perfect health. It was discovered that among the Okun people like other Yoruba, medical care was a family based issue where everybody participated and met their various medical needs by employing traditional African herbal practice through divination of *Ifa* oracle by the Babalawo and herbalist, *Elegbogi*. We also observed the effort of the colonial government in providing health care services to Okun people through Dispensaries and the training of Dispensers as well as Mobile Clinics since the 1930s.

The activities of Christian Missionaries in providing health care to Okun people since 1930 through mobile clinics and later hospitals were also discussed. Focusing specifically on the SIM hospital, Egbe and St. John's Catholic Hospital, Kabba, it was discovered that the hospitals had provided quality medical care to Okun people since 1930 and 1956 respectively through maternity and out-patient services, run initially by Christian Missionary Doctors and Nurses. As their operation expanded, they relocated to their present and more spacious sites with more staff.

It was noted that services are rendered without religious discrimination at subsidised rates, supported with drugs from local and international NGOs in Nigeria, Canada, USA and Germany. Despite the many challenges of low patronage and funding, the self-sustaining hospitals are still functioning well in meeting the medical needs of Okun people. Therefore, the study concludes that the Sudan Interior Mission and the Roman Catholic Mission have contributed immensely to the development of medical care in Okun land since 1930 and 1950 respectively.

References

1. R.K., Udo, *Geographical Regions of Nigeria*, (Oxford, Oxford University Press, 1970).
2. E., Kraft-Askari, "Social Organisation of the Owe", *African Notes, Institute of African Studies*, Ibadan, Vol. 2, No. 3, April 1965; A., Obayemi, "States and Peoples of the Niger-Benue Confluence Areas," in I., Obaro (ed) Ground *Work of Nigerian History*, (Ibadan, Heinemann Educational Books, 1980), 144-149
3. M.A.Y., Lewu, "Nupe Incursion: Captives and Refugees Question in Okunland, 1833-1934", Unpublished PhD thesis, Department of History and International Studies, University of Ilorin, Ilorin, 2016, 94.
4. E.A., Ayandele, *The Missionary Impact on Modern Nigeria: A Political Analysis, 1842-1942*, Longman Nigeria, 12.
5. M.A.Y., Lewu, "The Contributions of the Roman Catholic Mission to Formal Education in Okunland, Nigeria, 1920-1976", *Journal of Arabic and Religious Studies (JARS)*, Published by the Department of Religions, University of Ilorin, Vol. 17, December 2003, 69-80
6. I. A., Paul, "A History of Health Care Services in Okun-Yoruba land, 1900-2000", Unpublished PhD thesis, Department of History and International Studies, University of Ilorin, Ilorin, 2015, 44
7. J. V., Taylor, *The Primal Vision*, (London, SMC Press, 1969), 159
8. G. E., Smith, Y*oruba Medicine and Religion*, (Ibadan, Ibadan University Press, 1980), 143
9. I. A., Paul, "A History of Health Care Services in Okun-Yoruba land, 1900-2000,"... 45
10. G. A., Mohammed, "The Development of Traditional Medicine in Nigeria, 1930-1955", M.A. Dissertation, Department of History, University of Ilorin, 1999.
11. O.T., Oshadare, & I. A., Paul, "Traditional Methods of Curing Mental Illness among the Owe People of Kogi State in Nigeria" in R. A., Olaoye,.

(ed) *History of Indigenous Science and Technology in Nigeria*,(Ibadan, Crest Hill Publishers, 2009), 228-235
12. P., Morley, "Culture and the Cognitive World of Traditional Medical Belief: Some Preliminary Considerations" in P., Morley, and W., Roy, (eds) *Culture and Curing*, (London, Peter Orven, 1978).
13. E. B., Idowu, *Olodumare: God in Yoruba Belief:* (London, Longman, 1962)
14. J. O., Lambo, "Medical Astrology as an Aid to Therapy", in Proceedings of International Symposium at the University of Lagos, 1973, 31-33
15. R. A., Olaoye, "African Culture in Perspective of Contemporary Science", in *African Culture, Modern Science and Religious Thought*, P. A. Dopamu, et al (eds), African Centre for Religions and the Sciences (ACRS), University of Ilorin, Ilorin, 2003, 243-253
16. I. A., Paul. "A History of Health Care Services in Okun-Yoruba land, 1900-2000,"... 49
17. R. A., Olaoye, "African Culture in Perspective of Contemporary Science", in *African Culture, Modern Science and Religious Thought*, P. A., Dopamu, et al (eds), African Centre for Religions and the Sciences..., 250
18. S. F. Olowojolu, Oral interview, the 75 year old retired banker was interviewed at his Offa Garage residence, June 20, 2017
19. G. W., Harley, *Native African Medicine*, (London, Frank Cass & Co. Ltd., 1970), 197
20. I. A., Paul. "A History of Health Care Services in Okun-Yoruba land, 1900-2000,"... 46
21. U., Maclean, U., *Magical Medicine: A Nigerian Case Study*, (London, Allen Lane, 1971), 26-28
22. P.A., Dopamu, "Scientific Basis of African Magic and Medicine: The Yoruba Experience" in Dopamu, *African Culture, Modern Science and Religious Thought*, P. A. Dopamu, et al (eds), African Centre for Religions and the Sciences,... 442-464
23. P.A., Dopamu, "Yoruba Magic and Medicine and their Relevance for Today," *Religions: Journal of the Nigerian Association for the Study of Religions*, Vol. 4, 1979, 5-6
24. J.O., Awolalu, and P. A., Dopamu, *West African Traditional Religion*, (Lagos: MacMillan Nigeria Publication Limited), 1979, 269-270
25. J.O., Awolalu, and P. A., Dopamu, *West African Traditional Religion*,...146-147
26. J.O. Awolalu, *Yoruba Beliefs and Sacrificial Rites*,(Longman Group Limited, 1979), 86-98
27. O. T., Oshadare, & O. A. Paul, "Traditional Methods Curing Mental Illness among the Owe People of Kogi State in Nigeria" in R. A. Olaoye (ed) *History of Indigenous Science and Technology in Nigeria*,...228-229

28. U., Maclean, Maclean, *Magical Medicine: A Nigerian Case Study*,... 32
29. M. A. Y. Lewu, " Women in the Economic Development of Oweland before 1900", B.A. Dissertation, Department of History, University of Ilorin, Ilorin, 1996, 22-23
30. *Annual Report, Department of Medical and Sanitary Services (ARDMSSS)*,1931
31. J.A. Owotunse,"The Role of African Agents in the Spread of Christian Missionary Activities in Oyi Local Government Area of Kwara State, Nigeria, 1900-1980", M. A. Dissertation, Department of History, University of Ilorin, Ilorin, 1987, 72.
32. J.C., Bulifant, F*orty Years in African Bush*,(Grand Rapids; Zondevan Publishing House Michigan, 1950), 10
33. Sophie DelaHaye, *Tread upon the Lion; The Story of Tommy Titcombe*, (Canada: Sudan Interior Mission), 20-21.
34. I. A., Paul, "The Beginning and Growth of Western Education in Okun-Yoruba land. 1903-1970. An M.A Seminar Delivered in the Dept. of History, University of Ilorin August 2008, 126.
35. Sophie DelaHaye, *Trend Upon the Lion*...... 20-21
36. S. B. Agaja, E*CWA Hospital Egbe: A Citadel of Blessing*, (FHB/Legacy Print, Ilorin 2008), 8-9
37. I. A., Paul, "A History of Health Care Services in Okun-Yoruba land, 1900-2000,"... 127-128.
38. Sophie DelaHaye, *Trend Upon the Lion*......23-24
39. S. A., Agbo, *ECWA Hospital Egbe, 1952-2002*, (Alanukitan Commercial Press, Nigeria Ltd.,Egbe), 6-7.
40. I. A., Paul, "A History of Health Care Services in Okun-Yoruba land, 1900-2000," 129.
41. S. B. Agaja, *ECWA Hospital Egbe*..., 8-10.
42. I. A. Paul, ... "A History of Health Care Services in Okun-Yoruba land, 1900-2000"130
43. S. B., Agaja, *ECWA Hospital Egbe*..., 11-13.
44. I. A., Paul, "A History of Health Care Services in Okun-Yoruba land, 1900-2000" 131
45. S. B., Agaja, E*CWA Hospital Egbe*........, 12-13
46. M., Martins "The Long Depression: West African Export Producers and the World Economy, 1914-1945" in I., Brown, (ed) *The Economics of Africa and Asia in the Inter-War Depression*, (London, Rutledge 1989).
47. E. O., Ochonu, *Colonial Meltdown: Northern Nigeria in the Great Depression*, (Ohio: University Press, 2009), 25-39.
48. E. O., Ochonu, *Colonial Meltdown*..., 26-28

49. S. B., Agaja, 60+, interview, Ilorin, 17th February, 2018; he was the Medical Director of the ECWA Hospital, Egbe for many years and now a Professor of Orthopaedic Surgery at the University of Ilorin Teaching Hospital (UITH), Ilorin. He is also the author of a comprehensive book on ECWA Hospital. Egbe.
50. I. A., Paul,. "A History of Health Care Services in Okun-Yoruba land, 1900-2000", 132
51. Sophie DelaHaye, *Trend Upon the Lion...*, 21.
52. S. A., Agbo, *ECWA Hospital Egbe,...*, 4
53. S. B., Agaja, *ECWA Hospital Egbe...*,10
54. S. S., Agbo, E*CWA Hospital Egbe, 1952-2000...*,12
55. S. S., Agbo, E*CWA Hospital Egbe, 1952-2000*, 12
56. S. B., Agaja, *ECWA Hospital Egbe...*, 8
57. S. A. gbo, *ECWA Hospital Egbe...*,9
58. S. B., Agaja, *ECWA Hospital Egbe: A Citadel of Blessing*, (FHB/Legacy Print, Ilorin 2008), 32-33
59. S. B., Agaja, *ECWA Hospital Egbe: A Citadel of Blessing*, 69.
60. The Revitalization of ECWA, Hospital, Egbe, n.d, 3
61. The Revitalization of ECWA, Hospital, Egbe
62. S. B. Agaja, *ECWA Hospital Egbe: A Citadel of Blessing*, (FHB/Legacy Print, Ilorin 2008), 32-33 (The Revitalization of ECWA, Hospital, Egbe, n.d), 3
63. S. B., Agaja, 60+ was interviewed in Ilorin, 17th February, 2018; he was the Medical Director of the ECWA Hospital, Egbe at the time the School of Nursing started readmitting students again. He is now a Professor of Orthopaedic Surgery at the University of Ilorin Teaching Hospital (UITH), Ilorin.
64. S. B., Agaja, *ECWA Hospital Egbe: A Citadel of Blessing*,... 81
65. S. B., Agaja, *ECWA Hospital Egbe*, 81 and 89
66. V. O., David, et al, ECWA School of Midwifery, Egbe, Kogi State, A handbook published by the school's management, n.d, 5
67. S. B., Agaja, *ECWA Hospital Egbe: A Citadel of Blessing*,...76
68. V. O., David, et al, ECWA School of Midwifery, Egbe, Kogi State, A handbook published by the school's management, n.d, 5
69. S. B., Agaja, *ECWA Hospital Egbe: A Citadel of Blessing*,. 77
70. V. O., David, et al, ECWA School of Midwifery, Egbe, Kogi State, A handbook published the school's management, n.d, 6
71. J. S., Obaro, "The Origin and Development of SIM/ECWA in Yagbaland, 1908-2008", M.A Dissertation, Dept. of History and International Studies, University of Ilorin, Ilorin, 2015, 73-74

Chapter Seven	Lewu, Ige & Afolabi, in Y.A. Quadri, Omotoye & R.I. Adebayo (Eds) Religion and Development in Nigeria London, Adonis & Abbey Publishers

72. J., Fowoyo, "The History and Impact of Roman Catholic Mission in Kabba, 1884-2000". Unpublished B.A. Dissertation, University of Ilorin, Ilorin, 2003, 62
73. J., Tolorunshagba, Interview. The Catholic Reverend Father, the Current Administrator of St. John's hospital, Kabba, 46 was interviewed at the hospital on Monday, May 1, 2017.
74. J. Fowoyo, "The History and Impact of Roman Catholic Mission in Kabba, 1884-2000"…55-58
75. A. Olumudi, interview, 70+ retired business woman, Odoero quarters Kabba, May 1, 2007.
76. M.C. Toluhi, "The Growth of Christian Churches, in Oweland since 1900: A Comparative Study of the Christian Missionary Society (CMS) and the Roman Catholic Mission (RCM)" Long Essay, Department of History, University of Ilorin, Ilorin, 1987, 65-66.
77. J.A., Owotunse, "The Role of African Agents in the Spread of Christian Missionary Activities in Oyi Local Government Area of Kwara State, Nigeria, 1900-1980"… 72
78. P. Mofolorunsho, interview, 60+, the Matron was interviewed in her office at St. John's Hospital, Kabba, May 1, 2017.
79. J. Tolorunshagba, Interview. The Catholic Reverend Father, the Current Administrator of St. John's hospital, Kabba, 46 was interviewed at the hospital on Monday, May 1, 2017.
80. P. Mofolorunsho, interview, 60+, the Matron was interviewed in her office at St. John's Hospital, Kabba, May 1, 2017.
81. Mofolorunsho, interview, 60+.
82. Mofolorunsho, interview, 60+.
83. Tolorunshagba, Interview. The Catholic Reverend Father, May 1, 2017.
84. Tolorunshagba, Interview.
85. Tolorunshagba, Interview.
86. Mofolorunsho, interview, May 1, 2017. May 1, 2017
87. Mofolorunsho, interview, 9

CHAPTER EIGHT

Christianity and Educational Development in Delta State, Nigeria

S.O. Aghalino
Department of History and International Studies
University of Ilorin, Ilorin, Nigeria
soaghalino@gmail.com
+2348039435843

Introduction

Religion is as old as mankind. Education, on the other hand, has been an indispensable tool in the perpetuation of religion. Education is a key factor in human development and was readily employed by the missionaries in their quest to plant Christianity and advance western civilisation[1]. Missionaries were the first to initiate the development of western education in Nigeria. Government participation first took the form of giving limited financial assistance to voluntary agencies and gradually developed into the recognition of education as the responsibility of government. Education from age long has been described as the system by which one generation imparts the ideals and cultural practices of its society to the next generation through an unending process. The prime place of education in the developmental efforts of nations has never been doubted all over the world. Religion and education seem to be inseparable as the oldest known educational systems in history shared two characteristics: they taught religion, and they promoted the traditions of the people. This implies that religion had begun ever since man became conscious of his environment.

There is balance of evidence to suggest that religion is instrumental to educational development. Right from the pre-colonial times, religion and education have been Siamese twins. In Delta, the region was exposed early to western education. This was not unconnected with the early contact of the people with the Europeans who exposed them to rudiments of Christianity and education, which was a handmaid of evangelisation. In this chapter, attempt is made to examine the historical role of religion in the educational development of Delta State. We are conscious of the fact that Delta state was created in 1991 and our usage of the word Delta may be suggestive of the then Delta Province. More importantly, we need to emphasise that our discussion here may be limited to the Urhobo and Isoko areas of Delta state, even though allusion may be made to the Ijo and Ndokwa areas for illustration. In specific terms, we highlight the coming of the missionaries and the planting of Christianity and the consequent establishment of schools and also examined some of their teething problems. An adjunct to the study is analysis of government take -over of schools and their subsequent return to missions as well as the rise of Pentecostal churches and their contributions to development. Our conclusion is adumbrated on the utilitarian role of religion in educational development in spite of the contemporary abuse of mission schools.

Conceptual Clarification

Religion: There is no consensus on the definition of religion. Ojo[2], has attempted to distill some definitions of religion. To him, Johnston and Samson see religion as 'an institutional framework within which specific theological doctrines and practices are advocated and pursued, usually among a community of like-minded believers [3]. Gwamna also defines religion as 'man's attempt to relate with supernatural force(s) as part of man's search for meaning, understanding and explanation of life[4]... According to Dopamu[5], religion has been part and parcel of man's existence and it is associated with the unseen. Religion is integrative; it functions to integrate society by providing social support and promoting social change. As an integrative tool, it was effectively used in the spread of the gospel[6].

Chapter Eight | S.O. Aghalino, in
Y.A. Quadri, Omotoye & R.I. Adebayo(Eds)
Religion and Development in Nigeria
London, Adonis & Abbey Publishers

Education: Education is widely recognised as key to national development[7]. Education has been defined in different ways by several scholars. For example, Nwagu defines education as 'the process by which every society attempts to preserve and upgrade the accumulated knowledge, skills and attitude; and guarantee its survival against the unpredictable and atimes hostile and destructive elements and forces of man and nature[8]. The Catholic Bishops of Nigeria in 1972 described education as consisting 'not only in the aggregate of all experiences that enlighten the mind, increase knowledge and develop abilities, it includes moral and religious education which help to develop attitudes and strengthen the will'[9]. Education is the process of facilitating learning, or the acquisition of knowledge, skills, values, beliefs, and habits. It is the act or process of imparting or acquiring general knowledge, developing the powers of reasoning and judgments, and generally of preparing oneself or others intellectually for mature life. Education is also conceived as the process of receiving or giving systematic instruction, especially at a school or university.

Development: The concept of development on the other hand is subject to many definitions. For example, Walter Rodney, defines it as a many-sided process[10]. At the level of the individual it implies increased skills and capacity, greater freedom, creativity, self- discipline, responsibility and material well-being. Education plays many roles in the society which are necessary for development. Development is described simply as the 'act, process or result of development of state of being developed, gradual advance or growth through progressive changes. Another concept of change is that of the mind leading to a complete mastery over nature in which case the humanity of man is no longer subjugated to nature. For those like the Latin American thinkers and theologians, development is seen in terms of liberation from poverty and oppression[11]. For our purpose, religion, education and development are geared towards the transformation of man from the state of nature and the need to make meaning out of an otherwise monotonous existence.

Religion and Educational Development in Delta Region before the Era of the Missionaries

For centuries, the reflection of the religious life of the people of modern day Delta State could be examined in the practical teaching and worship of their titular traditional gods and Supreme being variously referred to as *Oghene,* for the Isoko and Urhobo, *Tamara or Oyin* for the Ijo, *Oritse, for the Itsekiri* and *Chukwu* , for the Ndokwa and Anioma people. Although, the belief systems and traditions of worship slightly differed from one ethnic group to another, they all had several things in common; long before the advent of Christianity in the state, religion dominated the roots of the culture of the areas as all activities and instruments of governance and survival were clothed in religious rituals, language and symbolism. On the other hand, the purpose of education in the traditional society was to set afoot man with functional skills that would help him live peacefully among others and contribute his quota to the overall development of himself and his community. Traditional education in the Delta area like in most pre-colonial Nigerian communities, was informal as all the members of the community were collectively involved and the youths generally learned by imitating the ways of life and activities of the elderly members of the society. It focused its expectations on usefulness to the community rather than to an individual. This, indeed, conformed with Fafunwa's observation that "Society used to accord priority to the inculcation of values of "social responsibility, political participation, job orientation and spiritual and moral uprightness in the citizens" [12]. In other words, traditional education among the various peoples of Delta state was utilitarian. This possibly informed Ozigi's contention when he stressed that:

> There is the traditional form of education which has existed in our own societies, as in other societies, for centuries. It has taught our children, formally or informally, how to behave as members of a group (family, clan, peer, community); the cultural values, norms and beliefs of societies (its traditions, history, legends, folklore, dance, music); and also how to produce certain things needed for the survival of the society food, clothes, tools, housing, crafts[13].

Chapter Eight	S.O. Aghalino, in
	Y.A. Quadri, Omotoye & R.I. Adebayo(Eds)
	Religion and Development in Nigeria
	London, Adonis & Abbey Publishers

Traditional education in Delta region was centred on culture and traditions of the Delta people with functionalism being the main guiding principle. Thus education was regarded as a means to an end and not an end in itself[14]. In traditional Delta region, even though people were not literate in the Western sense, emphasis was strongly placed on education from infancy to adulthood via the processes of indoctrination, imitation, training and initiation. Hence, the word *Ewune* among the Isoko, and *Eyono,* among the Urhobo, which means to learn. Learning is comprehensive in its scope as it covers a wide range of issues which include religion, farming, agriculture, specialisation in craft, politics, character training, trade, fishing, apprenticeship, etc. In all of these activities, emphasis was placed on societal values such as respect for elders, honesty, hard work, integrity, good manners, obedience, discipline, tolerance, selflessness, home keeping, a sense of reciprocal obligation to others and to nature, and more importantly, willingness to conform to ancestral precedents. Children and adolescents were engaged in participatory education through myths, folklores, rhymes, drama, proverbs, ceremonies and festiva[15]. In point of fact, traditional education in Delta region, as elsewhere in the Niger Delta, combined physical training with character-building and manual activity with intellectual training. At the end of each stage, the child was given a practical test relevant to his experience and level of development and in terms of the job to be done. In sum, traditional education in Delta was in conformity with Fafunwa's seven cardinal goals of traditional education which were predicated on the desire to:

- To develop the child's latent physical skills.
- To develop the characters.
- To inculcate respect for elders and those in position of authority.
- To develop intellectual skills.
- To acquire specific vocational training and to develop a sense of belonging and participation.
- To develop a sense of belonging and participate actively in family and community affairs.
- To understand, appreciate and promote the cultural heritage of the community at large[16].

The point to note is that, before the coming of the missionaries and western-style education, traditional education among the people sought to transmit to younger generation the values on which ensured the survival and continuation that was worthwhile in the society which had organic and synchronic relationship between the living, the dead and those yet unborn.

The Advent of Missionaries

The origin of Western education Nigeria could be traced to the era of the Christian missionaries who had established contacts with this part of the country as early as the 15th century. This early effort began with the Portuguese who ventured into the coastal area in about 1472. Indeed, the Portuguese missionaries operated in the kingdom of Benin between 1515 and 1538 at the invitation of the Oba of Benin[17]. However, these early efforts in the area failed completely to displace the traditional religion. In spite of this, the Portuguese missionaries achieved some measure of success in Warri where, from the 1570s[18], they began to make considerable impact on the Olu, that is, the paramount ruler of Warri. It is relevant to note that, this early missionary effort did not endure as the religion never spread beyond the court. But this changed in the nineteenth century with a renewed determination to plant the gospel. Indeed, the Christian missionaries who came to West Africa in the nineteenth century were keenly aware of the failures of earlier missionary activities. Spurred on by T.F. Buxton's *The African slave trade and its remedy* published in 1839, and the evangelical revival of John Wesley in Britain, missionaries were eager to reach as many African societies as they could[19]. The work of T.F. Buxton was instrumental in convincing the British public to finance the Niger Expedition of 1841[20]. More so, it was believed by the 'Humanitarians and the Philosophers of the Age of Reason that the solution to the teething problem of abolition of the obnoxious trans-Atlantic slave trade', was to be found partly in Christianity which it was hoped would open the minds and eyes of the people to see the evils of the nefarious trade[21]. It is a fact of common knowledge that among Christian missions, education and evangelisation were inseparable. As it was the objectives of the early Christian missionaries to convert the 'heathen' or the benighted Africans to

Christianity via western education, this was promoted right from the beginning. Even though the various missions adopted different approaches to the implementation of their policies, they all regarded literacy education as an indispensable tool in the course of evangelisation. Yet it should be grasped that missionary education was designed to aid religion - to enable converts to read and have greater understanding of the Bible. But even then, parents favored the schools established more than the religion because of the opportunity of learning useful such as reading and writing of English and Portuguese and Arithmetic, etc. which the schools provided.

The necessity of having African converts who would be able to carry on the missionary work from the coasts to the hinterlands created an important link between education and missionary activity. Thus, mass education was necessary to expand the supply of missionaries in Nigeria, and elsewhere in tropical West Africa[22]. The different Christian missions used school as an organ of religious instruction, character formation, skill acquisition and initiation into the three elements of reading, writing and arithmetic. The first government financial contribution to education in Nigeria was recorded in 1877 when the Lagos administration made a grant of 200 pounds to each of the three missionary societies working in the Colony[23]. With the creation of the Protectorate of Southern Nigeria in1900, government opened a primary school in Benin City in 1901.

In a bid to get the converts into the new faith (Christianity), missionaries formally went into the establishment of schools on a large scale. For a long time, the Christian missions (i.e. the CMS, Roman Catholic Mission, Baptist Mission, Africa Church Group) dominated the educational scene of not only the Niger Delta region but the entire Nigeria. It could also be noted that each denomination emphasised its own importance and spared no pains at proving that one denomination was better than the other. As these denominations moved further into the hinterland, they established schools for the training of the catechists, teachers, deacons, priests and interpreters. Later on, education was provided for the training of people who would assist the colonial administrators in subordinate positions as clerks, artisans, assistant engineers, dispensers, etc.

Chapter Eight	S.O. Aghalino, in
	Y.A. Quadri, Omotoye & R.I. Adebayo
	Religion and Development in Nigeria
	London, Adonis & Abbey Publishers

To a very large extent, the colonial government treated education with relatively less importance and never accorded it the due priority it deserved[24]. So haphazard were the priorities of that government that education received attention only 'after the building of prisons and police barracks'. This trend should, however, not be too surprising because … ' initially and for long, the colonial administration placed the emphasis on the military …campaigns among the people while giving the advancement of education a low priority…'[25].

Thus, the colonial administration could not achieve as much improvement of the educational system, above that which they inherited from the missionaries. The British officials were more guided by consideration of effective colonial administrative control, consequent upon which they had a myopic view of education. In a nutshell, government intervention in educational development was ineffective initially, at least up to the second decade of the 20th century. Even after this period, education was restricted both in scope and in quality to the base level requirement of the regime, and was structured in such a way as not to constitute a challenge to the hegemony of the imperial order. In the circumstance, education in Nigeria up to the era of internal self-rule in the area was neither free nor universal. So grave was the situation that parents, guardians and relatives had to make great sacrifices to see that their wards got as much education as they could afford, for this was the well-paved road to a well-paid job.

As rightly observed by Ademola Ajayi, whatever the myopia of the British colonial educational policies when compared with the Christian Missionary venture, it is difficult to deny completely the fact that in their own little way, the British authorities did contribute in building on the foundation of mass educational culture, which the missionary societies had earlier laid. Both agencies, therefore, helped to soften the ground for mass popular education in later years[26]. In order for us to get the specific effort at the establishment of schools and their roles in national development, it is relevant for us to examine some cases from the Isoko and Urhobo areas of Delta state. What we have done in the preceding section is a general appraisal of the coming of the Missionaries and the spread of western education.

Development of Mission Schools in the Isoko/Urhobo Areas of the Delta Region

Western education was a veritable handmaid of evangelisation employed diligently by the missionaries in Isokoland as was the case in many other places in Nigeria. It is a well-known fact that missionaries played a crucial role in the spread of Western education. It is also true although to a lesser extent, that other interest groups - colonial administration and local African initiatives were also important in the planting of Western education in Nigeria. For the Isoko people, the missions should be given the credit in the process of the establishment of schools. Two missionaries namely James Welch and J. Hubbard were instrumental in the gigantic education scheme of 1929. Indeed, Welch appears to be a household name in Isoko, as he was seen as the pioneer of Western education in the sub-region. He put in place a blueprint for the evangelisation and subsequent establishment of schools in Isoko. The schools that were established functioned within the limits of fund and other attendant problems. In the midst of the euphoria for schools to be established, the local people, it must be emphasised, played their own part in the management and funding of the schools established by the missionaries.

It was not until 1911 that the gospel was spread to Isoko[27]. It was common knowledge that it was quite recently that the church preceded the effective presence of the British colonialists in Nigeria. But the Isoko case has shown that British rule preceded the spread of Christianity. In contrast to areas like Warri and Sapele, it took a very long time before Christianity could be planted in Isoko. The delay in the missionary penetration of Isoko was not unconnected with the general delay in the spread of Christianity into most parts of the then delta region[28]. Long distance traders to Patani must have also heard about Christianity when they exchanged their palm oil and kernel for European goods at the United African Company (UAC) and Messrs John Holt and Co. Factories. Hubbard posits that Christianity got into Isoko through three channels. These channels, were Ughelli, Igbide and Uzere. It would appear that this is an oversimplification of a complex issue[29]. Emerging evidence has shown that apart from these sources, some villages got introduced into the "white man's religion" from other places. For example, in Owhe clan, most people were converted to Christianity from places outside the clan. Emevor and the Ozoro clans received Christianity when men and women from these areas flocked to Ughelli to meet one Evware to be taught the ways of the "new God". A clerk attached to the Native Court at Uzere played a vital role in the establishment of the C.M.S. Church there.

The church got to Igbide through the effort of a woman named Bribinae, who earlier on, had been converted to Christianity at Patani. The Roman Catholic Mission was not widespread in Isoko. Nevertheless, this variant of Christianity reached Isoko in 1918, six years after the arrival of the C.M.S. Christianity was established at Uzere through the initiative of the court clerk. But when one Alexander Obuseri, an ex-serviceman from Ase paid one Adaka of Uzere a visit, both of them attended the only C.M.S. church there in spite of the fact that Alexander was a Roman Catholic. After the service, he made a sign of the cross. By this singular act he was expelled from the church. The expulsion may not be unconnected with the fact that they saw the sign of the cross as a savory of pagan practices. Alexander then left the church with his sympathisers and founded a Catholic church adjacent to the C.M.S. church at Uzere. From Uzere the Catholic Church spread to the rest of Isoko through one Odhu, the church reached Ilueologbo, (now Owhelogbo) wherein Okoloko who had separated from the C.M.S. at Ozoro, nourished the faith.[30]

The spread of Christianity to Isoko was rapid and this could be attributed to a number of factors. Most of the converts did so out of their conviction that being members of the Church, they could be freed from the demand of their titular gods that have been oppressing them. Indeed, contrary to the observation of Hubbard that the liberty exhibited by the "White fathers" was enough to prepare the ground for the spread of Christianity, what the people hoped to gain from conversion made the people to embrace Christianity. For example, the sick expected to be healed, those barren yearned for children and those held down by the gods longed to be released from their clutches.

The Missions and Education before the Advent of Welch

The work of conversion and evangelisation was followed closely by educational activities. In the field of education, it was the C.M.S. that blazed the trail. For instance, it was the C.M.S. that produced the first orthography of Isoko language and gave the public the first vernacular literature. St. Mark's gospel was translated into Isoko in 1918 while the other gospels followed in 1921.[31] At the initial period, the missionary tried to establish some schools, but there were no regular teachers However, a method was devised whereby some itinerant teachers were employed and such teachers stayed for a short period in various villages, and did such teaching as they could within the time available. Vernacular schools followed itinerant schools. Some schools were established by the C.M.S. through the initiative of Aitken between 1917 and 1925. These vernacular schools were attached to the churches, and they provided their instructions in Isoko language. Teachers' qualification in these early schools was not well defined as some possessed only Standard Two Certificate and others, even less. With time the staffing situation improved. It was not until 1923 that a regular school was opened in Isoko by the R.C.M. This school was later closed down because of a number of reasons. Uppermost, was the paucity of qualified teachers. Nevertheless, this school was reopened in 1937. In 1925, a central school was opened by the C.M.S. at Ozoro. The mission envisaged that the school should serve as centre of learning not only for reading and writing, but also for teaching agricultural practices and handicraft.[32]

The Advent of James Welch

The advent of James Welch in 1929 marked the beginning of effective educational work in Isoko. A comprehensive scheme was planned in 1929 and was intended to come into operation in 1931. In this plan, it was envisaged that eighteen schools would be built in the Isoko and Urhobo area. In this scheme, three categories of schools were identified: First Grade schools which were to read up to Standard Two. At the beginning of this scheme, the only first grade schools was at Ozoro and as it has been stated earlier, it was closed down and its pupils transferred to Uwheru. Second grade schools were established at Aviara and Uzere; while Third grade schools were opened at Ikpidiama, Irri, Iluelogbo and Edhene. More of the third grade schools were located at Oleh, Bethel, Emevor, Olomoro, Ellu, Emede, Orie-Irri, Igbuku and Igbide[33]. From all indications, the Catholic mission seemed not to have favoured the kind of education scheme envisaged by the C.M.S. especially as the C.M.S. hoped to appeal to the Native Authority for financial aid. Among Catholic circles, there was the insistence that if the Native Authority (NA) was to be involved in any way then provisions should be made for religious freedom in such schools.

The fear of the R.C.M. was that the C.M.S. could use the schools to win converts to their disadvantage. Father Heeley, the Catholic superintendent at Warri, saw the C.M.S. antic, and sought to frustrate their endeavours[34]. In this light, Oswald Gerrard, in his Annual Report for 1933, complained that the R.C.M. was making a real endeavour to "divide the work in Isoko". In these circumstances, the C.M.S. did not find it easy to get government approval for their education scheme in Isoko. Even the N.A. became rather suspicious and apprehensive of the C.M.S. initiative. The bitterness of the N.A. towards the C.M.S had to do with the fact that the CMS often protested to the government against the decisions of the Native Courts, which they claimed, went contrary to the religious beliefs of their adherents. In 1930 for example, the C.M.S. denounced a Native Court's decision in favour of handing over a widow to her deceased husband's brother as laid down in Isoko culture. The N.A. would have loved to thwart this elaborate venture of the C.M.S., which was bound to increase their influence in Isoko. But, the NA was in a dilemma, because the NA could not deny the urgent need of education in Isoko. The alternative to C.M.S. schools was Native Authority schools and the NA did not have the funds. Indeed. P.V. Main, the Assistant District Office (A.D.O), at Ase, supported the C.M.S. initiative, although some of his superiors were less enthusiastic.

To avoid further antagonism from the colonial state and the R.C.M. Welch decided to provide the funds for building the schools. He also provided apparatuses and other ancillary needs of the nascent schools. Welch was prepared to let some of the schools start in vernacular and later convert them to regular schools, as staff became available. To avert possible friction with the Isoko people, Welch made sure that the school calendar was so arranged that school children could assist their parents during the most pressing period of the respective occupational season.

As noted earlier, one of the problems that confronted the grandiose scheme of the C.M.S. was the paucity of qualified teachers. To this end, probationary teachers received lectures on Sundays from the few certificated teachers who came from Igboland. Reverend M.C. Letham, came to Isoko to assist Aitken in this task before the advent of James Welch. Aitken and Letham trained some natives who were posted to these schools as evangelists and teachers. They gathered young men who had studied outside Isoko to assist in training of teachers. Some of these people who studied outside Isoko that were co-opted by Aitken included Samuel Efeturi, Etetie Daniel, Dioko Joseph Igboro and Oriki. Teachers were given in-service training. All teachers were made to assemble at Oleh yearly for two months to receive general training in "African education." The teachers were taught how to relate Arithmetic to everyday life. An Isoko specialist in handicraft taught the teachers, who later imparted such skills to their pupils. More so, the teachers were taught the art of making baskets, chairs, and bookshelves.

James Welch went a step further by organising lectures for the teacher on the need for proper sanitation. Until quite recently, female education in Isoko, as was in most parts of Nigeria, tended to lag behind. In Isoko, the C.M.S. also blazed the trail in female education. Miss Jewith and Miss Smith were in the forefront in the pursuit of female education in Isoko. These two English ladies came to Isoko from the Iyenu hospital in 1930 to organise a medical centre at Bethel. Consequently, they established the Girls Training Home at Bethel where they also trained girls in domestic science. The first set of girls passed out from the centre in 1933. Female education was further given impetus with the establishment of Isoko central school at Oleh in 1936. This was a mixed school, and had hostel facilities for boys and girls.

In addition to regular lessons, the girls were taught cookery and needlework[35]. Perhaps, acting on the initiatives of the CMS, and probably with the fear that the gigantic C.M.S. educational scheme in Isoko, the R.C.M. may lag behind and become inconsequential, the R.C.M. and other missionary bodies followed the trail of the C.M.S. as they established their own schools. The African Church, for example, made some attempt at establishing schools at Okpe, Ellu and Ofagbe but failed as a result of the antagonism of the people who preferred the C.M.S. schools. Nevertheless, the African Church succeeded in opening some schools at Umeh, Owodokpokpo and Anibeze. The Christ Apostolic Church, on the other hand, opened a school at Irri[36]. The dearth of qualified teachers more than ever, stared glaringly at the missionaries, to the extent that it almost crippled their educational scheme. In this light, effort was made to establish teachers training colleges. J.M. Curr, who was the Superintendent of the C.M.S. fought hard to open a Teachers' Training Centre at Oleh in 1939.

However, six years later, the school was converted to a Grade Three Teacher Training College. Indeed, in 1957, St. Michael's College, Oleh, as the school became known, awarded its first Higher Elementary Teachers Certificate. The Roman Catholics were not to be out-paced. They also entered the teachers' education schemes, when they established a college for that purpose at Ozoro in 1956. This was the famous St. Joseph's College. In 1956 also, the CMS took up the initiative to venture into the establishment of a Secondary' Grammar School. This, it did, with the establishment of the James Welch Grammar School, at Emevor. This School was fittingly named after the pioneer of Western education in Isoko. Toeing the line of the CMS, the RCM opened its own Secondary Grammar School at Ozoro on March 9, 1957. To reflect its Catholic character, the school was named Notre Dame College[37]. In the Urhobo area, a Central school was opened at Okpare, and another at Uwheru in 1931. After the 2nd world war, particularly in the 1950s, primary schools increased in number. When in 1955, the Universally Free Primary Schools were introduced together with Secondary Modern Schools, the CMS built Modern Schools at various towns and villages in Delta. The table below is explicit on the proliferation of Mission schools in the Delta area.

Table 1: Selected List of Mission Schools in Delta State

S/N	Name of School Established	Date
1.	Africa Church Grammar School, Ekakpamre,	1965
2	Anglican Girls Grammar School, Ozoro ,	1969
3	Anglican Girls Grammar School, Ughelli,	1960

Chapter Eight | S.O. Aghalino, in
Y.A. Quadri, Omotoye & R.I. Adebayo(Eds)
Religion and Development in Nigeria
London, Adonis & Abbey Publishers

4	Anglican Grammar School, Okpare Water-side,	1964
5	Baptist High School, Eku	1968
6	Baptist High School, Orerokpe	1964
7	James Welch Grammar School, Emevor	1957
8	Notre Dame College, Ozoro	1957
9	Our Lady's High School, Effurun,	1960
11	St Kevin's Grammar School, Kokori	1963
12	St Vincent's College, Okwagbe	1963
13	St. Ambrose College, Usiefun	1963
14	St. Peter Clavers College, Aghalokpe	1950
15	St. Enda's Grammar School, Agbarho	1964
16	St. Ita's Grammar School, Sapele	1964
17	St. Joseph's College, Ozoro	1955
18	St. Malachy's Grammar School, Sapele	1959
19	St. Theresa's Grammar School, Ughelli	1966

Source: B. George, Unethical Practices and Management Option in Mission Schools as Perceived by Teachers in Delta State' *Global Journal of Management and Business Research*, Vol.4, No.4, 2017, p.7 and author's field work.

Management and Funding of the Mission Schools

Initially, Reverend M.C. Letham and J.D. Aitken supervised the teachers until they eventually left Isoko. James Welch took over from their people in 1929 when he arrived in Isoko. Welch came to Isoko highly determined to organise Western education in the area. It is important to note that James Welch, before coming to Isoko, wrote a long essay on "West African Education" for the award of the Diploma in theory and practice of education of the Durham University. Thus, Welch was well equipped with the task ahead of him. But his effort at effective management of schools in Isoko was limited by the education code of 1926[38]. As it were, with the introduction of education code, schools were also classified into grades A, B, C and D. This was done for the purpose of winning grants from the government. It also laid down the minimum rates to be paid to teachers in assisted schools. One other provision was that all assisted schools and non-assisted schools were to be opened for government inspection at any time without warning. Also, schools could be closed down for sufficient reason established by the appropriate authority[39].

In spite of the incursion of the colonial state, James Welch succeeded in initiating a large percentage of Isoko children into proper formal education. In order to carry along the whole segment of Isoko society, Welch incorporated the elders into the administration of the schools by asking them to set up schools committees. The headmasters of the schools regularly consulted these committees each time they needed one form of assistance or the other. The Bishop had the prerogative to appoint managers and supervisors of schools. He also had the right to appoint an education officer, who was based at Warri. Every District had a manager of schools. The supervisor of schools closely followed the managers. In Isoko area, M.A. Marioghae was the first supervisor of Schools. The Missions bore the brunt of the financing of the schools at the initial period. Nevertheless, as time wore on, they charged nominal fees. For example, between 1938 and 1942, infants' classes were one shilling. Standard 1-3 two shillings while Standard IV was five Shillings. The missions subsidised the fees charged with money realised from church dues and harvest sales. Teachers" salaries were paid according to the limited resources available.

Indeed, in 1930, some teachers' salaries stood at seven shillings six pence. By 1935, however, teachers' salaries were fixed according to the classes the teachers were handling. As it were, Assistant Third Year pupil teachers were paid One Pound while certificated teachers were paid Three Pounds. But in 1946, certificated teachers' salaries were fixed at Seven Pounds per month. As should be expected, the school fees and church dues collected for running these schools were inadequate. As such, the missions called on the elders of such villages where schools were established to assist by putting up some school structures, like building of classrooms and staff-quarters. The missions diligently employed this method as a pre-requisite before new schools could be established. In some villages, land was given out free. At Iluelogbo for example, the parcel of land the C.M.S Church was built on was given out free to the Mission. In order to alleviate the financial crisis of their wards and the missions, some communities paid school fees collectively. In 1949, Ikpidiama and Canaan did this for their children in the schools, while Aviara and Idheze did the same to assist the mission schools in

1950 and 1951 respectively.[40] In Isoko, as in other parts of Nigeria, government gave some form of financial assistance to approved elementary schools. This assistance was in form of grants-in aid. Initially, the grants were given in lump sum. However, in 1949, the colonial government put three schools on the assistance list in Isoko. But as the financial burden of these schools increased, government advised the Native Authorities to introduce education rates.

Thus, the Native Ordinance was amended to make it legal for Native Authorities to levy rates to support any school operating within their sphere of influence[41]. As it were, the Urhobo-Isoko Federal Native Authority enacted the Education Rate by-law in 1952. By this law, it made it mandatory for every adult male residing or carrying out business within the area of its jurisdiction liable to pay the annual education rate of four shillings. The collection of this levy continued until the introduction of the free Universal Primary Education in 1955 by the Government of the old Western region of Nigeria. From the foregoing, it could be seen that the management and funding of the established schools was a Herculean task for the missions. But aside from this problem, the missions also contended with the initial antagonism of the Isoko people. The school programme was opposed at the initial period because the Education Ordinance of 1926, stipulated that teaching in primary one or two classes must be done in the appropriate Nigerian language. This clause in the Ordinance infuriated the Isoko people whose children were in these schools. They felt, after all, education was meant to learn the English Language and the White man's ways. At least, this was their narrow perception of Western education. To this end, most parents withdrew their children from these schools.

Government Takeover of Schools

A number of interrelated factors conspired to influence government takeover of mission schools. After the civil war, there was a new thinking in government circles to take over mission schools in order to instill secular ideals and values into public education. This position of the Federal Government is also strongly attested to in the National Policy on Education when it was clearly stated that:

Education in Nigeria is no more a private enterprise, but a huge government venture that has witnessed a progressive evolution of governments' complete and dynamic intervention and active participation. The Federal Government has adopted education as an instrument par excellence for effecting national development.[42]

But government's claim is seriously contested by scholars when it is alleged that, the quest to give secular education is a smokescreen. According to Nwokolo, the decision to take over schools from the missions was meant to punish the missionaries whose humanitarian organisations like (CARITAS) assisted the Biafran agitators during the civil war[43]. The overnight flight of relief materials to the affected areas during war angered the Nigerian government at that time. This action, the government alleged, was responsible for the prolongation of the thirty months civil war which was meant to be a two-week "police action" as was envisaged, to end the war.

Arising from government intervention in education, she decided to give unconditional grants to the mission school, which was used to proliferate mushroom schools in villages. Earlier, the sources of funds for the mission schools mainly came from the grants from the main missions abroad and/or donations from groups and individuals outside the country, including local Christian and parents who were later paying for their children. This singular exercise, often marked as the costliest mistake ever made by government, signaled the collapse of quality of education cum the disappearance of morality and character building from the school system. Ever since, many groups and individuals have kept agitating that since schools are centres of excellence, as well as stronghold for character building, handing over of schools back to their missionary owners would hopefully revamp the standard back to what it used to be, since the inception of Western education.

Nevertheless, the decision to take over the missionary school was made by the military government in 1973 after the excruciating thirty months civil war in Nigeria. In 1972, a meeting was held between the military governor of Midwest state Dr. Samuel Ogbemudia and the Proprietors of private schools in the state. In that meeting the government indicated its intention to take over primary and secondary schools from private owners with an arrangement put in place to pay

Chapter Eight	S.O. Aghalino, in
	Y.A. Quadri, Omotoye & R.I. Adebayo(Eds)
	Religion and Development in Nigeria
	London, Adonis & Abbey Publishers

compensation to the private owners. The Catholic Mission which objected to the move refused to take compensation but instead advocated that government should build their own schools to take care of the teeming population.[44]

With the government mind made up, primary and secondary schools belonging to the Catholic and other missions were taken over by the government in 1973 in spite of the protest from the missions and old Boy/Girls Associations of the affected schools. With the takeover of those schools by the government, the quality of education in the affected schools began to nosedive in terms of teaching and learning, infrastructure as well as values. This move by the government has remained the bane of primary and secondary school education development in Nigeria till date. Schools that knew no strikes before began to experience incessant strikes, school buildings- classroom, staff quarters and boarding homes became seriously dilapidated and in perpetual state of decay. The learning environment not only became un-conducive but also grossly non-habitable as school children were made to learn under leaking roofs and in some cases, bare floors. The Government inability to meet the ever growing demands and challenges of the educational sector forced it to have a rethink in its initial policy to take- over of the schools.

In the light of the above, the military Government of the then Bendel State in 1984, under the administration of Brigadier J.T. Useni invited genuine participation of private individuals and organisations in the running of secondary schools in the state. Government had realised that it could not alone run schools and provide enough school for the education for the teeming masses needed it. This decision came only about eleven years after the takeover [45]. In December 1985, the government agreed to return ten secondary schools to the Bendel State Catholic Mission. Of the ten schools returned, four were in present Edo state and six schools in the present Delta state. But this process of return of schools could not materialise because of the frequent changes in government as well as the eventual creation of Delta state. The Catholic mission continued to press for the return of Catholic schools and in 1996, the then Military Governor of Delta State, Group Captain Ibrahim Kefas promulgated the law-Edict No. 3 of 1996 returning the six

Secondary schools earlier approved by the military Government of J.T. Useni, back to the Catholic Mission. This decision was followed with a protest from the other missions who also wanted their schools returned to them. The Delta state Chapter of Nigeria Union of Teachers (N.U.T) headed by then Reverend, and now Bishop T.J. Edewor and some communities spear-headed the agitation for the complete and non-selective return of mission schools to their rightful owners. In view of the uproar and incessant agitations that accompanied the initiative, the Governor, Colonel David Dung in 1997, suspended the return of the schools "until enough consultation" was made.

The Catholic mission did not rest in the quest for the return of their schools as they continued with the request. They met with then Governor of Delta State, Chief James Onanefe Ibori who subsequently set up a panel headed by Prof. B.I.C. Ijomah to examine the issue of return of schools and discus with relevant stakeholders on the request. The report of that panel was not made known until the Emmanuel Uduaghan's administration set up another panel in 2009 with Bishop T.J. Edewor as the Chairman. The report of the Bishop Edewor panel was given a favourable consideration and this led to the return of 40 (forty) secondary schools to the missionaries in 2011 with the Catholic Mission taking back twenty seven (27) schools, the Anglican Mission had eight(8) schools, Baptist Convention had four(4) schools and a school to the African church[46]. During the schools handover, the then Governor, Dr. Uduaghan asserted that the return of the schools to the missions would improve the standard of education in the state and create room for healthy competition as his administration was poised to also improve the standard of public schools in the state. Considering the capitalist inclination of present day Churches, it is hoped that the old glory and standard that characterised the then mission schools would still be dedicatedly pursued and revived.

Pentecostal Churches

The emergence of Pentecostal Churches in the 1970s is a revolutionary phase in the history of religion and educational development in the Delta area. While opinion is divided on the origin of Pentecostal churches in Nigeria, Omotoye aligned with Dada when he stressed that Pentecostalism is not alien to the Nigerian Christians… and, "that the

Chapter Eight	S.O. Aghalino, in
	Y.A. Quadri, Omotoye & R.I. Adebayo(Eds)
	Religion and Development in Nigeria
	London, Adonis & Abbey Publishers

phenomenon of spirituality is not a monopoly of any race or tradition"[47]. It is believed that it was the late Arch-Bishop B.A. Idahosa that introduced televangelism to Nigeria. The prosperity teaching of Arch-Bishop Idahosa was a foundation that other Pentecostal evangelists such as Bishop David Olaniyi Oyedepo, Pastor Adeboye, Oritsejafor and others built upon. In Delta state as elsewhere in Nigeria, The Living Faith Church has to its credit a conglomerate of Nursery, Primary, Secondary and Universities. The nursery and primary schools are under the name Kingdom Heritage while the Secondary section is named Faith Academy. These schools are found in all the nooks and crannies of urban centres in Warri, Asaba, Ughelli, Kwale and Oleh.

The importance of the establishment of schools has shown that it provides employment to a reasonable number of people, most especially the youths who are roaming the streets of the country. Heroes of Faith Church has also established, The Heroes Academy, Ughelli and the Eagle Height International Montessori established by Pastor Ayo Oritsejafor of the Word of Life Bible Church, Ajamomugha, Warri. Again, the World of Life Church, Warri, established the Eagle Height University (EHU) at Omadino, Delta Sate. With the proliferation of Churches, came also the mushrooming of pseudo- mission schools. There is hardly any street in most of the urban centres of Delta that a variant of churches and their schools are not seen. It is however observed that unlike the colonial mission schools that preceded the rise of Pentecostal mission schools, the tuition fees being paid in the contemporary mission schools are exorbitant and beyond the reach of the common man in the society. The capitalist inclination of the contemporary mission schools has raised doubt whether they are advancing the course of development or perpetuating underdevelopment. Nevertheless, it is to the credit of contemporary missions that they have uninterrupted academic calendars and curriculums that are consistent with developments in the 21st century.

Conclusion

Missionary education contributed to wealth and reversal of fortunes as exposure of individuals to missionary activity is positively associated with the individual living in a wealthier condition [48]. This position is in contrast to Ali Mazrui's claim that the role of missionary schools in Africa was paradoxical in that they created what he called 'techno-cultural gap' that did not make for significant social development. While it is granted that quasi-religious education was given by the missionaries, effort was made to put in place medical services, even though this was ancillary to evangelisation[49]. As it where, Mission doctors and health personnel used medicine as a bait to get converts in their membership drive. They established dispensaries, 'bush' hospitals and clinics as adjuncts to the church. The legacy of this strategy in Christian ministries who operate free health services within the church but also use medicine as a means of evangelism in their outreaches is till date sustained. Health facilities and sick bays are prerequisites in the establishment of all schools today and their ability to provide effective medication remain another consideration for parents' choice of school or institution.

Consequent upon the primary aim of the missionaries to transform indigenous ways of thought, there emerged a new life in which the individual and his relation to God, his means of livelihood and his wife and family would take primacy over traditional beliefs, in ancestral spirits, primitive methods of subsistence, extended kinships and polygamy. With the embrace of Christianity therefore, Christian values and ethics were introduced. Monotheism was emphasised and new identities (unity and solidarity) formed. Some obnoxious practices associated with the traditional religions had been criticised and condemned. The teachings (biblical standard) in the ever increasing churches today are not in any way different from the emphasis laid by the missionaries. Most inhabitants of the state practice Christianity and very few, Islam and the traditional faith. This is not to however deny high level of syncretism among the people as the people and their culture are inseparable.

Similarly, the trend of religious and educational development seems to have borrowed from the legacy of the foreign missions in the sense that hardly is there any church established today that does not begin its own school sooner or later. Again, each denomination equally struggles to have its mission secondary and higher institutions at either the state or national levels respectively. Similarly, one major development in the region is the creation and growth of the *élite* along socio-cultural, religious, professional, and political lines. New forms of associations ranging from small savings club to multi-purpose religious unions, reshaped traditional ties for city purposes. Cities, being the centres of education and employment of the educated *élite* as well as of political awareness eventually became the centres of nationalist activities. The introduction of western education and values had raised competent educated *élite* who are not only at the helm of affairs in administration, education, commerce, politics, entertainment, music, etc but are also in high proportion of such positions today. However, it must be pointed out that many of these *élite* belong to two worlds. While some remain indigenous in their thinking and way of life, they at the same time cherish the European ideals such as foreign civilisation, sense of justice, form of government and custom. The blend has suggested co-existence between the foreign and indigenous traits as well as possible modifications in some areas.

The role played by the private individuals and voluntary bodies in the educational development of the state cannot be over-emphasised. Education is one of the engine rooms for measuring the developmental height of a state. The comparative giant strides made towards quality assurance and improved standard did encourage the thriving of private schools as parents have always sought to provide quality education for their children irrespective of the cost. The proliferation of schools in the State evidently attests to the ever growing consciousness of the people to acquire Western education as well as to yield to the position of the Federal Government's provision, contained in the National Policy on Education that:

> Education is an expensive social service which requires adequate financial provision from all tiers of Government for a successful implementation of the educational programmes. …Government's ultimate objective is to make education free at all levels. The financing of education is a joint responsibility of the Federal, State and Local Governments. In this connection, Government welcomes and encourages the participation of local communities, individuals and other organization[50].

It is on this note that it should be reemphasised that one of the major ingredients of a nation's prosperity is education as well as the biggest asset for skills acquisition for future development. Since education is a dynamic instrument of change, constant review of all-round development or policies pertaining to pre-primary education, primary education, secondary education, higher education including professional education, technical education, adult and non-formal education, special education and teacher education become indispensable in order to ensure its adequacy and continued relevance to national needs and objectives. On the whole, the success of any system of education is hinged on proper planning, efficient administration and adequate financing.

References

1. S. Ademola Ajayi, Christian Missions and Evolution of the Culture of Mass Education in Western Nigeria, *Journal of Philosophy and Culture* 3, no.2 (June 2006): 33-54
2. R. J. Ojo, Religion, National Transformation and the Nigerian Society: Some Reflections, *International Journal of Philosophy and Theology* 2, no.2 (2014):165-184
3. Johnson D. and Sampson, C. (eds.) 1994. *Religion: The Missing Dimension of Statecraft* (New York: Oxford University Press), 4.
4. J. D. Gwamna, *Religion and Politics in Nigeria* (Jos: African Christian Textbooks, 2010), xi.
5. P.A. Dopamu, 'In the Service of Humanity', being a farewell lecture at University of Ilorin, (Ilorin: Unilorin Press, 2009), 7
6. F. Barasa and J. Misati, The Role of the Church in the Development of Education in Kenya: Expanding Education through Evangelization. *International Journal of Current Research* 4, no 12 (2012): 097-102.
7. M.A. Nwagu, UPE: Issues, Prospects and Challenges, available online at www.christianpost.com/news/education-and-development-in-nigeria-7129. Retrieved on 15/7/2017
8. M.A. Nwagu, UPE: Issues, Prospects and Challenges.
9. A.A. Omoruyi, Impact of Catholic Mission in Nigeria. Available online at: https://www.linedin.com/pulse/amazon-go-brings-retail-experience-21st-cebtury-brians-solis. 8/7/17.
10. A.A. Omoruyi, Impact of Catholic Mission in Nigeria.
11. W. Rodney, *How Europe Underdeveloped Africa* (Abuja: Panaf Publishing, 1972), 1.

Chapter Eight	S.O. Aghalino, in Y.A. Quadri, Omotoye & R.I. Adebayo(Eds) Religion and Development in Nigeria London, Adonis & Abbey Publishers

12. S.B. Mala, "Religion and Development: The Case for Christian-Muslim Joint Responsibility", in I.A.B. Balogun, P. Ade-Dopamu, et al.(eds.) *The Place of Religion in the Development of Nigeria* (Ilorin: Department of Religions, University of Ilorin), 1988.
13. A.B. Fafunwa, *History of Education in Nigeria* (London: George Allen & Unwin, 1974). See also, S.O. Aghalino, 'Isoko Under Colonial Rule' (Unpublished MA Thesis, University of Ilorin, Ilorin, 1994), Chapter Two.
14. A. Ozigi, & Ocho, L., *Education in Northern Nigeria* (London: George Allen & Unwin, 1981).
15. O. Uyeri, 'A History of Western Education in Isokoland", (Unpublished M.A. Thesis, University of Ibadan, Ibadan, 1974), 96.
16. S. Erivwo, *A History of Christianity in Nigeria, the Urhobo, the Isoko and the Itsekiri* (Ibadan: Daystar, 1979).
17. A.B. Fafunwa, *History of Education in Nigeria*
18. S. Ademola Ajayi, Christian Missions and Evolution..., 34
19. S. Ademola Ajayi, Christian Missions and Evolution
20. T.F. Buxton, The African Slave Trade, and Its Remedy, J. Murray, 1840
21. Ajayi, J.F.A., *Christian Missions in Nigeria, 1841-1891: The Making of a New Elite* (Ibadan: Longmans, 1965), 7-8; B. Sundkler, and C. Steed, *A History of the Church in Africa* (Cambridge: Studia Missionalia Upsaliensia University Press, 2000), 224.
22. S. Ademola Ajayi, Christian Missions and Evolution...
23. Ajayi, J.F.A., *Christian Missions in Nigeria, 1841-1891...*; G.O.M. Tasie, *Christian Missionary Enterprise In the Niger Delta 1864-1918*, Studies on Religion in Africa, Brill, 1978; E.A. Ayandele, *The Missionary Impact on Modern Nigeria, 1841-1914*, Ibadan: Longmans, 1966; O. Nduka, *Western Education and the Cultural Background* (Oxford University Press, 1964); O. Dozie and R. Pongou, Historical Missionary Activity, Schooling, and the Reversal of Fortunes: Evidence from Nigeria.
24. U.U. Okonkwo and Mary-Noelle Ethel Ezeh, 'Implications of Missionary Education for Women in Nigeria: A Historical Analysis', *Journal of International Women Studies* 10, Issue 2 (2008): 186.
25. S. Ademola Ajayi... Christian Missions and Evolution...

26. S.O. Osoba and A. Fajana, "Education and Social Development in the
Twentieth Century", in O. Ikime (ed.) *Groundwork of Nigerian History* (Ibadan: Heinemann, 1980).
27. S.O. Osoba and A. Fajana, Education and Social Development.
28. S.O. Aghalino. 'The Spread of Christianity in Isokoland: Local Initiatives and Responses, 1910-1930', *Journal of Arabic and Religious Studies* 14, (2000): 29. See also, A.F.C. Ryder, "Missionary Activities in the Kingdom of Warri in the early nineteenth century", *Journal of the Historical Society of Nigeria* 11, no.1 (1960): 1-24; See also O. Ikime, "The Coming of C.M.S. in the Itsekiri, Urhobo and Isoko Country", in *Nigeria Magazine,* 86 (1965): 211.
29. A.F.C. Ryder, 'Missionary Activities in the Kingdom of Warri…
30. J. Hubbard, *The Sobos of the Niger Delta* (Zaria: Gaskiya Corporation, 1948), 279.
31. Aghalino, S.O., "Impact of Christianity on the people of Owhe Clan 1911-
1990", B.A. Lond Essay, Bendel State University, Ekpoma, 1990.
32. S.O. Aghalino, Impact of Christianity…
33. S.O. Aghalino, Impact of Christianity…
34. National Archives Ibadan, (NAI), Ughelli Papers: File No. 118 1930, 8.
35. National Archives Ibadan, (NAI), Ughelli Papers: File No. 118 1930, 8.
36. O. Ikime, *The Isoko People* (Ibadan: Ibadan University Press, 1972), 50.
37. O. Ikime, *The Isoko People…* 77
38. O. Ikime, The Isoko People…
39. J.E. Uyeri, 'The Development of Education in Isoko Division, 1910-1960, M.A. Thesis, University of Ibadan, 1976.
40. J.E. Uyeri, 'The Development of Education in Isoko Division, 1910-1960…
41. J.E. Uyeri, 'The Development of Education in Isoko Division, 1910-1960…
42. Ughelli Papers: File 1223/1930.
43. Federal Republic of Nigeria, *National Policy on Education,* (Lagos: Federal Ministry of Information, 1981).
44. J.I.L. Nwokolo, Issues of Our Time: Selected works of Chief J.I.L.,

Nwokolo, Asaba: His Bride Ventures, 2013.
45. J.I.L. Nwokolo, Issues of Our Time: Selected works of Chief J.I.L., Nwokolo
46. I. Awulor, As Missions Take Over Schools in Delta, available online at thepointernewsonline.com/?p=1272. Retrieved on 15/7/17
47. R.O. Omotoye and E.O. Opoola, 'The Church and National Development: A Case of the Living Faith Church (Winners Chapel'. Available online at http://www.censur.org/2012/Nigeria.htm
48. R.O. Omotoye and E.O. Opoola , 'The Church and National Development
49. O. Dozie and R. Pongou, Historical Missionary Activity, Schooling, and the Reversal of Fortunes: Evidence from Nigeria, available online at https://www.aeaweb.org/conference/2015/retrieve.php?pdfid=874.Retrieved 15/7/2017.
50. Federal Republic of Nigeria, *National Policy on Education,* (Lagos: Federal Ministry of Information, 1981), 49.

CHAPTER NINE

The Impact of Christianity (Sudan Interior Mission) on Igbomina Land, Kwara State, Nigeria

Daniel, Mary Taiye
*Department of Religions,
University of Ilorin, Ilorin, Nigeria
danielmarytaiye@gmail.com
+2348062598033*

&

Abolarin, Isaac Adeshina
*ECWA Theological Seminary
Igbaja, Kwara State, Nigeria
abolarinisaac@gmail.com*

Introduction

Over the years, religion has been seen as an instrument of promoting conflict and war, to a very threatening level, instead of as an instrument for building blocks for peaceful co-existence in the society. This has made some to question the relevance of religion in this age. According to Malomo, religion in Nigeria today has been devilled with religious intolerance and disharmony culminating in wanton destruction of lives and property.[1] He cited so many instances of religious violence from year 2001 to date especially in Northern Nigeria.

At the global level, the story is not different. The September 11 terrorist attack on the United States of America quickly comes to mind. The list is endless of various religious conflicts in many parts of the world. This is why Shadrack Best sees religion as becoming a divisive issue that has constituted a growing conflict flash point not only in Nigeria but the whole world at large.²

However, religion has been and would still be an agent of social-economic transformation of any society, including Nigeria. The benefits of religion in the society can never be over emphasised. The evil seen in religion is as a result of the adherents of different religious groups not practicing it as it should be. Religion has no evil in itself, after all religions teach against evil practices in the society. All religions encourage religious tolerance, peaceful co-existence and love. In agreement with this submission, Oderinde noted that if people (adherents of various religions) apply their religions to their social, emotional, economic, intellectual and spiritual life, there would be unity and peaceful co-existence in all societies.³ In other words, the religious violence and uproars witnessed so far are not caused by religions but by the inability of the Muslims and the Christians to follow strictly the teachings of these religions.

The impacts of religion in Nigeria are enormous. This chapter focuses on the impacts of the Sudan Interior Mission (SIM), one of the major Christian Missionary Agencies in Igbomina land, Kwara state.

The Igbomina People: A Historical Survey

The Igbomina people are also called *Ogbonna*. They are a sub-ethnic group of Yoruba people who occupy some parts of Kwara-South and the Northern part of Osun State, Nigeria and speak a dialect also called *Igbomina or Igbonna*. In Osun State, Igbomina people live in Ifedayo and Ila Local Government Area Councils. ⁴ In Kwara State, they live in Irepodun, Ifelodun and Isin Local Government Areas of the State. Some major Igbomina cities/towns in Osun State are Oke-Ila, Orangun, Ora, and Ila Orangun. In Kwara State, which has the majority of Igbomina people, some major towns are: Omu-Aran, Idofian, Igbaja, Share, Ganmo, Amoyo, Ajase-Ipo, Oke-Ode, Isanlu-Isin, Ekun Mesan Oro, Oro-Ago, Babanla, Iwo, Oke-Onigbin etc.⁵

The origin of Igbomina people is still a subject of historical conjecture. However, we agree with Dada who indicated that available oral evidence and scanty written records explain that some Igbomina migrated from Ile-Ife, the cradle of human civilisation according to the Yoruba mythology, while others are said to have migrated from other established Yoruba kingdoms such as Oyo.[6] Closely related to this is the tradition which says that the area now called Igbomina land was given to and founded by *Orangun* of Ila as his own share of inheritance from his grandfather, *Oduduwa,* the purported progenitor of the Yoruba race.[7] *Orangun* was the second son (and the fourth child of *Okanbi*), the only son of *Oduduwa*, he (*Orangun*) founded Igbomina through the use of *Ogbo.* It was this *Ogbo* that was supposed to know the way to the bank of River Niger, the ultimate destination of this itinerant way-farer, hence the name *Ogbomo ona* i.e. *Ogbo* knows the way, which became Igbomina with the passage of time.[8] However, Ibitoye noted that there exists also a tradition in Omu-Aran which claims the possession of similar *Ogbo* as that in Orangun's custody.[9] We, however, noted that the duplication of *Ogbo* is closely associated with leadership rivalry in Igbomina land since the possession of the genuine *Ogbo* would have stronger claim to the leadership and headship of the entire Igbomina land.

However, Igbomina people have traditions that attempt to explain the origin of their common language (Yoruba), culture and political institutions from descent through a single ancestor, Oduduwa. They share to a degree, a common culture and social life that can be classified into two distinct sub-groups based on dialectic variations. The two dialectic groupings in the land are the *Mo yee* and *Mo san* groups. The *mo yee* includes Oro-Ago, Ile-Ire, Ora, Oko/Ola, Oke-Ode,and Agunji districts, while the *Mo san* groups comprise Ajase-Ipo, Igbaja, Isin, Omu-Aran, Oro, Esie, Omupo, Idofian, Ila-Orangun and mostly those areas that constitute the southern outpost of Igbomina.[10] Each group possesses a dialect slightly different from the other. Nevertheless, they are mutually intelligible. The headquarters of Igbomina is Ajase-Ipo in Irepodun Local Government, Kwara State.

The Sudan Interior Mission (SIM) in Igbomina land

The Sudan Interior Mission (SIM), just like the Sudan United Mission (SUM) was borne out of the burden of the Sudan. This mission was not from an ecclesiastical organisation as the Church Missionary Society or the Church of England or like other Church Mission Boards, such as the Baptists, the Presbyterians, the Methodists and the Catholic Missions.

SIM was borne and founded by some individuals who had the burden to take the Gospel of Christ to places where it had not been preached. Today, this non-denominational mission has become a renowned Christian denomination in Nigeria. According to the trustees of ECWA, her name was changed to Evangelical Church of West Africa (ECWA) in 1954 in an attempt to indigenise her. In 2010, her name was equally changed from Evangelical Church of West Africa to Evangelical Church Winning All.[11] This was done in order to accommodate other branches opened outside Africa, particularly in the United States of America.

The sole objective of the SIM was to open the Sudan which includes Igbomina land to the Gospel of Christ. Sudan, in this context does not mean the Sudan in East Africa, but a geographical or vegetation region in West Africa, South of the Sahara that is characterised by the Savannah vegetation of level land covered with low vegetation, treeless or dotted with trees or patches of wood.[12] In short, Sudan, here, refers to the land of the Black people from West to East of Africa between the Equator and Sahara desert that are yet to receive the gospel of Christ. It was the belief of the Mission that the gospel was incomplete until it gets to the people in the 'dark world' i.e. the black people in the Sudan who are yet to become Christians.[13] However, Turaki added that the word 'Sudan' is an Arabic word meaning 'the land of the black.'[14] Nonetheless, what is important here, is that the name Sudan in this context only refers to the land of the black people who were yet to accept Jesus as Lord and Saviour.

One wonders how easy and convenient it was for the white men and women to leave their 'comfortable' countries to come into places labelled as 'the white main graveyard'.[15] The mandate of Jesus to go and preach the gospel to the whole world (Matt 28:19-20) must be the great reason for this missionary enterprise. Fleck sees this call as faith in action where people who obey this command change their spiritual lives forever.[16]

The vision that gave birth to SIM was of a Scottish Canadian woman named Mrs. Margret Gowans in the 1890s.[17] She had a great burden for the Sudan, having learnt that millions of people lived therein without the knowledge of Christ in the interior. After praying, she passed the burden of the Sudan to her son, Walter Gowan and Rowland Victor Bingham, an English Canadian. These two men were later joined by Thomas Kent, an American. They arrived Badagry on December 4th 1893 without any sponsorship. Olatayo submitted that "even though, they knew that it was a venture that could lead to the loss of their lives, still they were determined to risk it to faith".[18]

At the beginning, they did not get enough support from local churches in their home countries. Not only that, they were told about the death of many missionaries who attempted to evangelise the Sudan, and that they and their unborn children would not be able to see the Sudan. However, these discouragements did not stop these missionaries from being obedient to the missionary call from God. The churches in America, Canada and Britain were reluctant to support them because they knew that many missionaries from the West had died in West Africa as they attempted to take the gospel to that land. It seemed to them that there was no value in supporting those who were likely to die soon.

Indeed, their coming to the interior part of Nigeria was a great risk of life considering the hot weather, transportation problem, shortage of food and finances, health challenges, etc. As noted by Fleck, these men reached Lagos with only about thirty British pounds.[19] They had no mission board at home to stand behind them. When giving the command to go and preach the gospel, Jesus gave his promise: 'And surely I am with you always, to the very end of the age' (Matt. 28:20 NIV). This led them to depend on God without any reservation. They left for Nigeria in the same manner that Jesus requested his disciples to go: 'Take no bag for the journey, or extra tunic, or sandal, or a staff, for the worker is worth his keep' (Matt. 10:10). When considering the lives of these three pioneers, it is easy to see how the SIM motto,' SIM by prayer,' developed. From Badagry they got to Lagos. Other missionaries discouraged them from embarking on the journey that could lead to their untimely deaths in the Sudan but they did not listen to their warning. Bingham's ill health made him to stay back in Lagos while Gowans and Kent left in April 1894 for the Lake Chad via Kano and got to Bida in June 1894. The roads were not good, the heat was excessive and they had much trouble keeping their carriers together.

Gowans was the first to die just almost after a year that they got to the Sudan. He died of dysentery at Girku, close to Zaria (Kaduna State) on the 17th November 1894.[20] Kent also took ill at Bida (Niger State) and died on the 8th of December 1894.[21] Only Bingham managed to survive and returned home. That ended the first attempt to open up the Sudan with the gospel of Christ. Not giving up on the Sudan, Bingham came back to Lagos on March 13th 1900 with two other missionaries: Albert Taylor and A. J. Moline. As it was with Apostle Paul, who said, 'for Christ's love compels us...,' (II Cor. 5:14), so it was with Rowland Bingham. However, this second attempt failed also as Bingham took ill with fever in Badagry and was rushed back home. The other two missionaries later joined him, they arrived England via the next ship. This ended the second attempt without any thing to show for.

The third attempt was the fruitful one that opened up the Sudan with the gospel of Christ in 1901. As at that time, Bingham had succeeded in having a council that would be sending missionaries to the Sudan. This group of missionaries: Mr. Albert Taylor, Mr. Charles Robinson, Rev. E. Anthony and Mr. Alex W. Banfield, were the first to be sent. They got to Patigi via River Niger on 15th March 1902. Thus, Patigi became the first preaching station for this mission in the central Sudan. This was because Patigi was the first town they settled in through River Niger. It was from Patigi that the gospel spread to Egbe and other towns among the Yagba people, in Kogi State through Rev. Tommy Titcombe called *Oyinbo Egbe* by the indigenes. From here, the SIM mission launched out to Igbomina land in 1912 through Rev. Guy William Playfair, popularly called *Oyinbo Oro* by the indigenes.

Thus, Oro-Ago became the cradle of the SIM/ECWA mission in Igbomina land. Before the coming of these white missionaries into the land, the indigenes knew nothing about the gospel of Jesus. They were all traditional worshippers except for some that were Muslims. The SIM Missionaries faced lots of persecutions from the Traditional worshippers and the Muslims in Igbomina land. Islam got to Igbomina land before the Ilorin onslaughts that began from 1835 C.E.[22] Some were attacked physically, while others were attacked spiritually and some even lost their lives in the process. Nevertheless, Christianity is a religion to reckon with in Igbomina land today. The introduction of this religion in to the Land has great impact on the lives of Igbomina people. Their ways of life were greatly influenced by the activities of these missionaries in the land. Their economic, social, and cultural lives were equally greatly influenced.

Chapter Nine	Daniel & Abolarin, in Y.A. Quadri, Omotoye & R.I. Adebayo(Eds) Religion and Development in Nigeria London, Adonis & Abbey Publishers

The Impacts of SIM / ECWA Mission on Igbomina land

The impact of SIM / ECWA on Igbomina land, Kwara State is enormous and could be felt in all ramifications of life of Igbomina people. Indeed, the impact of Christian missionaries in Nigeria as a country can never be over-emphasised.[23] Many scholars have written a lot on such impacts. Among them are: E.A Ayandele in a book titled *Missionary Impact on Modern Nigeria* 1842-1941[24] and E.A Odumuyiwa in a paper titled "Christianity, Governance and Development: A case study of Nigeria in the 21st Century."[25] From all indications, it becomes clear that Igbomina people were not exposed to western civilisation before the coming of the SIM and the Church Missionary Society missionaries into the land beginning from 1912. Thus, for a better and objective evaluation of the impacts of SIM / ECWA on Igbomina land, it is necessary to examine the religious, educational, socio-cultural and economic impacts of this mission in the land under study. This justifies the fact that religion (Christianity) is a veritable instrument of peace, unity, cohesion and development not only in Igbomina land, but Africa as a whole.

Educational Impact

The development of Western Education in Igbomina land cannot be treated in isolation from traditional forms of education in the land. Traditional education was a way of life before the advent of Western education that was introduced by the Christian missionaries.[26]
SIM/ECWA and CMS are the agents of Western Education in Igbomina land, Kwara State. However, it has been noted by some scholars that the Christian missions in Nigeria including SIM have not hidden their intention that establishment of schools was meant for evangelism. Such scholars include Fafunwa who indicated that the primary aim of the early Christian missionaries was to convert the 'heathen,' or the 'benighted' to Christianity via education.[27] Omotoye also added that:

> This was a strategy adopted by the early missionaries to win converts to their various missions. The Christian missionaries have been consistent

and dogged in their aspiration of the establishment of schools in this regard.[28]

As far as these missionaries were concerned, human intelligence is to be cultivated as an instrument of understanding Christian message. Faith, which enabled man to hold fast to God grows out of the conviction induced by intelligence. Before the coming of Playfair into Igbomina land, a few indigenes had gotten opportunities to travel to other parts of Yoruba land, such as, Abeokuta and Lagos and had learnt that western education brings with it western civilisation. As a result, Playfair's effort to introduce western education was welcomed at least by those who were aware of it. In Yoruba land, according to Ayandele, western education was looked upon as the only agency that could bring about the social revolution that Nigeria envisaged.[29] So, it is not surprising that mission schools were eagerly welcomed.

Dosumu notes that early development of education in Igbomina land owes much of its success to the emergence of mission communities in 1918 established by SIM/ECWA at Oro-Ago, the Catholic Mission in late 1930s at Oro and the United Missionary Society (UMS) at Share in early 1940.[30] There were other mission organisations, but they did not establish mission outposts because their members operated from various towns and villages outside Igbomina land. We perceive that western education has revolutionary influences in Igbomina land and by extension, the whole country, Nigeria. Like in all other parts of Africa, such as Kenya, Malawi, and South Africa, western education was a product of missionary work.[31] Until the approach of independence in 1960, the Christian missions in Igbomina land were the first and the only organisation willing to provide western education to the people.

The period between 1930 and 1960 was significant in the development of primary education in Igbomina land. This was a period of transition from church oriented education to a full-fledged primary education long demanded by the people. That is to say other subjects beyond reading, writing and Christian religious knowledge, were introduced into the School curriculum. By the middle of 1950, there had been many mission-based primary schools in Igbomina land.[32] Thus between 1913 – 1965, SIM/ECWA had up to forty five primary schools across Igbomina land. Among them were Primary Schools in Oro-Ago, Agbeku, Alabe, Atiran, Eggi Oyopo, Elesin Meta, Odo-Eku, Ola, Oke-

Ode, Patako, etc. Adult education programmes was equally established especially in those towns and villages where the SIM Missionaries settled, such as, Oro-Ago, Igbaja, and Omu-Aran. Secondary education was developed after the primary education. Teachers' Colleges were established in Igbaja in 1944 and Omu-Aran in 1948. The theological College/Seminary was established in Igbaja in 1942. This was the first seminary of SIM/ECWA in Nigeria.[33] A College of Education was also established in 2014 at Igbaja by ECWA Theological Seminary Igbaja, Kwara State.

Many Nigerians have benefitted from western and theological education introduced by the SIM/ECWA mission in Igbomina land. The former Deputy Governor of Kwara State, Chief Joel Afolabi Ogundeji, was a product of the SIM Teacher's College at Igbaja, Rev. Dr. J. B. Lawal, former Provost of ECWA Theological Seminary Igbaja and Professor Yusuf Turaki former Provost of Jos ECWA Theological Seminary were both products of ECWA Theological Seminary, Igbaja. The bulk of the educated Civil Servants and professionals in the land and beyond had their humble beginnings from mission education programmes and institutions in the land.

Thus, the major contributions of Christian missions in the area of education has been in literacy, social, moral and spiritual up-bringing and general development of the people and societies, even though the mission favoured Theological education over general (secular) education. This was one of the reasons for Government take-over of mission and church schools in the late 1960's and early 1970's.

Socio – Cultural Impact

The socio-cultural heritage of a society inter-alia embraces norms, morals, beliefs, attitude, taboo, superstitions, religion, festivals etc. Afolabi in his book titled: *Igbomina land in the context of Yoruba History*, noted that quite a lot of these and the like have been bequeathed to descendants of Igbomina people over years by words of mouth (verbally) and by imitations.[32] So, it is obvious that Igbomina as a group of Yoruba people have their indigenous beliefs before the commencement of the activities of SIM/ECWA in Igbomina land.

The passage of life (naming, puberty, marriage and death ceremony) of Igbomina people has been greatly influenced by the activities of SIM/ECWA in the land. The ceremonies attached to all these differ from what it had been before the coming of the western civilisation that was introduced by the missionaries. English wears are now worn by Igbomina people, people now live in modern houses. This was not so before Guy Playfair stepped into Igbomina land.[33] According to a write-up in the 90th Year Anniversary Booklet of SIM/ECWA in Iwo-Isin, mud houses with thatched roofs with small windows and palm frond or guinea corn stalk doors gave way to modern block houses and corrugated iron sheets when Christianity came in to Iwo in 1924. Round family long room houses with *Ilo* suddenly gave way to two, three or four flats and storey buildings in the town as well.[34] Motherless babies were no longer buried along with their dead mothers in Oro-Ago and environ. Indeed, the establishment of Orphanage Homes in Igbomina land by the SIM missionaries was an outstanding impact and contribution of the mission to the development and welfare of Igbomina people. Among the babies rescued from being buried with their dead mothers at birth was S.K.S. Olubadewo, a wealthy man who was the first person to own an aircraft in Igbomina land, and Janet Funmilayo Ibitoye, a former Principal of ECWA Nursing School Egbe.[35]

The abilities of the people to know how to read and write brought great enlightenment to them. Playfair was the first to have a bicycle in Igbomina land Kwara State.[36] From here, transportation system in the land got significant improvement. The custom of isolating those with leprosy to die all alone was put to an end in the land since 1943 when a lepers' home was opened in Omu-Aran by the SIM missionaries.[37] Thus, rehabilitating lepers, which is today a government policy is altogether a heritage inherited from the Christian mission. The custom and practice of killing of twins was put to an end in Igbomina land through the activities of these missionaries. Like Mary Slessor in Calabar,[38] the SIM Missionaries in Igbomina land fought and won the battle against this barbaric act. They would collect such babies and raise them up under their own roofs.[39]

Another outstanding influence of Christianity on Igbomina land was adding or introducing new names to some Igbomina towns and villages. Owode-Ofaro in Ilere District, Ifelodun Local Government was an example here. The name of this community was Ofaro before an SIM

Missionary Miss Dick (popularly called *Ebun Oyinbo*) stepped in to the town and advised them to migrate from the hill top and settle on the plain land on 26th November 1945. She added *Owode* (literary translated: money has come) to the name of the town as we have it today Owode-Ofaro.[40]

Linguistic development of African indigenous language was another heritage from the Christian mission. While the European Missionaries can be well criticised for their cultural imperialism, they did positively well in the development of Nigerian indigenous languages and helped in the translation of the Bible into many local languages. Guy Playfair was the first to introduce Igbomina people of Kwara State to Yoruba alphabet and helped in documenting many oral traditions and customs of the people.[41]

Medical Services

SIM/ECWA was the first agent to introduce modern medicine into Igbomina land Kwara State. This mission body built dispensaries, maternity homes and leprosarium centres in the land. The superiority of this modern medical care to the traditional medicine was apparent in the land. Turaki noted that the SIM was the largest contributor in Northern Nigeria towards fighting diseases and ailments.[42] The missionaries started treating the sick ones in their homes and later built dispensaries to cater for the increasing demands of medical services.

At its introduction, the Whiteman's medicines *Ogun Oyinbo* and medical practice were accepted by the people with great suspicion and contempt, but as time went on, the people grew to accept them. However, SIM Medical services in Igbomina land were also used as a tool for the propagation of the Gospel in the land.[43] Those who came for treatment were first of all preached to. We observe that the medical work of the SIM was as wide as the spread of mission stations in Igbomina land. This explains why mission medical work had great impact upon the people and the society and was indeed the strongest mission activity in the land. Between 1902 and 1960, SIM/ECWA in Nigeria had about 110 dispensaries and treatment centres in the Mission Field. Three out of these were in Igbomina land between 1912 and 1947. The one in Oro-

Ago was established in 1912, the one in Igbaja was established in 1933, and the one in Oke-Ode was established in 1947.[44] Dispensaries were later opened at Babanla, Agunjin, Ora, Omu-Aran to mention but a few. Prominent among the pioneering Nurses were Miss. Moulding, Miss. Margaret Lang, and Mrs. Playfair.[45] Later, indigenes were trained as nurses and posted to different dispensaries in and outside Igbomina land.

The impact of medical services on the Igbomina people can never be over-emphasised. People were taught hygiene and how to give first aid treatment. This reduced the death rate among the people drastically in the land. Health Education was given from time to time and free medical services were administered. Immunisation was also given from time to time to the people.[46] Thus, immunisation which is today sponsored by Nigerian government is altogether a heritage inherited from the Christian missionaries.

However, regardless of the impact of these medical services of the SIM/ECWA on the land under study, we note that only very few of these dispensaries and maternities survive till date. They are the one at Igbaja and the one at Omu-Aran (renamed Herbold Hospital), and the leprosarium Hospital at Oke-Igbala Omuaran. Reasons for this were poor management and the establishment of local government clinics and state Hospitals in Igbomina land. The charges of these government clinics and hospitals were lower than what the missions charged. For this reason the government clinics and hospitals got more patronage than the missions. Thus, ECWA could not sustain this legacy from SIM.

Economic Impact

Christianity and economic advancement have long been in partnership not only in Igbomina land but anywhere the religion is practiced. SIM/ECWA has not only preached against indolence but condemns it and encourages her members to be industrious. In the area of Agriculture which is the major source of economic development in Igbomina land, SIM/ECWA has done a lot to its improvement. Igbomina people are predominantly farmers. At the arrival of Playfair in to the land, he introduced new crops like tomatoes, mangoes, vegetables, American maize and cross breed cotton to Oro-Ago community. The non-converts also got involved in planting of these newly introduced species.[47] Elaborate training were given by the SIM Missionaries in the land in new farming techniques along with western education. Hunting techniques were also improved on. It is on record that Playfair was the first to use a rifle for hunting games in Igbomina land.[48] All these put together improved food production in the land, especially with the establishment of ECWA Rural Development (ERD).

Apart from agricultural development that was championed by SIM/ECWA mission in Igbomina land, tailoring, carpentry and bricklaying were introduced to the land by the SIM Missionaries. Tailoring was introduced by Mrs. H.E. Mouldling, Miss. K. M. Dick and Miss. S. J. Buller in the 1930s. The first house to be roofed in Igbomina land Kwara State with corrugated iron sheet was in 1936 by J. K. Adeniyi, the first SIM convert in Igbomina land.[49] Many people, even outside Igbomina land came to Oro-Ago to learn these modern professions. This did not only improve the economic status of the land but aided the spread of the gospel because those apprentices became Christians and went back to their villages and towns to spread the gospel. Among such people were Olokoba Oluode, an indigene of Babanla. He learnt bricklaying in Oro-Ago and became one of those who introduced Christianity into Babanla around 1925.[50]

Today, SIM/ECWA is involved in programmes that bring more economic development, not only in Igbomina land but Nigeria at large. One of them is called People Oriented Development of ECWA (P.O.D.). Its Headquarter is in Jos, with staff in all ECWA District Church Councils throughout Nigeria. Wells are being dug for different communities, toilets are being erected for the villagers, and even houses are being built for them. Also, Church and Community Mobilisation Process, (CCMP) is an arm of People Oriented Development (POD) of ECWA. CCMP helps in empowerment of the people in the community. Among those empowered was Mrs. Abifarin, a widow, from Iwo-Isin in 2013 via this programme.[51]

ECWA has many Nigerians that are gainfully employed under her. The number of Pastors and other staff members who work in the three District Church Councils of ECWA in Igbomina land is over 300.[51] ECWA Theological Seminary Igbaja has more than sixty Nigerians that are gainfully employed. The College of Education and ECWA Staff Nursery and Primary Schools in the land equally provide employment opportunities for the citizenry. The Seminary and Radio ELWA Igbaja have brought much popularity to Igbomina land and Kwara State as a whole,[52] and have improved the social and economic status of the land.

Conclusion

From the foregoing discussion, it can be concluded that the impacts of SIM/ECWA on Igbomina land Kwara State are enormous. The effects are reflected on different aspects of life and the social institutions in Igbomina land. It is observed that her impacts on the education, medical, economic and socio-cultural life of the people under study are positive. We however, agree with Salami who observed that Nigerians (Igbomina people inclusive) were introduced to Christianity and taught Christian truths that were heavily tinged with Western culture, [53]but with the passage of time, especially in the 21st century, Christianity has been contextualised. Thus, we would like to recommend that ECWA must work very hard to sustain all SIM heritages, especially the Medical Services that have almost faded away.

References

1. E.O Malomo, *Christianity and Politics in Nigeria Context*, (Ilorin: Amazing Grace Print-Media, 2016), 144.
2. S, G Best, "Religion and Religious Conflicts in Nigeria," *Journal of Political Science*, 2no3, (December, 2001), 63.
3. J. T. Oderinde, *Introduction to Sociology of Religion*, (Ilorin: Dehna and Sons Press, 2004), 8.
4. En.wikipedia.org/wiki/Igbomina tribe. Accessed on 12th August, 2014. 12.
5. En.wikipedia.org/wiki/Igbomina tribe. Accessed on 12th August, 2014. 13.
6. O. E. Dada, *Indirect Rule and Educational Development in Igbomina land 1900-1960*.
7. O. E Dada, Indirect Rule and Educational Development in Igbomina land (1900-1960), (M.A Dissertation submitted to the Department of History, University of Ilorin, 1999), 2.
8. O. A. Dada, *A Brief History of Igbomina, gboona* (Ilorin: Matanmi & Sons Publishing Co. Ltd. 1985), 1-10.
9. Dada, *A Brief History of Igbomina, gboona*...33.
10. ECWA Ministers' Hand Book, (Jos: Challenge Publications, 2011), 2.

11. E. O. Ibiloye, *The Igbomina Migrant Community in Lagos 1893-1983* (Unpublished Ph. D Thesis submitted to the Department of History, University of Ilorin, Nigeria, October, 2007), 61.
12. Dada, *A Brief History of Igbomina, gboona*...63-64.
13. *The Maiden a Publication of ECWA Theological Seminary Igbaja, 2012, xxvi.*
14. Y. Turaki, *An Introduction to the History of SIM/ECWA in Nigeria 1893-1993* (Jos: Challenge publication,1993), 45
15. I. Fleck, *Bringing Christianity to Nigeria; The Origin and Work of Protestant Mission,* (Jos: African Christian Textbook Publication, 2013), 11.
16. Fleck, *Bringing Christianity to Nigeria;* 12.
17. Fleck, *Bringing Christianity to Nigeria;* 13.
18. D. I. Olatayo, *ECWA, The Root, Birth and Growth* (Ilorin: Ocare Publication, 1993), 3.
19. Fleck, *Bringing Christianity to Nigeria:* 207.
20. O. Aboyeji, Trend in the Religion Experience of Igbomina People (1800-200), (Unpublished PhD Thesis, Department of History, University of Ilorin, Ilorin, March 2015), 145.
21. Y. Turaki, *An Introduction to the History of SIM/ECWA in Nigeria 1893-1993,* 55.
22. Turaki, *An Introduction to the History of SIM/ECWA* 55.
23. J.F.A. Ajayi, *Christian Mission in Nigeria, 1841-1891* (London: Longman, 1965), 9.
24. E. A. Ayandele, *The Missionary Impact of Modern Nigeria, 1842-1914: A Political and Social Analysis* (London: Longmans Group Ltd; 1966), 329 – 350.
25. E. A. Odumuyiwa *'Christianity, Governance and Development: A case study of Nigeria in the 21st Century,'* in Nigerian Association for the study of Religions (NASR) R. A. Raji et al (Ago-Iwoye: NASR, 2006), 209.
26. J. T. Dosunmu, *'Historical Development of Western Education Among the Igbomina people of Kwara State in* www.Unilorin.edu.ng/Journals/education/ije/June 1984, 1
27. A. B. Fafunwa, *History of Education in Nigeria,* (London: George Allen and Union, 1981), 15.
28. R. W. Omotoye, 'Communication and Universality of the Gospel in Yoruba land," in *Science and Religion in the Service of Humanity,* Ade P. Dopamu et al (Eds), (Ilorin: The Nigerian Association for the study and Teaching of Religion and the Natural Sciences (NASTRENS) and Local Societies Initiative (LSI), 2006), 40.

29. E. A. Ayandele, *The Missionary Impact of Modern Nigeria, 1842-1914: A Political and Social Analysis*...340.
30. J. T. Dosunmu, *Historical Development of Western Education Among the Igbomina people of Kwara State*...3.
31. J. C. Bulifant, *Forty Years in the African Bush*, (Grand rapids: Zondervan Publishing House, 1980), 56-66.
32. F. Afolabi, *Igbomina land in the context of Yoruba History*, (Lagos: Michael Adebayo Com. Service, 2006), 26.
33. P. Baba, *The History of EMS of ECWA 1948–1998*, (Jos: EMS of ECWA Publication, 2013), 11 – 15.
34. A Pamphlet written to commemorate the 90th Year of SIM/ECWA in Iwo-Isin, Isin L.G.A Kwara State 1984-2014. 2014:25.
35. *The Ancient paths: Christianity in Oro-Ago and Environs 1912 – 2012.* A publication of the planning committee of the centenary celebration of Christianity in Oro-Ago 2012, 20 – 21.
36. *The Ancient paths:*.. 43.
37. *The Ancient paths:*... 31.
38. Ayandele, *The Missionary Impact of Modern Nigeria,*... 256.
39. Ayandele, *The Missionary Impact of Modern Nigeria,*... 258.
40. *The Ancient paths:*... 43 – 46.
41. The Biography of Late Pa Elder (Prince) Peter Adenigba Akande Awolola and Late Ruth Wura-Ola Abike Awolola in Commemoration of the 70th Birth Day Celebration their Son Elder Awolola Adebisi Olatunji, May 2016: 7-8.
42. Y. Turaki, *An Introduction to the History of SIM/ECWA in Nigeria*... 173.
43. *The Ancient paths:*...... 36.
44. Y. Turaki, *An Introduction to the History of SIM/ECWA in Nigeria*... 172-173.
45. J.C Bullifant, *From Pagan Child to Christian Mother: The Story of the Oro-Girls Bible Schools*, (Toronto: SIM Publication), 77-80.
46. Interview with Dr. J.B Lawal, former Provost of ECWA Theological Seminary, on 24th November, 2014 in the school.
47. *The Ancient paths:*..... 42.
48. *The Ancient paths:* ...39.
49. Interview with pa. Joseph Dosunmu, a native of Babanla who is in his early 80s, on the 21st September 2014 at his residence, Ile-Olu, Babanla.
50. Mrs. Abifarin was empowered by ECWA Ita-Aisa Ilorin in 2013 through CCMP. She sells bean cake *Akara*. She is now self-reliant. She is Igbomina, from Iwo in Isin Local Government Area of Kwara State.
51. A. A. Duya, *ECWA Compedium and Fact Finder*, (Lagos: Victory Signs International, 2013), 1104- 1123.

52. E. A. Adebiyi, *The History of Radio Eternal Love Winning Africa (ELWA) Igbaja, Nigeria*, 2010, viii.
53. S.S. Salami, 'Decolonization of Christian Theology in Africa: The Role of Theological Institutions' *Christianity and African Society Journal*, vol.3 (Ibadan: Book Wright Publisher, 2013), 206 – 207.

CHAPTER TEN

Islam and the Attainment of the Sustainable Development Goals (Sdgs) in Nigeria

Akeem A. Akanni
*Department of Religious Studies
Olabisi Onabanjo University
Ago-Iwoye, Nigeria
akanniakeem2050@gmail.com
+2348033561743*

Introduction

The Sustainable Development Goals (SDGs) couched in seventeen (17) goals and one hundred and sixty-nine (169) targets are a proposed set of global priorities relating to future international development.[1] They replaced the eight-point agenda Millennium Development Goals (MDGs) conceived and adopted by one hundred and eighty-nine (189) member states of the United Nations in collaboration with twenty-three (23) other international organisations in 2000 to address the socio-political and economic challenges facing the people of the world. But alas, the year 2015 set as the target date for the realisation of those social needs and priorities ended with relative success recorded[2]. Like the Millennium Development Goals (MDGs), the target date of 2030 was set for the attainment of the overall Sustainable Development Goals (SDGs), although there are different earlier dates set for the attainment of some of the specific goals. As a pro-active measure, the means of achieving these goals within the stipulated times set for each of them as well as for the totality of the goals were also set by the world leaders who set them or else they become like the Millennium Development Goals (MDGs) and a new set of goals and target date(s) would have to be set again. Hence, the last of the seventeen goals of the Sustainable Development Goals (SDGs) requires that "the means of implementation of the goals be strengthened and that the global partnership for sustainable development be revitalised"[3]. It follows therefore that not only must all hands be on deck to ensure the realisation of these goals but also that all resources must be driven towards the attainment of the SDGs. It is for this reason that this chapter advocates the exploration of religion, and in this particular situation, Islam as a widely practised religion in Nigeria for the attainment of the Sustainable Development Goals (SDGs) in the country and by extension, across the globe.

The Sustainable Development Goals (SDGs)

For more than two decades, the question of sustainable development has been the concern of world leaders. This led to the declaration of the Millennium Development Goals (NDGs) by the United Nations (UN) in the year 2000 with over one hundred and eighty-nine (189) member states of the United Nations and twenty-three (23) other international organisations signing the "Declaration"[4]. The goals were targeted at eradicating extreme poverty and hunger, achieving universal primary education, promoting gender equality and empowering women, reducing child mortality, improving maternal health, combating HIV/AIDS, malaria and other diseases, ensuring environmental sustainability and developing global partnership for development. According to Sachs, this global attempt to package these priorities into easily understandable measurable and time-bound objectives helps promote global awareness, political accountability, improved metrics, social feedback and public pressures for those needs[5]. The end of year 2015 was set as the target for the realisation of those goals[6]. The relative success recorded on the MDGs at the end of the fifteen year incubation period set for it by its propagators led to the formulation of the Sustainable Development Goals (SDGs). The UN conference on sustainable development held in Rio de Janerio in June 2012, and UN General Assembly (UNGA) held in September, 2014 prepared a solid foundation for the SDGs and finally agreed in the UNGA held in September 2015 on the following seventeen point goals as the SDGs:

Figure 1: Sustainable Development Goals (SDGS)

S/N	GOAL
1	End poverty in all its forms everywhere
2	End hunger, achieve food security and improve nutrition and promote sustainable agriculture.
3	Ensure healthy lives and promote well-being for all at all ages.
4	Ensure inclusive and equitable quality education and promote life-long learning opportunities for all.
5	Achieve gender equality and empower all women and girls.
6	Ensure availability and sustainable management of water and sanitation for all.
7	Ensure access to affordable, reliable, sustainable and modern energy for all.
8	Promote sustained, inclusive and sustainable economic growth, full and productive employment and decent work for all.
9	Build resilient infrastructure, promote inclusive and foster innovation.
10	Reduce inequality within and among countries.
11	Make cities and human settlements inclusive, safe, resilient and sustainable.
12	Ensure sustainable consumption and production pattern.
13	Take urgent action to combat climate change and its impacts.
14	Conserve and sustainably use the oceans, seas and marine resources for sustainable development.
15	Protect, restore and promote sustainable use of terrestrial ecosystems, sustainably manage forests, combat desertification.
16	Promote peaceful and inclusive societies for sustainable development, provide access to justice for all and build effective, accountable and inclusive institutions at all levels.
17	Strengthen the means of implementation and revitalise the global partnership for sustainable development

Source: Derek Osborn, Amy Cutter and Farooq Ullah [7].

Although, seventeen goals have been identified as achievable in order to attain sustainable development across countries of the world, each of these goals has its specific targets. The targets totally require that by 2030, issues relating generally to hunger, accommodation, healthy living as well as peaceful co-existence among all peoples of the world would have been maximally addressed if not totally resolved. The first goal, for example, has five specific targets which border on (i) eradicating extreme poverty for all people everywhere, currently measured as people living on less than $1.25 a day, (ii) reducing at least, by half the proportions of men, women and children of all ages living in poverty in all dimensions according to national definitions, (iii) implementing nationally appropriate social protection systems and measures for all so that by 2030, a substantial coverage of the poor and the vulnerable would have been achieved, (iv) have equal rights to economic resources, as well as access to basic services, ownership and control over land and other forms of property, inheritance, natural resources, appropriate new technology, and financial services including microfinance and (v) building the resilience of the poor and those in vulnerable situations, and reducing their exposure and vulnerability to climate-related extreme events and other economic, social and environmental shocks and disasters[8].

Goal two, like one, also has five targets. These are: (i) ending hunger and ensuring access by all people, in particular the poor and people in vulnerable situations including infants, to safe, nutritious and sufficient food all year round (ii) ending all forms of malnutrition, including achieving by 2025, the internationally agreed targets on stunting and wasting in children under five years of age and addressing the nutritional needs of adolescent girls, pregnant and lactating women, and older persons, (iii) doubling the agricultural productivity and incomes of small-scale food producers, particularly women, indigenous people, family farmers, pastoralists and fishers, including through secure and equal access to land, other productive resources and inputs, knowledge, financial services, markets and opportunities for value-addition and non-farm employment (iv) ensuring sustainable food production systems and implementing resilient agricultural practices that increase productivity and production that help maintain ecosystems, that strengthen capacity for adaptation to climate change, extreme weather, drought, flooding and other disasters, and progressively improve land and soil quality (v) maintaining by 2020, genetic diversity of seeds, cultivated plants, farmed and domesticated animals and their related wild species, including through soundly managed and diversified seed and plant banks at national, regional and international levels, and ensuring access to and fair and equitable sharing of benefits arising from the utilisation of genetic resources and associated traditional knowledge as internationally agreed[9]. In fact, each of the seventeen goals has specific targets that must, according to the document signed by all member states, be accomplished within specific period but not exceeding 2030[10]. Those targets indicate specific areas where particular and adequate attention should be paid in order to achieve the goals to which they are attached.

A critical look at the goals and the specific targets however, shows some kind of interesting and puzzling revelation. Generally, it is pleasing to observe that the goals and the targets are well-intended, well-formulated, and ambitious. However, one notices a kind of duplication and overlapping in them. For example, there is clear overlap between Goals 1, 5 and 11 just as Goal 1 also overlaps with Goal 2, 3, 4 and 6. The underlining factor here is the need to end poverty in all its dimensions as Goal 1 whereas, Goal 2 also requires that hunger is ended. Although, the specific objectives of each of Goals 1 and 2 show where attention should be paid, one wonders if hunger is not directly related to, and even constitutes the basis for, measuring poverty. In a similar very vein, Goal 3 which requires ensuring healthy living and promotion of well-being for all at all ages is similar to, if not the same as Goals 4, 5, 6 and 11 all of which generally call for ensuring inclusive and equitable quality education and life-long learning opportunities for all, achieving gender equality and making cities and human settlements inclusive, safe, resilient and sustainable. It is for these reasons that Leowe and Rippin consider the formulation of some of the goals as unfortunate and their operationalisation as quite challenging[11]. They also see the goals to be too broad, aiming to cover too many topics and therefore face too many trade-off[12]. They therefore recommended a rewording of the goals to remove similarities and be much more concrete[13]. Nonetheless, the goals and their targets are, in our view, quite expressive of the situations in many countries of the world, including Nigeria and are therefore, worthy of being vigorously pursued within the stipulated time(s).

Chapter Ten | Akeem A. Akanni, in
Y.A. Quadri, Omotoye & R.I. Adebayo
Religion and Development in Nigeria
London, Adonis & Abbey Publishers

The Sustainable Development Goals (SDGs) and the Nigerian Nation

A quick rundown of the seventeen Sustainable Development Goals (SDGs) shows that all issues relating to them concern the Nigerian nation. One does not need a soothsayer to know that poverty, food insecurity, unhealthy living, poor education, gender, inequality, women disempowerment, poor sanitation, absence of power and energy etc. are all issues facing the country. Other issues affecting Nigeria include poor economic growth, unemployment, poor industrialisation, youth restiveness, climate change, deforestation, erosion and abuse of the environment. Many scholars have critically looked at these in their works and recounting these here will amount to re-stating the obvious[14]. Suffice it to stay therefore that all these are what the Sustainable Development Goals (SDGs) are aimed at eradicating across countries of the world by the year 2030. It therefore follows that those issues are realities with regard to Nigeria just like many other nations.

Religion as an Instrument for the Attainment of the Sustainable Development Goals

In setting the Sustainable Development Goals, the member states also requested that other sections of the society must join hands with the government to ensure the realisation of the SDGs[15]. In that wise, religion becomes a veritable tool for the attainment of the Sustainable Development Goals (SDGs). This is anchored to the functional theory of religion which states that there is an interaction between religion and society within which it functions. Religion as it were, performs a variety of social functions. It affects the social behaviour of the individual and influences other facets or social institutions in the society.

The functional theory of religion maintains that religion persists as a critical vehicle for humanity to attain its evolutionary goals as specie[16]. Consequently, religion is indispensable for man as regards his life in society and his individual personality. As Gofwen, contends, religion reinforces the collective conscience of society, which is requisite for social order and stability[17]. It also does the duties of both world-building and maintenance[18]. It thus works through the dialectic of self and society by creating a system of symbolic order that revolves all potential conflicts of the individual with the norms and intentions of those to whom he must remain loyal and trustworthy.

Also, religion is related to economic activities because without it, certain kinds of economic behaviour would not seem rational and consistent. According to Onwu, the prophets possess charisma and speak out for the oppressed and promise a re-ordering of economic properties[19]. Besides, these prophets upheld and lived by the truth. Therefore, on the strength of religion, religious leaders confront their audience at every moment. Religion also enables people to see meaning and purpose of life[20]. Through the description of man's status in the scheme of things, man is able to develop a sense of direction. The functionalist theory of religion also contends that religion inculcates morals in man as a result of self-abnegation. Since the Sustainable Development Goals are on all issues relating to the welfare of human beings, religion thus becomes a veritable tool for the attainment of the SDGs. How Islam as a religion does this is the focus of the next section of the chapter.

Islam as it Relates to the Sustainable Development Goals (SDGs)

The Sustainable Development Goals set to achieve are all that Islam teaches. The first goal, for example, seeks to end poverty in all its forms everywhere across the world. In doing this, all religions particularly Islam not only sees poverty as incompatible with human nature[21] but also as something that must be tackled headlong through social safety instruments like *Zakat* (Islamic tax)[22] and *Sadaqah* (voluntary charity). Though, the perception of Islam about poverty is that, it can only be alleviated and possibly not eradicated, the Qur'ān abhors it so much that it condemns infanticide and abortion due to poverty[23] and assures the poor of God's ability to enrich them no matter the level of their poverty[24]. In fact, it sees both the poor and the rich as of equal standing before God[25], urging the rich to give part of their patrimony to the poor in order to receive mercy from Him[26]. It specifically commends those who help the poor out of their poverty.[27]

In a similar manner, Islam has addressed the second of the Sustainable Development Goals which is ending hunger and ensuring food security. Apart from the general condemnation of poverty and the enjoyment of *Zakat* and *Sadaqat* as means of ending it, it specifically addresses hunger by ordering the giving of food as a virtue as well as vitiation for certain wrong doings. In Qur'ān 90:14-16, it sees "the giving of food in the day of privation (hunger) to the orphans or to the indigent (down) in the dust" as a virtue that a Muslim should imbibe rather than seeing his possessions as products of his own efforts. As vitiation for certain wrong doings however, the giving of food is enjoined when a Muslim deliberately breaks a day's fast in the month of Ramadan[28], when he breaks his vow[29] and when he compares his wife's back to his mother's[30], a practice the Arabs adopted to abandon and divorce their wives. Additionally, Islam also enjoins a Muslim to give as much as two-thirds of his sacrificial animal during the *'id al-Adha* (the festival of animal sacrifice) to the poor,[31] just as he/she is enjoined to give food items common to his/her locality as charity at the end of Ramadan fast (but before the observance of the *'id* (festive prayer)[32]. All these are Islam's approach to specifically end hunger and demonstrate how Islam creates an enabling environment for the attainment of the second SDG Goal and has been assisting the nation in taking care of the less-privileged ones in the country.

Islam's approach to the third goal which requires that healthy living and well-being be promoted is the advice it gives that man should not be the cause of his own death. Qur'ān 4:26-29 states: "Do not kill/destroy yourself for verily Allah has been to you Most Merciful". Additionally, the Qur'ān urges Muslims to eat what is good only, placing restrictions on food that are proven by science today as injurious to human health. Such foods include dead animals[33], liquor consumption[34] and swine[35] among others. The Qur'ān also urges Muslims to eat proportionally and to avoid over-eating[36]. In a number of traditions, the Holy Prophet Muhammad also advised Muslims to avoid over-eating. For example, he said: "if you must eat, make sure you fill one third of your stomach with food, one third with water and one third for yourself (i.e leave it empty for the purpose of breathing).[37]

Goal four of the Sustainable Development Goals states that equitable and quality education as well as life-long learning opportunities must be provided for all. Interestingly, in Islam's viewpoint, education is the lost property of every Muslim and must be acquired wherever he/she finds it[38]. Muslims, male or female are enjoined to acquire sound education as the Qur'ān classifies the educated and the uneducated as belonging to different levels[39]. The educated is also specially recognised by God Almighty in the Qur'ān and considered as belonging to the category of angels and the prophets[40]. In fact, premium is placed on education in Islam and for Muslims to the extent that it constitutes the first theme upon which the revelation of the Glorious Qur'ān began[41]. The Qur'ān stresses further that all forms of education must be acquired, using the Adamic example as a yardstick[42]. Both the Qur'ān and the Hadith are emphatic on the fact that both sexes are to be educated[43].

The fifth of the Sustainable Development Goals (SDGs) calls for achieving gender equality and empowerment of all women and girls. In Islam's perspective, both sexes are of equal standing before God[44], though it equally recognises that they play different roles and as such should possess different instruments to play those roles. For example, in family matters it gives the headship to the man and equally requires him to be the breadwinner of the family[45]. In a similar vein, it makes the woman the superintendent of the home and equally gives her the necessary tool to play this role[46]. In all of these, Islam gives special recognition and needed power to both sexes. For example, the woman is to breastfeed the baby while the man is to provide moral and financial support for this[47]. Even where this responsibility is being contracted out to someone else, the Qur'ān makes it clear that the man is to be responsible for the financial responsibility[48]. Beyond these special natural responsibilities and the corresponding rights and privileges, Islam places both sexes on equal pedestal. Both sexes are treated on equal basis spiritually, socially, economically, culturally, etc. The woman has the right to own properties just like the man[49]. In specific areas, however, Islam further empowers women and girls as Goal five of the Sustainable Development Goals envisages. Qur'ān 4: 4 gives her the right to specify what she wants for *"mahr"* (dowry) and to collect same for her personal use. This is not even to be taken back at the point of divorce except it is initiated by the woman in which case Islam seeks to prevent divorce at the slightest provocation[50]. The Qur'ān also encourages Muslims to bestow gifts on their wives which must not also be taken back in case of divorce[51]. Islamic jurisprudence further gives her the right to dictate conditions for her consent to a marriage proposal, including allowing the would-be-husband the right to polygamy or not[52]. The woman is also empowered to say "yes" or "no" to the marriage of her daughter to a suitor in the concept of "*kafaa*" (compatibility)[53]. She is entitled to all her rights including feeding and accommodation for three menstrual cycles in the count-down to divorce, if the occasion arises[54]. She is equally given the right to the custody of her children till adulthood in case of divorce[55], unless and except it is established by a court of (Islamic) law that she is morally bankrupt and could endanger the lives of the children[56] and in which case the right goes to other women in her family, beginning with her mother, grandmother, sister etc before consideration is given to women in the husband family or husband himself[57]. Such is the equal opportunity and empowerment that Islam gives to the woman and the girl-child that Prophet Muhammad had to say: "whoever is given a female child and raised her to be righteous/virtuous will be with me in the paradise like this – he then raised two fingers of his hand together"[58]

Goal six is concerned with availability and sustainable management of water. In this regard, the Qur'ān mentions water in many ways, first as the source of life of all creatures[59]. It also recognises two bodies of flowing water[60], one palatable, the other salty and bitter[61]. It also talks about God's throne being spread over the waters[62] as well as water coming from the sky[63]. Islamic scholars have also identified the qualities of water through colour, taste and odour, because water is central to worship in Islam (i.e. *As-salat*)[64]. They have also spoken about the management of water, saying the less quantity of water used for ablution, the more commendable it is[65]. On the sanitation aspect of the goal, Islam imposes the ten acts of *Fitrah*[66] on every Muslim. These involve using the tooth-stick, snuffing water in the nose, cutting the nails, washing the finger joints, plucking the hair under the armpits, and cleaning one's private parts with water among others[67]. The ablution (Qur'ān 5:6) as well as the (five types of) *ghusl* spiritual bath) imposed in Islam[68] are all geared towards sanitation and clean environment. Similarly, Islam stipulates that one must not defecate by the road side[69] nor under a tree that provides shade for people[70]. These are sanitary measures put in place by Islam all of which fall under project Goal Six of the Sustainable Development Goals (SDGs).

Goal seven is about ensuring access to affordable, reliable, sustainable and modern energy for all. The targets of this goal clarify the focus of this goal better. They explain that energy here refers to solid fuel, crude oil, natural gas, nuclear and renewable energy sources. This, by explanation means all means of generating fire, power and light. The Qur'ān's modest way of addressing this goal is the recognition of the sun which is the source of (solar) energy today as God's gift of light-giving device to humanity.[71] In another verse of the Glorious Qur'ān, God is spoken of as the one who made the earth explorable for man[72]. Man is therefore challenged to "traverse through its tracts and enjoy of the sustainable which God has furnished him with" (Qur'ān 62: 10). These and other verses mean that God has deposited all kinds of resources in the earth for man to explore for his use, which include generation of power and energy from all sources.

Goal eight requires the promotion of sustained, inclusive and to a sustainable economic growth, full and productive employment and decent work for all. In the Glorious Qur'ān, there are numerous verses with economic implications generally for humanity and specifically for Muslims. For example, Muslims are enjoined to give full scale and weight[73], avoid hoarding of goods[74]. Muslims are further encouraged to support one another with interest-free loans to encourage productivity and to eschew usury/interest in all its forms on such loans[75]. The Qur'ān further requires that the one taking the loan should dictate the terms of the loan[76], get the payment of the loan re-scheduled if-repayment is difficult[77] and even wright off the loan as bad debt if payment becomes imperceptible[78]. The Qur'ān also desires that the bankrupt be supported to get back to business[79] and requires that all economic transactions be documented in the presence of at least two witnesses[80]. Muslims are also enjoined, through the sayings of Prophet Muhammad to pay living wages to their workers[81] and not to give responsibilities that are beyond their capacities to them to do[82]. It is also an Islamic economic principle to pay the labourer his wages when due[83]. Modern Islamic economists have also argued that the proceeds of *Zakat* can be used to establish industries where Muslims can work and earn their livelihood[84]. All of these address goal eight of the Sustainable Development Goals which requires the promotion of sustained, inclusive and sustainable economic growth, full and productive employment and decent work for all.

The focus of Goal nine of the Sustainable Development Goals is to build resilient infrastructure, promote inclusive and sustainable industrialisation as well as foster innovation. The Qur'ān is replete with the accounts of earlier generations of people who built massive infrastructure in their cities and towns[85]. Qur'ān 40:21 for example specifically urges its readers to travel through the lands and seas and see for themselves (the remnants of such) great edifices. There are accounts of those who fortified their towns and cities with walls and fences[86]. There are also accounts of Prophet Ibrahim and Ismail who came together to build the Ka'bah[87] referred to as the first building on the surface of the earth[88]. The early Muslims of the days of Prophet Muhammad were also said to have dug a ditch round the city of Madinah to fortify it against the attacking enemies of Makkah[89]. Such historical accounts are bound to motivate the modern man to build resilient infrastructure and industrialise his society. Besides, the Qur'ān challenges its readers to use their God-given talents saying "can't you reason,"[90] "won't you ponder".[91] Such verses of the Qur'ān are meant to challenge people to foster innovation which brings about industrialisation and development..

Goal Ten aims at reducing inequality within and among countries. The Qur'ān in unequivocal terms denounces such inequality saying all men are of the same origin[92]. It also teaches that though there may be differences in our colours, language and ethnicity, such natural differences are meant for identification purposes alone[93]. Consequently, all forms of barrier be they natural or artificial or as regards language, ethnicity or culture are of no consequence in Islam. The Islamic religion advocates reduction and indeed elimination of discrimination on the basis of culture, language, ethnicity etc. The Prophet Muhammad in his farewell message is reported to have said that there is no superiority of the white over the black or of the black over the white[94]. It is in this spirit that all its tenets are geared towards unity of mankind i.e. the congregational observance of the canonical five daily prayers (*Salat*), the unitary form and time of fasting and *Hajj* (Pilgrimage to Makkah) as well as the allowance of taking the *Zakat* of one place to other places of dire need[95].

In furtherance of Goal Ten, Goal Eleven seeks to make cities and human settlements inclusive, safe, resilient and sustainable. On its part also, Islam also teaches that all people of the earth are one[96]. Both the Qur'ān and hadith teach that differences in language, religion and or culture should not constitute barriers to human settlement. Qur'ān 2: 62

for examples sees Muslims, Jews, Christians and indeed people of any religion as one. The Qur'ān also says that all people of the world were originally created one and that they became divided along linguistic, cultural and religious lines according to the wish of God[97]. The example of the Madinan city established by Prophet Muhammad where Muslims, Jews and Christians lived together in peace based on mutual agreement is also opposite here[98]. The Islamic principle of guaranteeing the safety of lives and properties of non-Muslims living in an Islamic state is also relevant here[99]. All these are Islam's way of projecting the ideals and concept of Goal eleven of the sustainable Development Goals (SDGs) which seeks to make cities and human settlements inclusive and safe.

Goal Twelve is to ensure sustainable consumption and production pattern. The Qur'ān accounts of the story of Prophet Yusuf's ministerial activities in Egypt with regards to seven years of bumper harvest and seven years of drought is of particular relevance here. His words in interpreting the King's dream show great ideas for modern day food security mechanism[100]. This, in modern terminology is external reserve whether in liquid or solid form and it is all that is needed to ensure sustainable consumption and production pattern. Thus, Islam as a religion has its own concept of what Goal Twelve of the sustainable Development Goals (SDGs) entails.

Goals Thirteen, Fourteen and Fifteen require that urgent action be taken to combat climate change and its impact, ensure the conservation and sustainable use of the oceans, seas and marine for sustainable development as well as ensure the protection, restoration and sustainable use of the terrestrial ecosystem, management of the forest and combat desertification. These three goals are related to the environment, the management of which there are well laid-down principles of law and practice in Islam. The ecological principles of Islam consist of (i) the belief that God is the Creator of the universe (i.e heaven, earth and all that are between them),[101] (ii) that in that creation, there is orderliness[102],(iii) that a flaw of any kind cannot be seen in God's creation[103], (iv) that man, as God's representative on earth[104] has the responsibility of maintaining and sustaining the orderliness in God's creation[105], (v) and above all, detailed information on how to relate with God's creatures individually and collectively in a manner that will guarantee the default orderliness are provided in the Qur'ān and the Hadith. In this regard, Qur'ān 18:54 states: "We have explained in details in this Qur'ān, for the benefits of mankind, every kind of similitude…". According to Ahmad[106], there are about one hundred verses of the Glorious Qur'ān on the environment and there are even more in the Hadith. Examples of such verses of the Glorious Qur'ān directly relating to the protection, preservation, exploitation and conservation of the environment include:

i. And the firmament has He raised high and *He has set up the balance in order that you may not transgress (due) balance*…(Qur'ān 55:7-9; 54:49 and 67:3)
ii. Then, We appointed you after them to be *Khalifah* (i.e vicegerent-overseer) on the earth so We might observe how you would act (Qur'ān10:14; 6:165).
iii. Do no mischief on the surface of the earth, after it has been set in order…(Qur'ān 7:56)
iv. O Children of Adam, eat and drink *but do not waste by excess*, for Allah does not love the wasters (Qur'ān 7:31)

Of the Hadith, the following are apposite:
i. Whoever brings (a piece of) dead land to life, for him, there is a reward for it, and whatever creature seeking food eat of it, then it shall be recorded as a voluntary act of charity for him[107]
ii. A woman was punished because she kept a cat tied until it died, and she was thrown into the Fire. She had not provided it with food or drink and had not freed it so that it could (at least) eat the insects of the earth[108]

Such are the provisions of the Qur'ān and the Hadith on the preservation and conservation of the environment. They are so comprehensive that Ahmad had to conclude:

Islam claims well laid down principles of law and practice as to the different aspects affecting the environment. Be it for seawater or drink, be it for the land or its products, be it food or drink, be it for the animals, birds or other species, be it for wind or air, be it for cleanliness or hygiene, be it for the sun or moon and for the forests, greeneries and minerals, Islamic law (*Sharī'ah*) is well laid for their use, conservation and development[109]

He continues:

> (The) Qur'ān does not only guide you on the five pillars of Islam,...but it incorporates in it divine wisdom on all matters of human concern....,even matters such as science, economy, ecology and environment...It includes mention of all the bounties of the Lord and indications of how humans must treat water, land animals, the species, greenery and air. If we follow that path the wastage, mischief, exploitation and imbalance in nature and society, and the pollution in the environment will be well contained by its ethical, social and legal norms[110]

Goal seventeen which requires that the means of implementing and revitalising the global partnership for sustainable development also has Islamic provisions that support it. Qur'ān 5: 3 for example stipulates that people should cooperate on what is good and righteous and not cooperate on what is bad and vicious. In a similar vein, the Qur'ān admonishes people to fear a disaster which, when it happens will not affect only those who by omission or commission are responsible for its occurrence (Qur'ān 8:25). Specifically in chapter 30: 41, it says whatever appears on the surface of the earth life disaster is as a result of what people living in it have caused with their hands. The verse reads: "(Whatever) corruption (that) has appeared on the surface of the land and sea (is as a result) of that which the hands of men have caused...". It follows therefore that man should work for the good of his society for which reason the SDGs were formulated. Again, the Holy Prophet Muhammad advised Muslims to attempt to correct the evils of the society by one of three means of physically doing something about it or speaking against it or at worst, reproach it with their minds if it will be difficult for them to use any of the first two means[111]. All these divine provisions which seek cooperation of people for good things that will benefit humanity such as the SDGs are Islam's subtle way of strengthening the means of implementation of the Sustainable Development Goals.

Islam and Development in Nigeria within the Framework of the Sustainable Development Goals (SDGs)

From the foregoing, one can see that there are adequate provisions for the realisation of the Sustainable Development Goals within the superstructure of Islam. This section therefore, highlights briefly how Islam has contributed to development in Nigeria as it relates to the SDGs One may observe with delight that the seriousness Muslims attach to practising the tenets of their religion gives reasons to say that the religion has contributed to development in the country. For example, in yielding to the call to establish regular canonical prayers which requires the performance of (spiritual bath and) ablution, Muslims have always provided water at their worship centres (i.e mosques). Because of governments' inability to meet the water needs of the people of the country, they have had reasons to sink boreholes which serve as sources of portable water not only for their religious purposes and for Muslim worshippers alone but also for domestic use of Muslims and non-Muslims alike as such boreholes are often made available for public use. At these worship centres also, they provide toilet facilities separately for male and female worshippers. These efforts, though religiously motivated, help in the attainment of the Sixth of the Sustainable Development Goals which requires that availability and sustainable management of water and sanitation be ensured for all.

In a similar vein, in yielding to various injunctions of the Glorious Qur'ān and Hadith, Muslims in Nigeria have been giving food as vitiation for certain wrongdoings such as when they deliberately break a day's fast in the month of Ramadan or break vows. They also, in responding to divine instructions regarding giving charity to the poor, give food and other items like unused clothes, shoes and bags to the poor and the needy around them. On daily bases, they are seen giving to poor and the needy who line up the streets and motor garages waiting for a helping hand. By that, they are contributing to the well-being of the down-trodden in the country in a way that the Sustainable Development Goals 1 and 2 which seek to end poverty and hunger envisage. Similarly, Muslims in Nigeria give part of their sacrificial animals during the *'id al-Adha* (the festival of animal sacrifice) to the poor. They are seen sending fresh meat of the animals to family members and friends who could not afford to kill one. In the month of Ramadan and upon its completion, they give foodstuffs common to their localities as charity as enjoined by their religion thereby also contributing to people's well-being in the country.

The religion of Islam can also be said to have contributed to development in Nigeria as it is assisting the nation in taking care of the less-privileged ones in the country if Muslims' attitude of paying *Zakat* as a religious and social responsibility is considered. There are accounts of the positive impact of *Zakat* on the people of this country, though the potentials of the instrument are yet to be fully optimised for the benefits of the poor in the country. Musa, Ashafa, Maigudu, Alanamu and Mustapha are few of the scholars of Islam in Nigeria who have documented the positive impact of *Zakat* on the people of the country. While Musa assessed the application of *Zakat* for the alleviation of poverty in Lagos state[112], Ashafa documented the role of *Zakat* in poverty alleviation in south-western Nigeria.[113] Maigudu appraised the performance of the Zamfara *Zakat* and Endowment Board in the utilisation of *Zakat* for poverty alleviation in Zamfara state[114]. Alanamu on his own evaluated the operations of *Zakat* in selected states across the country[115]. The concern of Mustapha was how government agencies in the northern part of the country had helped in the better administration of *Zakat* for poverty alleviation among the people of the region[116]. All of these scholarly works attest to the unquantifiable contributions of *Zakat* to people's well-being in the country.

The contributions of Islam to development in Nigeria as they relate to the SDGs can also be viewed from the perspective of helping one another with interest-free loan. It is on record that, in yielding to this Qur'ānic injunction, Muslims in the country have come together to form Islamic cooperative societies through which they have assisted the poor and the needy. Many who had no capital to start businesses from which they could earn their living have been helped to do so through such mutual efforts of the Islamic cooperative societies. Ajani-Muritala has given a vivid account of how people have benefitted from the Islamic cooperative societies regarding wealth creation, welfarism and assets acquisition[117]. All these and many more are Islam's simple way of contributing to development in Nigeria as it obtains within the framework of the Sustainable Development Goals (SDGs).

Muslims have also established hospitals. The need to secure the privacy of female Muslims who may seek medical care from their non-*Mahram*[118] as taught by Islam necessitated the establishment of such Muslim hospitals. Although, there are still very few of such hospitals, a good number of them abound in the country at the instance of certain individuals and Muslim organisations. The Jamat Ahmadiyyah is known to be at the forefront of this in the country. It has such hospitals in Lagos and Ijebu-Ode among other places. Such contributions of Muslims in Nigeria are in tandem with Goal Three of the Sustainable Development Goals (SDGs).

The contributions of Islam to development in Nigeria can also be seen from the perspective of education. As enunciated above, Islam places high premium on education for both sexes. For this reason, Muslims in the country have also established schools at all levels of education – nursery/primary, secondary and tertiary - in order to provide qualitative education for their children. They are particularly challenged by the use of western education to christianise their children and wards. They therefore established schools where they could give western and Islamic education to their own and by that, have helped in the realisation of Goal Four of the Sustainable Development Goals (SDGs).

Again, Islam could also be said to have contributed to development in Nigeria as the concept relates to the Sustainable Development Goals (SDGs) if the application and operations of *Sharī'ah* in some states of the country are considered. Though, not without some challenges as non-Muslims particularly Christians in the country challenged its constitutionality, the application and extended scope of the operations of the *Sharī'ah* legal system in the country have helped in the realisation of Goal Sixteen which requires the promotion of peaceful and inclusive societies and particularly, the provision of access to justice for all. A good number of cases that would have been taken to the conventional English courts and which would have been there for years due to technicalities and over-stretch of the courts' facilities and personnel had been taken and dispensed of in the *Sharī'ah* courts. Besides, cases like those relating to Muslim marriages, divorce and custody of children which Muslims would naturally like *Sharī'ah* pronouncements on, based on the teachings of their religion not to submit to any legal system except the *Sharī'ah* (Qur'ān 5: 45-47 and 45: 18) as against the provisions of the customary or English courts now have places to hear them to the satisfaction of

Nigerian Muslims. This, in no small measure, is a contribution to development in Nigeria.

Towards Further Attainment of the Sustainable Development Goals (SDGs) with Islam in Nigeria

On how to further use the Islamic religion to work for the realisation of the goals within the Nigerian context, it suffices to say that since each of the goals of the SDGs has verses of the Glorious Qur'ān and words/practices of the Holy Prophet Muhammad supporting it, one good way of employing Islam (for which both are sources of legislature) for the realisation of the goals is to encourage the teaching and practice of this religion in the country. Although, already a highly Muslim populated country, the attainment of the SDGs in Nigeria can be further enhanced by the proper practice of Islam in the country. This may not necessarily mean the building of mosques by governments but it may require that governments, at all levels put in place policies and programmes that will encourage the practice of the religion. For example, government could issue directives that Muslim faithful, regardless of their number should be allowed to practise the tenets of their religion such as observing the five daily prayers or the *Jum'ah* prayer within the confines of their places of work as a group of people. The timing of these prayers could also be declared officially free for Muslim faithful to be able to do them according to the laws of the religion that instituted them. Muslim faithful who are salary-earners who wish to take their annual leave in the month of Ramadan may also be allowed to do so. The present situation whereby workers are at the liberty of the managements of their establishments and their respective bosses to observe these religious tenets during working hours will not augur well for the realisation of the SDGs. Such government policies would help in the attainment of the SDGs as such Muslims would be able to do their religious biddings, many of which are what the SDGs are aimed at achieving anytime anywhere and at the right time. Again, provisions for practising those tenets such as water could also be made available and accessible.

Another way of utilising the Islamic religion for the attainment of the SDGs is for the government of the country to make provisions that will facilitate the practice of the social structure of Islam by Muslims. It has been observed that Islam addresses the problem of poverty and hunger with a number of social safety nets. These include *Zakat* (Islamic tax), *sadaqah* (charity), *kaffarah* (expiation for sins) among others. *Zakat* for example is, according to Islamic principles, to be administered centrally by the Islamic government. Since Muslims in Nigeria, like most of their counterparts across the world live under non-Islamic governments, it would require governments' efforts to help them put in place institutions that will facilitate the practice of this tenet. One good way of doing this is to legislate in favour of payment of *Zakat* by Muslims. Though some states in the northern part of the country already have agencies or ministries that handle the collection of *Zakat*, it could become a national affair whereby a federal agency of government of the country may be established for this purpose. Muslims who show evidence of paying *Zakat* may also be exempted from paying the conventional tax as a way of forestalling double taxation on Muslims which is the present situation in Nigeria. Doing all these for Muslims in the country will not be too much in the name of achieving the SDGs. The government of Nigeria may also have to establish *Shari'ah* courts where none exists in the country and expand the scope of operations of these courts where they already exist. This is with a view to allowing for proper practice of the Islamic principles particularly those relating to human and women's rights as well as family matters. Some of the goals of the SDGs require that women be empowered and as could be seen in the analysis above, a good number of these rights and priviledges are embedded in the Islamic marital laws, upon which *Shari'ah* courts alone should and could adjudicate.

Another means of using the Islamic religion for the attainment of the SDGs is for Islamic clerics particularly those that lead congregations of Muslims to use the pulpit to advocate the SDGs. Government could seek collaborations with the Islamic organisations to reach the large Muslim populace where issues relating to the SDGs will be advocated. Doing so would and should not constitute a problem for the leadership of the Islamic organisations as all issues addressed by the SDGs have bases in and relevance to Islam as demonstrated above. All they need do is get acquainted with the SDGs and their various targets and identify relevant portions of the Glorious Qur'ān and Hadith that support them to prepare their sermons. The Imams also have to practically demonstrate what they teach and preach as a way of getting the messages down the hearts of members of their congregation.

Government in Nigeria could also collaborate with Islamic organisations and Muslim professional bodies to organise conferences, symposia and workshops on the objectives of the Sustainable Development Goals (SGDs). The Nigeria Association of Teachers of Arabic and Islamic Studies (NATAIS) will be particularly relevant here. The Islamic perspective on each of the SDGs and the role of Muslims in achieving them could form themes of such conferences and seminars. The specific roles of the Muslim youths and Muslim women could also be addressed at such seminars and workshops. There is no doubt that efforts in these direction will greatly further help in the attainment of the SDGs in Nigeria.

The realisation of the SDGs in Nigeria through Islam could also require the encouragement of the teaching of Islamic Studies at all levels of education in the country. The current National Policy on Education which makes Islamic Studies an elective course at the Senior Secondary School could be reviewed to give the course a compulsory core subject status that must be taken and passed in the West African School Certificate Examinations and its equivalents, at least by Muslim students. More teachers of the subject could be employed to fill vacancies where they exist while schools with Muslim children should also be provided with such teachers. Some steps could also be taken further to incorporate aspects of the course into the General Studies courses taken by all students of tertiary institutions in the country. It will be an understatement to state that teachers of this subject would be expected to highlight the Islamic provisions on the Sustainable Development Goals, which is the main reason why the teaching of the subject is being given priority and attention. It follows therefore that such teachers must be versatile and well-read to be able to showcase the beauty of Islam vis-a vis the contents of the Sustainable Development Goals. As a corollary to the above, the curriculum of the subject at all levels may have to be reviewed to reflect the contents of the SDGs.

Conclusion

It has been demonstrated from the foregoing that there are not only adequate provisions relating to the Sustainable Development Goals in Islam but also that the practice of the religion has engendered development in the country in one form or the other. However, it is the candid opinion of this writer that the teaching and practice of the religion in Nigeria could further be exploited for the attainment of the SDGs in the country and anywhere else the religion is practised in the world. Though the Sustainable Development Goals have 2030 as the maturity date, it is the view of this writer that the opinions expressed in this chapter will, forever be relevant. This is because, like the Millennium Development Goals (MGGs), the likelihood of the attainment of the Sustainable Development Goals (SDGs) by the target year (i.e 2030) is slim, going by reports from countries[119]. Thus, like the MDGs, the SGDs will also have to be recaptured under another name and since they concern human needs and development about which Islam will always have something to say as demonstrated above, the continued relevance will always be there. After all, the claim that there is no issue of human concern that the Qur'ān does not address has been proven with the issues relating to the SDGs, all of which have one Qur'ānic verse or Hadith addressing them. Two things are obvious from this; one is that, that the SDGs as the products of the minds of the entire leaders of the world as representing the pressing needs of humanity are all located in the divine sources of Islam shows that Islam is in tandem with human nature and is therefore God's way of worship set for human beings on the surface of the earth. Second, that no matter how long humanity runs away from the truth of Islam due to blackmail, slander and name-calling or even misrepresentation, it remains the only truth that humanity will come back to appreciate for its relevance to human nature.

References

1. Umberto Pisano, Lisa Lange, Gerald Berger and Markus Hametner, *The Sustainable Development Goals (SDGs) and their Impact on the European SD Governance Framework: Preparing for the Post-2015 Agenda*, ESDN Quarterly Report No. 35, ESDN Office, Institute for Managing Sustainability: Vienna University of Economics and Business, (Vienna, Austria, 2015), 16
2. United Nations *GEO5: Global Environment Outlook – Environment for the future we want*, Nairobi, http://www.unep.org/geo/pdfs/geo5/GEO5_report_en.pdf, 2012, 25
3. National Planning Commission, Sustainable Development Goals 2016-2030; National (Preliminary) Report, Government of Nepal (National Planning Commission), (Singha Durbar, Kathmandu, 2015), 33
4. National Planning Commission, (2015), 56
5. J. Sachs, *End of Poverty*, (New York: The Penguin Press, 2012), 123.
6. Derek Osborn, Amy Cutter and Farooq Ullah, *Universal Sustainable Development Goals: Understanding the Transformational Challenge for Developed Countries: Report of a Study by Stakeholder Forum*, Stakeholder Forum, 2015, internet material accessed on 25 (January, 2016), 45
7. Derek Osborn, Amy Cutter and Farooq Ullah, (2015), 46
8. Umberto Pisano, Lisa Lange, Gerald Berger and Markus Hametner, 34
9. Umberto Pisano, Lisa Lange, Gerald Berger and Markus Hametner, 36
10. Markus Leowe and NicoleRippin, *The Sustainable Development Goals of the Post-2015 Agenda: Comments on the OWG and SDS Proposals*, Revised Version, 26 February, German Development Institute 2015, www.d.e.gdi.de
11. Markus Leowe and Nicole Rippin, *The Sustainable Development Goals*, 26
12. Markus Leowe and Nicole Rippin, *The Sustainable Development Goals*, 27
13. Markus Leowe and Nicole Rippin, *The Sustainable Development Goals*, 27
14. For example, see L. I Akintola "Nigeria: the *Qur'ānic* Parable of a Poverty-Free Country", in R. A Raji (ed.) *Religion, Governance and Development in the 21st century*, (Ilorin: NASR), 2006. See also D. A Egbeolowo "The Role of Islamic Moral Teachings in Changing the Fortune of Nigeria", *Orisun: Journal of Religion and Human Values*, 9 (9), 2010. See also L. I Akintola, "Nigeria at Fifty: An Islamic Perspective", a column in *Nigerian Compass*, 1st, October, 2010
15. Markus Leowe and Nicole Rippin, 2015, 76

16. N. Onwu, "Religion as a Unifying Factor in Nigeria: Problems and Prospects" in Sam Babs Mala and Z.I. Oseni (eds) *Religion, Peace and Unity in Nigeria*, (Ibadan: Nigeria Association for the Study of Religions, 1984), p 157.
17. R.I. Gofwen, *Religious Conflicts in Northern Nigeria and Nation-Building: the Throes of two decades 1980-2000*, (Jos: Human Rights Monitor, 2004), 87
18. Onwu, "Religion as a Unifying Factor in Nigeria", 158
19. Onwu, "Religion as a Unifying Factor in Nigeria", 159
20. J. Omoregbe, *A philosophical Look at Religion*, (Lagos: Joja Educational Research, 2002), 97
21. Qur'ān 9:28
22. Qur'ān 9:60
23. Qur'ān 6:151; 17:31
24. Qur'ān 24:32
25. Qur'ān 4:135; 49:15
26. Qur'ān 2:271
27. Qur'ān 59:9
28. Qur'ān 2:184
29. Qur'ān 5:89; 16:91; 60:12; 66:2
30. Qur'ān 33:4; 58:2-4
31. Qur'ān 22:33-37
32. Sabiq Sayyid, *Fiqh as Sunnah*, (Bayrut: Dar al-Kitab al Arabia, vol. 2, 1973), 56
33. Qur'ān 6:145
34. Qur'ān 5:90; 2:219 & 4:43
35. Qur'ān 6:145; 16:115
36. Qur'ān 7:31
37. The Prophet Muhammad is also reported to have said: "The stomach is the tank of the body and the veins go down to it. When the stomach is healthy, the veins come back in a healthy condition but when it is in a bad condition, they returned diseased". For details, see Afzalar Rahman, *Muhammad: The Educator of Mankind*, (London: The Muslim Schools Trust, 1980), 29& 46
38. AbdurRahman I. Doi, *Islam in Nigeria*, (Zaria: Gaskiya Corporation Ltd) 1984, 286. For a good number of these *ahadith*, See Abdullah Sahin, *New Directions in Islamic Education: Pedagogy & Identity Formation*, (U.K: Kube Publishing Ltd, 2013). Also https://www.islamicquotes.net/blog/?cat=3 Accessed on 21st January, 2017
39. Qur'ān 39:9
40. See imitrust.net/index.../Islamic-scholars.quotes...productivemuslim.com accessed 15th January, 2017

41. Qur'ān 96:1-5
42. Qur'ān 2:30
43. https://www.islamicquotes.net/blog/?cat=3 Accessed on 21st January, 2017
44. Qur'ān 49; 13
45. Qur'ān 2: 233
46. Qur'ān 2: 233
47. Qur'ān 2: 233
48. Qur'ān 2: 233
49. Qur'ān 4:11-12
50. Qur'ān 4:25
51. Qur'ān 2:229
52. M. Abdulati, *The Family Structure in Islam*, (Lagos: Islamic Publications Bureau, 1981), 122
53. Abdulati, *The Family Structure in Islam*, 123
54. Abdulati, *The Family Structure in Islam*,123
55. Abdel Rahim Omar, *Family Planning in the Legacy of Islam*, (London: Routledge, 1992), 44.
56. Abdel Rahim Omar, *Family Planning in the Legacy of Islam*, 44
57. Abdel Rahim Omar, *Family Planning in the Legacy of Islam*, 44
58. Abdel Rahim Omar, *Family Planning in the Legacy of Islam*, 44
59. Qur'ān 21:30; 24:45; 25:54
60. Qur'ān 25:53 and Q 55: 19&20
61. Qur'ān 35:12
62. Qur'ān 11:7
63. Qur'ān 2:64
64. Y.A Quadri and I.O Oloyede, *Islamic Jurisprudence: Al-'Iziyyah for the English Audience*, (Ijebu-Ode: Shebiotimo Publications), 1990, 28
65. Quadri and Oloyede, 1990, 28
66. *Fitrah* here, according to Siddiqi refers to the inner sense of cleanliness in a man which is a proof of his moral and mental health. For details, see Abdul Hamid Siddiqi, *Sahih Muslim*, Vol. 1, (Beirut: Dar al Arabia, 1972), 159
67. Abdul Hamid Siddiqi, 160
68. These are i) Spiritual Bath upon entering the fold of Islam, ii) the bath after the stoppage of the birth blood (*Nifas*), iii) the bath undertaken after legal sexual intercourse (*Jannabah*), iv) the bath undertaken upon the stoppage of a woman's menstrual period (*haydah*) and v) the bath done

for the corpse of a deceased Muslim before burial (*Janazah*). For details, see Quadri and Oloyede, *Islamic Jurisprudence*, 29

69. Abdul Hamid Siddiqi, 159
70. Abdul Hamid Siddiqi, 1 Abdul Hamid Siddiqi,159
71. Qur'ān 91:1&2
72. Qur'ān 67:15
73. Qur'ān 83:1-6
74. Qur'ān 9:34-35
75. Qur'ān 4:61,30:39 and 2;275
76. Qur'ān 2:282
77. Qur'ān 2:280
78. Qur'ān 2:280
79. Qur'ān 9:60
80. Qur'ān 2:280
81. M. U. Chapra, "Objectives of the Islamic Economic Order" in Khurshid Ahmad (ed.) *Islam: Its Meaning and Message*, (Lagos: Islamic Publications Bureau, 1986), 186
82. Chapra, *Islam: Its Meaning and Message*, 1986, 187
83. Chapra, *Islam: Its Meaning and Message*, 1986,187
84. F.R Faridi, "Zakat and fiscal policy", in K. Ahmad (ed.) *Studies in Islamic Economics*, (Leicester: The Islamic Foundation, 1980), 22
85. Qur'ān 6:11, 22:46, 27:69, 29:20-22
86. Qur'ān 30:9&42, 35:44, 47:10
87. Qur'ān 2:127
88. Qur'ān 3: 96
89. Muhammad Haykal, *The Life of Muhammad*, (Lagos: Islamic Publications Bureau, 1982), 173
90. Qur'ān 51: 21
91. Qur'ān 47: 24
92. Qur'ān 2:231 and Qur'ān 10:19
93. Qur'ān 49:13
94. For details, see Haykal, *The Life of Muhammad*, 145
95. C. Hamilton, The *Hedaya*, (New Delhi: Nussrat Ali Nasri for Kitab Bhauvan, 1979), 122
96. Qur'ān 2:231 and Qur'ān 10:19
97. Qur'ān 10:99
98. Haykal, *The life of Muhammad*, 185
99. Saleh Hussain Al-Aayed, *The Rights of Non-Muslims in the Islamic World*, (Riyadh: Dar Eshbelia for Pub. & Dist.2002), 5
100. Qur'ān 12:47-49
101. Qur'ān 42:29

102. Qur'ān 55:3-9
103. Qur'ān 67:3
104. Qur'ān 2:30
105. Qur'ān 10:14; 6: 165.
106. Aktaruddin Ahmad, *Islam and the Environmental Crisis*, (United Kingdom: Ta-Ha Publishers Ltd, 1997), 186
107. Ahmad, *Islam and the Environmental Crisis*, 186
108. Ahmad, *Islam and the Environmental Crisis*, 186
109. Ahmad, *Islam and the Environmental Crisis*, 159
110. Ahmad, *Islam and the Environmental Crisis*, 172
111. Y.A. Quadri, *The Traditions of the Prophet*, (Ijebu-Ode-Shebiotimo Publications, 1995), 27
112. A. W. Musa, The Application of *Zakat* for the Alleviation of Poverty in Lagos State, (M.A Dissertation, Department of Religious Studies, Lagos State University, 1998)
113. S. A. Ashafa, Practice of *Zakat* and Poverty Alleviation in South-Western Nigeria (Unpublished PhD Thesis, Department of Religions, University of Ilorin, 2016)
114. A.A Maigudu, "Alleviating Poverty in Nigeria: An Appraisal of the Role of the Zamfara Zakat and Endowment Board" in Haruna Salihi *et.al* (eds.) *Sharī'ah, Democracy and Governance in Islam*, (Kano: International Institute of Islamic Thought, 2011), 142- 167
115. A. S. Alanamu, Zakat as a Social Mechanism in Selected States of Nigeria, (Unpublished Ph.D Thesis, Department of Arabic and Islamic Studies, University of Ibadan, 2010)
116. I. Mustapha, "The Role of Government Agencies in the Administration of *Zakat* in some Selected States of Northern Nigeria" (Unpublished Ph. D Thesis, Department of Islamic Studies, Usman Dan Fodio University, Sokoto, 2010)
117. Abdusalam A. Ajani-Muritala, An Assessment of Islamic Cooperative Societies in Selected States in Yoruba land, Nigeria, (Unpublished Ph. D Thesis, Department of Religions, University of Ilorin, 2015).
118. Islam stipulates that a Muslim woman must not be alone with a person of the opposite sex who by the Islamic law can marry her. This is technically called *dhi – mahram*. It also specifically warns against such loneliness even with close relations such as brother –in- laws. For details, see Quadri, *The Sayings of the Prophet*, 1995, 20 &39
119. Umberto Pisano, Lisa Lange, Gerald Berger and Markus Hametner, *The Sustainable Development Goals (SDGs) and their Impact on the European SD*

Governance Framework: Preparing for the Post-2015 Agenda, 2015,16; United Nations *GEO5: Global Environment Outlook – Environment for the future we want*, 2012, 25; National Planning Commission, Sustainable Development Goals 2016-2030; National (Preliminary) Report, Government of Nepal (National Planning Commission), 2015, 33; Sachs, *End of Poverty*, 123; Derek Osborn, Amy Cutter and Farooq Ullah, *Universal Sustainable Development Goals: Understanding the Transformational Challenge for Developed Countries: Report of a study by Stakeholder Forum*, Stakeholder Forum, 2015, 45

CHAPTER ELEVEN

The Impact of Sokoto Caliphate on Post-Colonial Political Development in Nigeria: A Focus on Selected Personalities

Muhammad Dahiru Shuni
Department of Islamic Studies,
Usmanu Danfodiyo University, Sokoto, Nigeria.
mdshunee@ymail.com
+2348161701011

Introduction

Sokoto Caliphate was founded by a great Islamic scholar in person of Shaykh Uthman Bn Foduye, whose ancestors had originally moved from Futa Toro into the central Sudan.[1] He was able to form a community along with his supporters and they preached against corrupt practices in the then Hausaland. At last they became very strong enough to oppose the corrupt kings and their supporters. At the beginning of the nineteenth century, from 1804-1810 CE, the Shaykh and his disciples went to war against the corrupt people in Hausaland and were able to defeat them. As a result of this Jihad waged by the Shaykh and his supporters, the Jihadists were able to establish a new Caliphate, and pure Islamic law prevailed in the entire Hausa land.

After the establishment of this Caliphate, the Shaykh decided to divide the territory between his two lieutenants (i.e. Shaykh Abdullah Bn Foduye and Sultan Muhammad Bello). Hence the eastern part of the Caliphate came under the control of Sultan Muhammad Bello, while Shaykh Abdullah was in charge of the western part of the Caliphate. This division of the Caliphate was made in 1812 CE.[2] Before the death of Shaykh Uthman Bn Foduye in 1817, Sultan Muhammad Bello who was in charge of the eastern part of the Caliphate was able to establish himself effectively towards succession and eventual leadership of the Caliphate.

Bello was among the prominent Sokoto Caliphate leaders who struggled for the establishment of the Caliphate. He was seen by many, as the builder of the Caliphate due to the fact that after the Jihad and the subsequent establishment of the Caliphate led by his father, he played a significant role not only in consolidating the achievements, but in expanding the Caliphate's territories. During his life time as renowned Islamic scholar, he wrote a number of works that have direct bearing on the lives of the society he lived in. These works concentrated more on the areas of politics and administration as he made them to be his subjects of focus. His father attested that his son, Bello, made politics to be his area of specialisation hence, anybody who wanted to know about the area should consult Bello's works.[3]

In addition to the works on politics and administration, Bello was a leader right from the time of the temporary division of the Caliphate in 1812 between him and Shaykh Abdullah (his uncle). Similarly, after the death of the Shaykh in 1817, Bello was elected as the new *'Amīr al – Mu'minīn*. He led for twenty years during which he tried to put into action some of the political ideas he expounded in his works.

Bello's leadership qualities such as justice, equality, humility, and sincerity had enabled him succeed in his leadership style. He implemented some of the political ideas of good governance that included preservation of religion, maintenance of security and promotion of the welfare of people among others. His programmes and policies on education, agriculture and health were other spheres his government succeeded in, as these areas impacted positively on the lives of his people by bringing prosperity and happiness to them.

The Northern political leaders on the other hand, had also left legacies for later generations in Nigeria. Their politics was ideological hence they played it with full sincerity; they were into it purposely to serve their people by not only emancipating them from the bondage of colonialism but also by bringing all that would make their lives to prosper socially, culturally, politically and above all spiritually. On the basis of this ideology among the Northern political leaders, they, on coming to power, introduced policies and programmes geared towards achieving their fundamental objectives. Their policies and programmes on education, agriculture and health were few areas where the good leadership of these Northern political leaders can be assessed or justified. On the basis of this background therefore, the chapter seeks to elaborate on the impact of political ideas and practices of Sokoto Caliphate particularly Muhammad Bello on post colonial political leaders in Northern Nigeria. Other personalities referred to were Sir Abubakar Tafawa Balewa, Sir Ahmadu Bello, the Sardauna of Sokoto and Malam Aminu Kano. These people were selected out of many either because of the leadership positions they held or because of the political role they played which helped in actualising the government of their time.

The Influence of Sokoto Caliphate on Northern Political leaders

It is the belief among many people that there was an influence of Sokoto Caliphate and Muhammad Bello in particular on the politics and leadership styles of the Northern political leaders. To reiterate that view, Adamu is worth quoting here when he said:

The Northern mentality, which is now a powerful political force in Nigerian politics, was not invented by the British or developed in a vacuum by the post-independence politics. It had, in our views its roots in the establishment and the management of the Sokoto Caliphate.[4]

Sardauna's view is in accord with Mahdi's statement that they had, during their time, retained features of the system of administration inherited from the Sokoto Caliphate tradition and he reiterated that there was no retreat from copying that system.[5] Balewa, too, concurred with Sardauna as he envisaged the evolution of a Nigerian democracy based on Nigerian experiences, history and culture which he believed, can effectively address local problems instead of imitating and applying other peoples' political experiences in the country.[6] In addition, the NPC's invocation of the name of Shehu *"Usmaniyya"* on the awards its government gave out to its own party members in recognition of their outstanding service to the region was a clear instance where the Caliphate influence on these Northern political elites can be noticed. While presenting that *Usmaniyya* medal to Abubakar Tafawa Balewa, the then NPC Prime Minister, Sardauna remarked that:

> Sir Abubakar would accept the medal not because of its value but because of his (Sir Abubakar's) loyalty and belief in the duties

performed by Shehu Usmanu Danfodio, and what they were doing in following Dan-Fodio's footsteps.[7]

This quotation reveals the very strong agenda of continuity between the Caliphate and the NPC government. Alhaji Ibrahim Imam, another recipient of the *"Usmaniyya"* medal, once suggested that Nigeria should have been renamed *"Usmaniyya"* with the coming of independence. At least, he proposed, the Northern region should bear the name.[8] All these statements were as a result of the influence of Sokoto Caliphate on the Northern political leaders in those days.

Likewise, it is probable that it was the influence of the Caliphate that made Mallam Aminu Kano to make a courageous statement before her Majesty at constitutional conference in London in 1953 to the effect that the British had institutionalised an autocratic, anti-people as well as anti-Islamic system of administration which was the dominant culture in the Northern region. Beside this, it is on record that Malam Aminu and his Party, the NEPU, focused their political struggle within the guidelines laid down in the Sokoto Caliphate founded by Shaykh Uthman and consolidated upon by his son Muhammad Bello both of whom were regarded as not only being true and great Muslims but also democrats whose democratic tenets were subsequently marginalised by the Colonialists.[9]

Similarly, stressing their ties to the leadership policies of the Jihadists, not through blood as some leaders from NPC were accused of, but through scholarship and piety, Alhaji Babba Dan Agundi, one of the outstanding figures in the NEPU party, remarked that:

> We (NEPU) were the legitimate successors of Usman Danfodio. Was Danfodio corrupt? He was always on the right side of justice. Emirs are grand children of the Shehu-That is what they were saying. We did not care about the emirs being the grand children of the Shehu, we cared about what was practised. They are his grand children but do not follow his leadership. So you see, **we that were trying to copy Shehu** are the real successors, not his so-called grand children. If they do not do as the Shehu did, just forget about them.[10]

All these statements illustrate that these Northern political leaders mirrored the Sokoto Caliphate leadership as in their political affairs. Furthermore, Sardauna said that their interest and love for the culture and traditions of the Caliphate would not deter them from being selective and from making improvements where possible from the traditions and culture they cherished (Sokoto Caliphate).[11] He averred that:

> ...It might be recalled the restoration of then pre-1900 era, modernized, polished, democratized, refined, but out of recognition, reconstructed, but still within the same frame work and on the same foundations comprehensible by all and appreciated by all. The train, the car, the lorry, the aeroplane, the telephone, the hospital... the school...have, transformed Uthman Danfodiyo's world, but the basis is still there.[12]

In addition to the above discussions, the influence of the Sokoto Caliphate and Muhammad Bello's ideas and practices on the Northern political leaders can be further discussed in the following areas:

Religious Influence

People believed that the Northern political leaders were committed to the spread and development of their religion, Islam.[13] Bello, one of the architects of the Caliphate believed that it is the responsibility of a leader to ensure the promotion and the protection of the religion of his people. His efforts in this regard were clear, as among the other things he did to promote the religion of Islam was the building of the two famous mosques in Sokoto: Shehu and Bello mosques. In addition, he encouraged the repair of many mosques and *Islamiyyah* schools. The direct impact of Sultan Bello's idea and practice toward the religion on the leadership of the first Republic was very clear. Sardauna had first of all confirmed that he had no power or honour which exceeded his religion (Islam), hence, he said that, he would never be a party to anything that would discredit his religion or make him deviate from it.[14]

Sardauna's idea about Bello's religious efforts impacted on him. First of all, he renovated the two mosques built by Sultan Bello. In addition, he also built another famous mosque in Kaduna and named it after Sultan Bello. Not only these, he ordered the construction and renovation of many mosques which he financed personally. Sardauna's conversion tours to pagan areas and the formation of Jama'atu Nasrul

Islam were clear to all and sundry. He also engaged some scholars in the translation of Sokoto jihad literature into Hausa language. All these could be attributed to influence he had from the Caliphate's religious policies and programmes.

On Political Influence

Abubakar Imam, one of the leading political elites in the north, explained that they used Sokoto Caliphate literature as their guide in most of their appointments. He affirmed that the Jihadists emphasised that it is incumbent upon a leader to choose learned men of integrity who are capable of advising the leader in the discharge of his responsibility.[15] The Caliphate's idea and practice in appointing state officials were based on merit and competency of the person to be appointed. This idea and practice had influenced the appointments made by Northern political leaders in the first republic as most of the appointments were made on the basis of merit laying emphasis on the experience of the appointees and also targeting younger ones who were qualified and had the necessary skills; the idea which Sarduana always emphasised. The Sardauna, according to Sunday Awoniyi, will not look at one's place of origin, his tribe or religion at all in appointments, but rather, one's capability, loyalty and commitment were what counted.[16]

Justice and Accountability

Justice and accountability were the cardinal principles of the Sokoto Caliphate's administration. The Jihadists tried to ensure just and accountable government, a government that was administered with justice regardless of one's economic, social, religious or political status. The influence of this idea and ideal on the Northern political leaders is noticeable in their struggle to liberate not only the Northern part of the country but Nigeria as a whole from the injustice and the bondage of colonialists who dominated the country and looted its resources. Hence, they tried to ensure that the legacies of justice and accountability inherited from Sokoto Caliphate and Bello's model of administration of justice were strictly followed.

Similarly, the Sokoto Caliphate resisted tyranny and corruption from the leadership circle. The Jihadists wrote works expressing their worries and condemnation of all sorts of injustice and atrocities from those in authority. Bello practically demonstrated how he detested injustice as some of his Emirs were queried, warned and some deposed for their injustice and maladministration.[17] These works and practices of Bello on this fundamental issue had impacted the leadership of the First Republic as they boldly showed their worries as regards the injustice from the Emirs and traditional institutions of their time. The injustice fought by Northern political leaders included abuse of public funds by traditional rulers, imposition of levies beyond the resources of their subjects, collection of gratification through their public offices and bribery among the judges. Malam Aminu Kano's struggle in the course of emancipation of the *Talakawas* in this respect is quite obvious. This of course would not be unconnected with the Sokoto Caliphate heritage.

Accountability and Service delivery

In this area, neither the Jihadists nor the early Northern political leaders were corrupt or unjust in their political and administrative practices. Sultan Bello for example, shunned corruption and accumulation of wealth, just as some Northern political leaders also shunned corruption and accumulation of wealth from state resources. Sardauna, for instance, in his effort to guard against using government resources for his personal benefit and to emulate Sokoto Caliphate leaders who used official lamp for official work and private lamp for personal work, never used any government asset for his private end, and if he did, Muhammad Jega (one of his private secretaries) confirmed that he would pay for it.[18]

On service delivery, it is the idea of Sokoto Caliphate leaders that a good government preserves the religion, maintains security, promotes the welfare of its citizenry, cares for the needy and fulfills the legitimate needs of its people. In order to ensure the implementation of this idea, Sultan Muhammad Bello articulated many programmes and policies geared towards the improvement of the welfare of his subjects. It was this idea and practice of Bello that made Sardauna to state that "he was impatient who would not be patient with all that lies before him and the responsibilities that have been placed upon him". He reiterated that all his time would be dedicated to his work. Not only this, Sardauna reassured that his entire life would be in the service of his people.[19]

The influence of Sokoto Caliphate's leadership style in service delivery was witnessed in the administration of the Northern political leaders especially in the First Republic. The leadership styles of Sir Ahmadu Bello and Abubakar Tafawa Balewa are good examples in this regard. Their government promoted rural water supply, roads, dispensaries, and schools among others. In a speech delivered during the opening of Kubani Bridge, Zaria in 1959, Sardauna recalled how rigorously they fought, in the House of Representatives, for its construction.[20]

Religious Tolerance/Accommodation

It is important to first of all recall that Muhammad Bello in particular, was moderate as far as religious belief is concerned. This can be attributed to his knowledge that Islam is a religion of moderation that tolerates and accommodates other religions. Sokoto Caliphate under Bello, was once diverse and heterogeneous; it was composed of multiple ethnic and tribal entities. But due to the idea of the then leadership, Bello left an exemplary trend in creating an atmosphere that ensured religious tolerance and peaceful coexistence with the people of other religion particularly traditional people who refused to accept Islam as their religion. The existence of *Maguzawa*[21] in the Caliphate under Bello was clear justification of such harmonious relationship that existed between Muslims and other people who followed other religions.

In addition to this, there was also contact with the Christian Europe by the Caliphate under Bello and the report shows that he exhibited religious tolerance and accommodation towards them. European explorers of the 19th century such as Hugh Clapperton who visited Sokoto during Bello's time (1824 - 1827) received excellent treatment and kindness.[22]

This legacy had influenced the political leaders of the First Republic to feel free with the European researchers such as Murray Last, Jean Boyd and host of other non-Muslim researchers. Similarly, Sardauna and other Northern leaders accommodated and tolerated non-Muslims during their time. That had permitted the construction of places of worship by the non-Muslims in areas like Kano and Zaria. Sardauna himself had once attended the Summit of Coalition of Protestant Missions in Nigeria held in Jos.[23]

Bello's and other jihadists' attitudes towards the followers of other religions and those who believed in traditional religions were emulated by Northern political leaders in the First Republic. The same spirit of peaceful co-existence and religious tolerance has been documented in their intra religious dealings. In dealing with non-Muslims, the Caliphal leadership adopted rules and regulations governing the treatment of non-Muslims under Islamic State. These included freedom of religion, freedom to practice their culture not harmful or offensive to the society and host of other rights. Awoniyi explained how the Northern political leaders were influenced by the idea saying that, even though Sardauna took his religion very seriously, he believed that one should hold on to his religion and let others hold to their own. He added that, should he work in the office on Sunday, there was possibility that Sardauna would come and ask if he had been able to go to the church for service.[24] When Jolly Tanko Yusuf and Dr. Ishaya Audu went to Sardauna and told him that they observed him going round and converting pagans to Islam, therefore, they too wanted to be given permission to do same, Sardauna granted them permission by saying "Good luck."[25] Not only this, Awoniyi recalled that, the Sardauna purchased copies of the New Testament Bible which was translated into modern English for him and his friends.[26]

Sultan Bello's idea of moderation while dealing with the adherents of other religions might have influenced the Northern political leaders as they accommodated and treated the followers of other religions with all sense of belonging. Sardauna's attitude towards the people of other religions was clear testimony to this as there were many people in his cabinet who were not Muslims. He had as his personal physician Dr. Ishaya Audu, Sunday Awoniyi as chief of his security, he also had Michael Audu Buba among his ministers as his right hand man. All these people were not Muslims, neither were they Hausa or Fulani, but they were accorded great respect and recognition in the administration of Northern leaders.[27] According to Awoniyi, one of the most sensitive positions in the then Northern civil service was that of the secretary to the executive council (SEXCO), the position he said, was held by some Christians uninterruptedly, namely Mr. S. Ade John, Mr. Silas Daniyan and his humble himself, Sunday Awoniyi.[28]

It was also the impact of religious tolerance and accommodation of Sokoto Caliphate's teachings that made Sardauna to appoint Sir Peter Achimugu to serve on the Penal Code Committee saddled with the responsibility of reintroducing the *Shari'ah*.[29] The significance of such political accommodation was noticed among the Christians in Sardauna's government as some of them were seen committed to the projects that have Islamic outlook. For instance, Sultan Bello Mosque Kaduna was built under the leadership of Ambassador Jolly Tanko Yusuf and George Ohikeri who was then the Minister for Works. This, they did, to accomplish the intention of Sardauna who informed him (Jolly Tanko) that he wanted the mosque built.[30]

Peace and Unity

The Sokoto Caliphate was able to hold together different tribes and ethnic groups with mutual understanding and respect. In the same vein, the Northern political leaders were also able to bind together different tribes and ethnic groups particularly in the Northern region under the same banner "One North, one people". It was said that out of 250 tribal groups in Nigeria, about 230 are found in the north but Sardauna was able to unify them into one entity.[31] It is equally important to know that, while the ideology of Sokoto Caliphate was primarily religious creed or Islam, which was not ethnic, tribal or regional, the Northern political leaders concern was nationalism and regionalism. Therefore, the issue of religion, ethnicity, and tribalism had no place in the political vocabulary of the Northern political leaders of the First Republic. According to Alhaji Wada Nas "no individual ever arose from the Nigerian political scene, who dedicated his life to the unity of his people as the Sardauna."[32] The idea essentially was inherited from the Sokoto Caliphate leadership especially from Bello who tried to see it done practically particularly when he experienced revolts within his Caliphate.

Concerning the state of peace in the Caliphate during Bello, Clapperton attested that *Shari'ah* was in force during Bello's time and as a result of peace in the Caliphate, it was discovered that a woman could travel with a casket of gold on her head from one end to another without fear.[33]

Northern political leaders placed high premium on justice, unity, welfare and primacy of the public interest. These were some of the political ideas of Sokoto Caliphate leaders which impacted on the lives and the leadership style of Northern leaders. On unity for example, the Jihadists dwell on its importance within the purview of their idea of community and in terms of the bond of truth that unites Muslims. The Northern political leaders on the other hand, conceived unity as a means to securing the well-being of the people living within the territorial boundaries of the country. Hassan Usman Katsina believed that only in unity can effective service be rendered to people.[34] On the basis of this belief, he, after his appointment as military leader in the northern region, embarked upon extensive tours of the region to meet the local rulers and people. The aim was to further the unity and progress of the region and country as a whole, without regard to tribal or geographical origin.[35]

Political Freedom and Right to Opposition

The Caliphate accommodated and tolerated differences of thoughts from individuals. People were allowed to express their views on issues related to the State. Shaykh Abdullah's opinion on some political issues such as drumming, administrative or traditional titles, wearing gorgeous attire by political officers were some of the examples where Abdullah held different views with Bello but still he was allowed to freely advance his arguments on these issues even though there had been serious academic debates on them. Bello's political diplomacy as well as the manner in which he approached the revolt of Abd al-Salam Bagimbane was another instance where administration of justice and the right to opposition manifested itself in the Caliphate. Abd al-Salam, who at one time had contributed to the success of the Jihad, was given the territory of Kware to administer after the demise of the Shaykh but he became more eager to have a larger territory. This made him an open enemy to the Caliphate under Bello. There were serious arguments and counter arguments between the two, which led Bello to compile a book[36] expressing what had happened between him and Abd al-Salam. The idea here is that, despite Bello's total control of the state army and other security in the Caliphate, he still tolerated and allowed the opposition to reign in his administration. Not only this, he had also used all avenues of diplomacy and dialogue between him and Abd al-Salam and continued to do so until when Abd al-Salam declared war against the Caliphate, the action which compelled him to use his military power to crush Abd al-Salam's revolt so as to ensure the defense of the Caliphate from his assault.[37]

This practice had impacted on the politics of Northern political leaders in the first republic. Sardauna, Balewa and others were co-actors in NPC and Aminu Kano, Lawan Dambazau and others were prominent in NEPU. Sardauna was on good terms with the native authority and the British; he was seen as their supporter. But Malam Aminu's main political targets were these two (native authority and the colonialists), yet, Sardauna's government continued to accommodate opponents like Aminu Kano despite all his criticism. Not only that, Sardauna appointed him as Resident Commissioner of Economic Development in the government formed by their political party, the NPC.[38]

Economic Policy of the State

In recognition of the importance of agriculture to state development, Sultan Bello made it a catalyst to technological and industrial developments. He ensured and massively supported agricultural and also ventured fully into it. There were leather materials exported to Europe and Morocco; there were also dying and chemical as well as sugar refining industries established in many centres in the Caliphate of Bello. He came up with positive policies and programmes in this sector aimed at bringing prosperity, and happiness to his people. His land policy had also made great impact on the development of agriculture in the Caliphate, as individuals could easily have access to land by merely seeking permission of a leader.

The Northern political leaders, particularly of the First Republic, were influenced by these ideas and the practices from Bello's administration. They promoted agriculture for food production and export. Sardauna for instance, established the Institute for Agricultural Research at Samaru and another modern farm at Bakura. While Bello had promoted local crafts, the Northern political leaders, and Sardauna in particular established and promoted modern textile industries, cement factories, tanneries and craft industries in leather and weaving in Sokoto, ceramics in Bida, shoe making in Maiduguri and many more industries in many parts of the North.

Bello encouraged his people to engage in faming and business to be self reliant. In the same vein, the Northern political leaders had ensured that people had access to the necessities of life and are treated in accordance with the demands of social justice and equality. The development of commerce by Northern political leaders was facilitated through governmental actions which could be either regulatory or productive and this of course, was similar to Bello's establishment of grain reserves or his introduction of a device for extracting sugar from cane which must have influenced these Northern politicians.

During their time, farmers were encouraged to adopt modern methods and techniques of agriculture and improved seeds were distributed to them more or less free of charge.[39] Right from the time he was in Rabah, Sir Ahmadu Bello had introduced his people to agricultural activities such as cultivation of dry-season crop, notably cassava, as a way of making people stay in the village during the dry season. Similarly, he had also popularised the cultivation of rice and sweet potatoes among his people in Rabah. All these were to make them self reliant.[40] There was also the growth of industries in the Northern region with the establishment of over 100 modern industries, enterprises ranging from textile mills to factories for the manufacture of tiles, furniture, stationary, mineral waters, footwear and many more.[41] This initiation led to the establishment of the Kaduna textile industry.

Conclusion

In conclusion, this chapter has shown that the Sokoto Caliphate influenced the leadership of the Northern political leaders especially in the First Republic. The influence was due to both religious and environmental factors. The Northern political leaders were Northerners and Muslims who were impacted by the socio-cultural and religious practices of their environment.

The environment where the Caliphate was established and ran according to Islamic teachings had impacted on the way of life of the Northern politicians generally. This of course, included their political struggles. Similarly, as practicing Muslims, they felt it mandatory upon themselves to ensure the protection of their religion and its development. They ensured that whatever they did was in consonance with the principles of the Sokoto Caliphate's political and administrative practices that were purely Islamic. They tried to ensure the protection of the

Northern region from any form of suppression and oppression that might come from any region. Their giant struggle before and after independence was clear testimony in this respect. All the efforts they exerted during that period were in the interest of the Northern region and the northerners. They wanted to ensure independence for all regions without seclusion of other segments of the country who could have been enslaved by other region. If it were not for that effort, the Northerners would have been turned to slaves of people from other region. Indeed, as Muslim politicians, they did all they could, irrespective of their political inclination, to ensure the protection of the image of Islam and Muslims in the North. Not only that, they had also tried their best in making sure that they copied the tenets of Sokoto Caliphate in the discharge of their political and leadership duties.

References

1. A.M Gada *A Short History of Early Islamic Scholarship in Hausaland*, (Sokoto: Department of Islamic Studies, UDU, Sokoto, 2010), 46
2. A.M Kani, "Dynamics of Administration: The role of Sultan Muhammad Bello in the Establishment and Consolidation of the Sokoto Caliphate" A paper presented at a seminar on the life and ideas of Amir al-Muminin Muhammad Bello, CIS, UDU, Sokoto (1985), 8.
3. U.Bn Foduye, *Najmu al-Ikhaawan* (M.S). (Sokoto: np. nd), 139
4. M. Adamu "Aspect of Economic and Social Development in the Sokoto Caliphate in the 19th Century" in H. Boboyi and A.M Yakubu, eds, *The Sokoto Caliphate: History and Legacies, 1904-2004*. (Kaduna, Arewa House 2006), 94.
5. A. A. Amune, *Work and Worship: Selected Speeches of Sir Ahmadu Bello*, (Zaria: Gaskiya Corporation Limited. 1986), 216.
6. A. O. Nwauwa and J.O. Adekunle (eds) *Nigerian Political Leaders*, (America, Goldline and Jacobs Publishing. 2014), 77.
7. J.T. Renolds, "The Politics of History: The Legacy of the Sokoto Caliphate in Nigeria", *Journal of Asian and African Studies*. Vol. XXXII, Number 1-2, (June, 1997), 57.
8. Renolds "The Politics of History...", 57
9. A. Feinsten. *African Revolutionary: The Life and Times of Nigeria's Aminu Kano*. (New York, Triatlantic Books, 1998), 352.
10. Feinsten, *African Revolutionary*, 59
11. Amune, *Work and Worship*, 19.
12. A. Bello, *My Life*, (Zaria: Gaskiya Corporation Limited, 1986), 227.

Chapter Eleven	Muhammad Dahiru Shuni, in Y.A. Quadri, Omotoye & R.I. Adebayo(Eds) Religion and Development in Nigeria London, Adonis & Abbey Publishers

13. S. Jami'u *Towards Diffusing Religious Tension in The Polity: Islam and Politics in Nigeria.1903-1983*. (Ilorin: Lavgard Investment ltd, 2012), 176
14. Amune, *Work and Worship*, 178.
15. J.N. Paden, *Ahmadu Bello Sardauna of Sokoto: Values and Leadership in Nigeria*, (London: Hodder and Stoughton, 1986), 193
16. A. Mohammed *Great and Curious things about Sir Ahmadu Bello Sardauna of Sokoto and Premier of Northern Region*, (Zaria: Moving Image Limited, 2015), 116
17. H.A.S Johnston, *The Fulani Empire of Sokoto*, (London: Oxford University Press, London, 1967), 181
18. Mohammed, *Great and Curious things about Sir Ahmadu*, 147
19. Bello, *My Life*, 238
20. Amune, *Work and Worship*, 49.
21. Maguzawa are the non-Muslim Hausa who have lived in Kano and Katsina for Centuries.
22. S. W. Junaidu & M. U. Bunza "Peaceful Co-Existence and Bridge Building in a Plural Society: The example of the Sokoto Caliphate" in A. Mika'il et-al (eds), *Islam and the Fundamentals of Peaceful Co-Existence in Nigeria*. (Sokoto: Sokoto State Government 2014), 220.
23. Junaidu & Bunza, "Peaceful Co-Existence and Bridge Building…", 225
24. Mohammed, *Great and Curious things about Sir Ahmadu*, 114
25. Alhaji Maitama Sule (Danmasanin Kano) an interview granted to *New Nigerian* Newspaper, 2016, Special edition on the 50th Commemoration of the death of Premier of the Northern Region Late Sir, Ahmadu Bello (Sardauna of Sokoto), 47
26. A. Mohammed, *Great and Curious things about Sir Ahmadu*, 114
27. Alhaji Maitama Sule (Danmasanin Kano) an interview granted to *New Nigerian* Newspaper, 47
28. Mohammed, *Great and Curious things about Sir Ahmadu*, 115
29. Mohammed, *Great and Curious things about Sir Ahmadu*, 116
30. Mohammed, *Great and Curious things about Sir Ahmadu*, 124
31. *New Nigerian* Newspaper, 2016, Special Edition on the 50th Commemoration of the death of Premier of the Northern Region Late Sir, Ahmadu Bello (Sardauna of Sokoto). 5
32. *New Nigerian* Newspaper, 5
33. Dixon Henham, Hugh Clapperton and Dr. Oudney, *Narrative of Travels and Discoveries in Northern and Central Africa in the Years 1822, 1823 and 1824*, (second edition, London, 1826), 53

34. T. Mahmud, "Leadership and Governance in Nigeria: The Relevance of Values" (London: Hudahuda/Hodder and Stronghton.1999), 265
35. A. O. Nwauwa and J.O. Adekunle (eds) *Nigerian Political Leaders*, 276.
36. See *Sard Kalam fi ma jara baini wabaina Abd al-Salam*. History and Culture Bureau Sokoto. Acc. No 31/3/9'28
37. M.U.Bunza "The Application of Islamic Law and the legacies in the Sokoto Caliphate, Nigeria. (1804-1903): Lessons for Contemporary Period." *Electronic Journal of Islamic and Middle Eastern Law*. Vol. 1 (2013), 95.
38. A. Feinstein *African Revolutionary: The Life and Times of Nigerian's Aminu Kano*, (New York: Triatlantic Books, 1998). 190
39. Amune, *Work and Worship*, 202
40. Nwauwa and Adekunle (eds) *Nigerian Political Leaders*, 36.
41. Amune, *Work and Worship*, 40.

Chapter Eleven	Muhammad Dahiru Shuni, in Y.A. Quadri, Omotoye & R.I. Adebayo(Eds) Religion and Development in Nigeria London, Adonis & Abbey Publishers

CHAPTER TWELVE

The Church and Socio-Economic Development of Ilorin Metropolis: a Case Study of Anglican Church in Ilorin, Kwara State, Nigeria

Rotimi Williams Omotoye
Department of Religions
University of Ilorin,
Ilorin, Nigeria
graquarters@gmail.com
+2348033933033

Introduction

The objective of this chapter is an highlight of the contributions of the Anglican Church to the socio-economic development of Ilorin metropolis. The history of the church cannot be dissociated from the historiography of Church history in Ilorin in particular and Nigeria in general. Since the focus of this book is on Religion and development, we delve into the contributions of the Anglican Church to Ilorin as a community.

The history and development of Christianity in Nigeria was in different phases. The first phase was the introduction of Christianity to Benin and Warri by the Catholic Portuguese Missionaries in the 15th century[1]. Many Church historians believed that the exercise was a failure because of some reasons that were identified in the expansion of Christianity in the area at that time. However, Omotoye opined that the 19th century Christian missionaries must have learnt some lessons from the pitfalls of the earlier missionaries. He based his argument on a Yoruba proverb which says that *"ẹni tó jìn sí kòtò, ó kọ́ àwọn tó kù lọ́gbọ́n"* "He who falls into a ditch teaches others some lessons"[2].

The second phase of Christianity was in the 19th century when the Mission Churches, such as the Methodist, Church Missionary Society (C.M.S.) later known as the Anglican Church, Baptist and Catholic were introduced to the religious space in Nigeria. The third phase was an era of emergence of African Independent Churches (Aladura), namely: Cherubim and Seraphim (C & S), Christ Apostolic Church (C.A.C.), Church of the Lord (Aladura) and Celestial Church of Christ (C.C.C)[3]. Another phase of Churches emerged in 1970's. These are Pentecostal Churches some of whose founders and headquarters are based in Ilorin. These are the Rhema church founded by Pastor George Adegboye[4], Strong Tower established by Evangelist Professor Timothy Opoola and New Testament Christian Mission led by Pastor Rahman Popoola[5]. There is a connectivity amongst all the churches introduced in different phases in Ilorin metropolis, because they recognised the Anglican Church as the first to be established in the city. Therefore, the Christian Association of Nigeria (C.A.N.) always ends the annual New Year prayer at St. Barnabas Anglican Church and the C.A.N. annual Palm Sunday procession used to take off and end in the Church. The last celebration of such Palm Sunday procession was held on 25th March, 2018.

The introduction of Christianity to Ilorin started in the middle of the 19th century. Rev. T.J. Bowen of the Baptist mission based in Ogbomoso visited the town in 1855 and met Emir Shitta who politely disallowed him from preaching the gospel because the town was referred to as the "city of Qur'ān". Bishop Samuel Ajayi Crowther who was a missionary in the Niger Delta also made an attempt to evangelise in Ilorin in 1857 and 1859 respectively[7]. He too was not given the support of evangelising in the town. The scenario started to change with the activities of itinerant Osomalo textile traders in Ilorin metropolis and its suburbs. Many of the traders were converted Christians from home[8]. Religion, especially spirituality and faith of an individual is important because it cannot be divorced from the personality involved. They went to Ilorin primarily to trade but they were also useful in evangelising the area. This is in compliance with the "Great Command" of Jesus Christ, "Go ye therefore and proclaim the gospel ..." Matthew 28:19. It is also recorded in Acts 1:8 that "you will be my witnesses in Jerusalem, Judea and Samaria and to the uttermost part of the world". The experience of the traders therefore was a fulfillment of the teachings of Jesus Christ.

| Chapter Twelve | Rotimi Williams Omotoye, in Y.A. Quadri, Omotoye & R.I. Adebayo(Eds) Religion and Development in Nigeria London, Adonis & Abbey Publishers |

Another episode that brought Christianity to Ilorin metropolis was the construction of Railway from the Southern region to the Northern area of the country[9]. Many of the workers of Railway Corporation employed were Christians in their communities before they were employed by the Railway Corporation. The railway Christian workers and Ijesa Osomalo Christian traders became useful agents of Christianity in Ilorin metropolis. Therefore, the two bodies prepared the ground for evangelisation of Ilorin metropolis. The Christians mostly from the Southern areas came together in a "Fellowship" of Christian community in Ilorin. The early Christians were protected by the British Colonial Government in 1900 onwards. Ilorin came under the Northern Protectorate governed by Lord Lugard. The latter became a Governor-General of the amalgamated Protectorates of the Northern and Southern protectorates in 1914. The policy of the government protected the interest of the minority in the Northern area. The Winnick Commission of enquiry of 1948 in the Middle Belt region was of a tremendous assistance to the survival of Christians and propagation of Christianity. [10].

The early Christians were meeting in the home of an Ijesa Christian named "Baba Ajia" in Itakure in 1910[11]. The fellowship expanded and grew phenomenally. The group formally requested for a piece of land from the Emir who granted them some plots of land at the present location of the Central Bank and extended to Sabo-Oke area where St. Barnabas Cathedral was located. It is necessary to mention that the early Christians came together to fellowship without any reference to denominationalism. Well, the prayer of Jesus Christ for the Church in John 17:11 was that they "may be one, as we are". Later events indicated that the initial fellowship became St Barnabas Anglican Church, Sabo Oke in 1912. Members who were not Anglican from birth started moving out of the group to start denominations of their choice. The movement led to the emergence of African Church, Baptist Church, Christ Apostolic Church, and Cherubim & Seraphim Church at different times.

Chapter Twelve | Rotimi Williams Omotoye, in
Y.A. Quadri, Omotoye & R.I. Adebayo(Eds)
Religion and Development in Nigeria
London, Adonis & Abbey Publishers

The Composition of Anglican Churches in Ilorin Metropolis

As said earlier, the foundation members of Saint Barnabas Anglican Church, Sabo-Oke were Ijesa Osomalo textile traders and some railway workers. The Church was named St. Barnabas Anglican Church, Sabo Oke. In the research work of Odunoye[12], other parish churches in Ilorin metropolis were serialised and mentioned. For example, All Saints Anglican Church, Taiwo Isale was established in 1962. However, the Church was badly devastated and affected by the impact of the Nigerian Civil war of 1967-1970. The church was an Igbo speaking church. Many of the worshippers deserted the church but it is back on track as a flourishing Igbo church and headquarters of Ilorin East Archdeaconry. St Paul's Anglican Church, Baboko was established in 1973 and now the headquarters of Ilorin Archdeaconry; while Mount Olives Anglican Church was established in 1980 and now serving as the headquarters of Mount Olives Archdeaconry. Bishop Smith Anglican Church, Gaa Akanbi was established in 1983 and is the headquarters of Bishop Smith Archdeaconry. Holy Trinity, Kulende too was established in 1983 and is the headquarters of Kulende Archdeaconry. St Peter's Adewole was established in 1984 and is presently serving as the headquarters of Adewole Archdeaconry. All Saint's Anglican Church, Eyenkorin is one of the oldest Anglican churches in Ilorin metropolis. It was founded in 1945 by the Ijesa traders. The Church was on the outskirts of the town before the expansion of Ilorin metropolis. It became the headquarters of Eyenkorin Archdeaconry in 2014. Our Saviour's Anglican Church, Olunlade was established in 2005 and it became the headquarters of Ilorin West Archdeaconry in 2015. Christ the King Anglican Church, Geri Alimi was established in 2001 and it became an Archdeaconry in 2015.These churches and others outside Ilorin formed an Archdeaconry which eventually became a formidable diocese. However, many of the existing Anglican Churches were not in existence as at the time the Diocese of Kwara was inaugurated in 1974, but they have become part of the history of existing churches in Ilorin metropolis as at the time of this research. Odunoye[13] quoted the deeds of relinquishment thus:

> Whereas in the year 1961, the Offa/Ilorin Archdeaconry Council was carved out of Ilesa Archdeaconry and was created the Offa/Ilorin

---

Chapter Twelve | Rotimi Williams Omotoye, in
Y.A. Quadri, Omotoye & R.I. Adebayo(Eds)
Religion and Development in Nigeria
London, Adonis & Abbey Publishers

Archdeaconry and in the same year the Lokoja Archdeaconry, the said Offa/Ilorin Archdeaconry covers the political area consisting of Ilorin Division, Oyun Division, Igbomina/Ekiti Division, Lafiaji/Patigi Division and Borgu Division, while the Lokoja Archdeaconry covers the political areas consisting of Kabba Division, Kogi Division, Dekina Division, Igbirra Division and Ankpa Division of Kwara state.

Ilorin/Offa Archdeaconry was merged with the Lokoja Archdeaconry to become a Diocese in 1974 with Diocesan headquarters located at St Mark's Anglican Church, Offa. The first Diocesan Bishop was Rt. Rev. Herbert Haruna. He maintained the headquarters until 1980 when the Synod of the Diocese of Kwara took a resolution of moving the headquarters to St Barnabas Anglican Church, Sabo Oke. The relocation generated controversy and name calling amongst the Offa Christians and others[14]. The reason adduced by the Synod was that the Diocesan Bishop should live in the state capital where he could easily meet the political leaders of the state. The Offa people were of the opinion that they should retain the headquarters because of the fact that Christianity was introduced to Offa before Ilorin.

Contributions of the Anglican Church to Ilorin Metropolis in the field of Education

The Anglican Church in Ilorin between 1974 -2018 was presided over by three Diocesan Bishops in succession. Rt. Rev. Herbert Haruna, 1974-1994, Rt. Rev. Jeremiah Olagbamigbe Fabuluje 1995-2005, and Most Rev. Olusegun Adedayo Adeyemi 2005- to-date[5] who is to leave office in 2019 after clocking the mandatory year of seventy. Christianity as a religion, especially the Anglican denomination, played a formidable role in the promotion of western education in Nigeria. In fact, Bishop Samuel Ajayi Crowther advised the missionaries to establish schools in their domains. It was a strategy of conversion by the denomination. Ade Ajayi believed that:

> The school was the chief method of evangelisation used by Samuel Ajayi Crowther. He introduced Christian Mission into new places by getting rulers and elders interested in the idea of having a school of

their own. And Crowther usually asked the senior Missionary at each station to give his chief attention to the schools[16].

Fafunwa and Omotoye also agreed with Ajayi's position in their earlier works. As at the time of introducing western education by the Christian missionaries to Ilorin, the community had been known as a centre of Islamic education. According to Balogun, "Ilorin had served as a useful training centre for Muslim scholars who helped to propagate Islam and Islamic education throughout Yoruba land"[17]. In other words, the community was a stronghold of Islamic education. However, the Christian missionaries remained focused and determined to succeed in the expansion of Christianity in Ilorin community. The Anglican Church therefore took the lead in this regard. One of the early teachers at St. Barnabas primary school who later became an Ambassador, Mr. Femi Aje in an interview, narrated the efforts of the church in championing western education in Ilorin. Mr. J.K. Ajayi and Venerable S. Akande who were amongst the early pupils of St. Barnabas primary school, Sabo-oke, also testified to the benefits the indigenes and non-indigenes of Ilorin acquired from the school.

The following schools were established by the Anglican churches in Ilorin metropolis between 1917-2018. A recent statistical data of the Anglican schools obtained at the Second Session of the Fifteenth Synod of the Diocese of Kwara held at the Cathedral Church of Saint Barnabas, Sabo Oke Ilorin between 12th -15th April, 2018 provided the data of Anglican schools as follows:

St Barnabas Anglican Primary school was established in 1917. The school celebrated her 100 years of existence in November 2017. The school has been divided into school A and B for administrative convenience. The second school was carved into school "B" in 1998.[18]

Saint Barnabas Anglican Primary school, Sabo-Oke (School A)

Classes	Pupil Enrolment
KG	33
1	53
2	50
3	54

Chapter Twelve | Rotimi Williams Omotoye, in Y.A. Quadri, Omotoye & R.I. Adebayo(Eds) Religion and Development in Nigeria London, Adonis & Abbey Publishers

4	54
5	52
6	37
TOTAL	333

Staff: both teaching and non-teaching: 28

Even though, the government had taken over the payment of monthly salary, recruitment and transfer of teachers in the school, the proprietor is still managing the school in collaboration with the Government.

St Barnabas Primary school B.

There are one hundred and twenty pupils in the school.

Bishop Smith Memorial College was established in 1957. In fact, the 60th year anniversary of its establishment was celebrated with pomp and pageantry by the Old students of the College between 22nd-26th November, 2017[19]. The staff strength of the Senior Secondary section goes thus: Teaching staff 62, Non-teaching 18; Parent Teacher Association (PTA) Mathematics teachers 3, Physics teachers 2, Night guard 1 and National Youth Service Corps members (NYSC) 9. Student population goes thus:

Class	Male	Female	Total
SS1	248	148	396
SS2	161	148	309
SS3	72	48	120
Total	481	344	825

Bishop Smith Junior Secondary School: The total number of students as at April 2018 was 920. Males 435 and females 485. The distribution goes thus;

	Male	Female
JSS1	140	160
JSS2	145	155
JSS3	150	170
Total	435	485

Chapter Twelve | Rotimi Williams Omotoye, in
Y.A. Quadri, Omotoye & R.I. Adebayo(Eds)
Religion and Development in Nigeria
London, Adonis & Abbey Publishers

The school has 38 teaching staff, 6 non-teaching staff, 22 N-Power staff employed by the Federal Ministry of Education and 5 NYSC members.

Bishop Smith Primary school emerged in 1962 (now A and B) for administrative convenience.

School A has 287 pupils; while the staff strength is 34 for both academic and non-teaching staff. School B has a population of 299 pupils made up of 156 boys and 143 girls. There are 25 teaching staff and 2 non-teaching staff.

St Barnabas Nursery/Primary School was established in 1991

Anglican Women's Guild Nursery/Primary School, Gaa Akanbi was established in 1994

Anglican High School, Gaa Akanbi came into existence in 2014

There are four permanent Academic staff, part-time 9 and one non-teaching staff

Anglican Grammar School, Ilorin was established in 1994

Permanent teaching staff are ten, part-time five, NYSC members 5 and Non-teaching three. The population of students was 65 as at April, 2018.

CLASS	MALE	FEMALE	TOTAL
JSS1	4	2	6
JSS2	2	5	7
JSS3	9	6	15
SS1	3	3	6
SS2	6	8	14
SS3	8	5	13
TOTAL	32	29	91

Bishop Smith Memorial Nursery/Primary School emerged in 1995
Women's Guild Vocational Centre (Day Care) was established in 1994
St Paul's Nursery and Primary School, Baboko was inaugurated in 1997
St Paul's Secondary School, Baboko came into existence in 2015
The statistical data of St Paul's Basic School goes thus:
1. K.G class — 17 pupils
2. Pre-Nursery — 26 pupils
3. Nursery One — 27 pupils
4. Nursery Two — 20 pupils
5. Reception class — 22 pupils
6. Basic One — 25 pupils

7. Basic Two — 31 pupils
8. Basic Three — 24 pupils
9. Basic Four — 24 pupils
10. Basic Five — 16 pupils
11. Basic Seven (J.S.S. One) — 10 students
12. Basic Eight (J.S.S. Two) — 10 students

The total population of the school as at April 2018 was 245 pupils/students in both primary and secondary sections of the school.
All Saints Nursery and Primary School, Taiwo, Ilorin was established in 2003
All Saints Anglican Model College, Ilorin was established in 2017
Holy Trinity Nursery/Primary School, Kulende came into existence in 1994
Mount Olives Nursery and Primary School, Fate road, Ilorin was established and later folded up because the church relocated to her permanent site. Another effort is being made to establish another Nursery and primary school. In fact, the construction of a two-storey building is in progress as at the time of this research.
Anglican Cathedral Nursery and Primary School, Sabo-Oke was founded in 2006
St Barnabas Junior Secondary School, Sabo-Oke, Ilorin was established in 2007
St Barnabas Senior Secondary School, Sabo-Oke, Ilorin was founded in 2014
The staff strength of St Barnabas Senior Secondary School, Sabo-Oke is 25 (consisting of 21 teaching and 4 non-teaching staff). As at April, 2018, there were five NYSC members, and four part-time teachers.
The population of students as at April, 2018 was 350.
Anglican Cathedral Secondary School, Sabo-Oke, Ilorin was established in 2016
Womens' Guild in the Diocese of Kwara is also providing functional Vocational centres for the public where computer training facilities are provided, Sewing and other trades are learnt.[20]
Henry Venn's Policy of Self-governing, Self propagating and Self-financing and the Church.

Henry Venn was the Secretary General of the Church Missionary Society (C.M.S.) for thirty years (1842 - 1872) and he propounded the theory of "Self –governing, Self- propagating and Self –financing" with the vision of assisting the Churches in Africa to succeed in future. The policy actually led to Native Pastorate and Indigenisation of the Mainline Churches in Nigeria, especially, the Anglican Church.

The retired Primate Jasper Akinola of Abuja Diocese championed the issue of investments by the Church of Nigeria in particular. He encouraged other dioceses to embark on such ventures, so as to assist in the economic viability and sustenance of the dioceses. In the past, the major source of financing the church was assessment fees paid by the members of the church. The economic recession and depression witnessed in Nigeria in particular after the fall of oil boom in World market in 1980's also affected the finances of the church. Even though, the Government of the Federal Republic of Nigeria said the country was out of recession, its effect is still being felt by Nigerians. Therefore, investments in businesses are ways out of the economic challenges in the church. The Anglican churches have been involved in some other investments that are yielding some revenues that are assisting the finances of the Diocese.

Investment in physical structure in Ilorin metropolis apart from assessment and money donations to the churches started with the second Bishop, Rt. Rev. Olagbamigbe Fabuluje (1995 - 2005) with a construction of ten locked up shops along Agba Dam road in Gaa Akanbi. Apart from the revenue generated between 1995-2005, it was an opportunity to take hold of the land of the church being encroached upon by trespassers of church land. Bishop Adeyemi built on the initial efforts of his predecessor by building another forty-five shops along the same route[21]. This is a source of income to the Diocese. However, there is a challenge of collecting agreed rents from the tenants majority of whom are not always willing to pay shop rents when due. A task force was set up by the Diocese in achieving the onerous assignment.

In 2012, Bishop Adeyemi built Peter Akinola Guest House named after the retired Primate Peter Jasper Akinola. It is located along Bishop Smith Secondary School, G.R.A, Ilorin. The Guest House contains thirty- six rooms of different sizes[22] (Luxury Suite, Crown suites, Luxury Double, Crown Double and Standard Rooms). Even though, the Guest

---

Chapter Twelve	Rotimi Williams Omotoye, in Y.A. Quadri, Omotoye & R.I. Adebayo(Eds) Religion and Development in Nigeria London, Adonis & Abbey Publishers

House is for business, strict Christian ethics are applied in the running of the institution. For example, alcoholic drinks are not sold, smoking is not permitted and women of easy virtues are not permitted to be brought in to the Guest House. It is necessary to note that the hotel business is highly competitive in Ilorin metropolis and some vices, such as sales of alcoholic drinks, cigarette smoking, harlotry, etc. are permitted in the conventional hotels. Nevertheless, investigation revealed that Akinola Guest House is performing above average in terms of revenue generation to the diocese in spite of the strict Christian rules. Investigation revealed that the establishment was making profit. The establishment is also a source of employment to some youths. At least twenty people are employed as staff and marketers in Ilorin metropolis. It also provides accommodation for visitors in the town. As an establishment which is growing gradually, it is believed that the number of workers would increase in the nearest future as the business is growing and expanding.

A Multi-purpose hall was erected within the compound of the guest house in 2015. The Venerable O.A. Aderogba is the Supervisor of the Guest House and the Multi-purpose hall.

Printing press

The Diocese of Kwara started a printing press business in 2011. It is located within the premises of the Arch-bishop's palace. Five permanent staff are serving in the establishment. The availability of printing press has made it easier for the diocese and churches to print books, Sunday programmes, tracts and bills for the propagation of Christianity within and outside Ilorin metropolis. The printing press is patronised by churches, individuals and organisations within and outside Ilorin metropolis. At Saint Paul's Anglican Church, Baboko a Quarterly Newsletter Bulletin was introduced in 2015 to propagate Christianity and news about the Church. A similar bulletin known as Olives Heights was introduced at Mount Olives Anglican Church, Pipeline road, Tanke, Ilorin in 2017.

Bishop Smith Water Business

The Diocese of Kwara also established Bishop Smith Table Water business as another source of revenue generation to the Diocese. Many business men and women are engaged in the business of water production; in fact, the Federal government had to set up National Agency for Food and Drug Administration and Control (NAFDAC) to monitor and assess the quality of water being produced for the general public. The Diocese of Kwara commenced operation of her table water business in 2015. The factory is a source of employment to the youths in the town and the profit being made annually is a source of revenue for the diocese. The production of Bishop Smith Sachet and Bottled Water was approved by NAFDAC because of its good quality. The NAFDAC number of the business outfit is C1-0309. Rev Adolphous Nzurike is the Manager of the Bishop Smith Water Business.

Bookshop and other Business Ventures

The Diocese of Kwara is running a C.S.S bookshop at Sabo-Oke in an apartment owned by St Barnabas Anglican Church to generate fund into the purse of the Diocese. Church books and materials are sold at the centre. It was opened in 2007.

Apart from the central yielding businesses in the Diocese, some churches in Ilorin metropolis also have sources of revenues. For example, Mount Olives Anglican Church, Tanke has a Multi-purpose Event Hall. Also, the first phase of Tick trees was planted as experimentation farm in 2017[26]. A Nursery and Primary school building is under construction in the church premises. Its foundation was laid by Archbishop Adeyemi on 30th December, 2017. Christ the King Church has a flat of building along Agba Dam road Gaa Akanbi for rentage and a building containing 40 rooms for rentage at Malete for students of Kwara State University. The Women in the Diocese also built a flat along Agba Dam road to generate revenue. The tenants are paying on an annual basis to the organisations.

Co-operative societies are encouraged to empower and assist members of such societies. There are three of such societies at Saint Paul's Anglican Church, Baboko and a functional cooperative society at

Mount Olives Anglican Church, Tanke. The Clergy in the Diocese also has a functional Cooperative Society which is assisting in having access to loans. Loans are being offered to members to embark on businesses to alleviate economic hardship.

The Diocese in 2017 gave about five hundred thousand naira to Widows (Women of Grace as they are called by the Diocese of Kwara) as soft loan to those who are interested in small scale businesses. Each person collected fifty thousand Naira from the revolving loan scheme and is expected to pay back within a record time. The number of beneficiaries varies from one church to another because the number of widows in each of the churches in the diocese is not the same. Apart from the Diocesan empowerment loan scheme, some Churches have other parish empowerment programmes for their members. In Mount Olives Anglican Church, an anonymous person donated a reasonable amount of money in 2016 and 2017 respectively for such an exercise. It is interest free for small scale business men and women in the church. The interviews conducted with some of the beneficiaries revealed that some are into petty trading in their homes. The amount being disbursed depends on the request of interested applicants. Investigation also revealed that majority of the beneficiaries took between fifty and hundred thousand naira each. As at February, 2018, at least fifty-five people had benefitted from the exercise. Some are selling food items, fast food, provisions, clothing materials, etc. The opportunities granted to the needy have improved the well-being of the beneficiaries as they can be financially independent.

Challenges in the church

A major challenge that all the Anglican churches are facing in Ilorin metropolis is inadequate economic stability. The church cannot be separated from the socio-economic hardship being witnessed in Nigeria. The economic challenge of recession, unemployment, unpaid salaries is affecting the income of the church.

The schools owned by the Churches are seen as humanitarian services to the society. Therefore, the fees being charged are minimal compared to other private institutions in the town. As of 2014/2015/2015/2016 academic sessions, survey was carried out on school fees of private schools at Baboko and Surulere areas of Ilorin by the education committee of St Pauls Anglican Church, Baboko. It was decided that the amount of money charged should be moderate so as to assist the "poor in the society". Consequently, the church authority decided to subsidise the school fees. It is necessary to mention that many of the early schools established by the church had been taken over by the state government. The churches in conjunction with other Christian proprietors of mission schools are in the High Court of Ilorin, seeking for release of such schools to the original owners. The missionaries believed that they are being marginalised in the running of such schools which they established as proprietors in the state. The missionary schools were taken over by the government in principle but the missionaries still claim the ownership of the schools. There is an understanding that the headship of such schools would be members of the owner churches. Event centres and production of table water have become a common business in Ilorin metropolis. Therefore, patronage is minimal and not too encouraging.

The establishment of many churches, especially Pentecostal churches in the nooks and crannies of the town is having adverse effect on attendance of Anglican churches in Ilorin. Many members of the Anglican churches have relocated to new sites where Anglican churches are not found. More importantly, some youths in particular are drifting to the Pentecostal churches where they believe that some opportunities and facilities are provided for them. In response to such challenges, the Anglican Church has put in place the opportunity for the youths to demonstrate their talents of leading some church programmes at least, once in a month. Some of them are appointed into various offices in the church, such as peoples' warden, verger, auditor and various committees.

Conclusion

The Anglican Church was the first Christian denomination to be established in Ilorin. The church established some mission schools which have contributed significantly to the educational development of Ilorin. Apart from education, the church has ventured into the provision of other socio-economic businesses, such as guest house, pure water business, printing press and bookshop business. In spite of the contributions highlighted in this study, the church is facing some challenges, especially in terms of funding and finances of some projects.

References

1. Rotimi Omotoye, "Christianity As a Catalyst For Socio-economic and Political Change in Yoruba land, Nigeria: An Account of a Church Historian" The One Hundred and Fifty-ninth (159th) Inaugural Lecture, University of Ilorin, Ilorin, delivered on 25th June, 2015, 6
2. Rotimi Omotoye, "Christianity As a Catalyst For Socio-economic and Political Change in Yoruba land, Nigeria: An Account of a Church Historian", 6.
3. Deji Ayegboyin and Ademola Ishola, *African Indigenous Churches An Historical Perspective*,(Lagos: Greater Heights Publications,1997)
4. Rotimi Omotoye, "Communication and the Universality of the Gospel in Yoruba land" in Ade P. Dopamu (eds)etal *Science and Religion in the Service of Humanity*, (Ilorin: Local Society Initiative and Nastrens, 2006), 42-43
5. Rotimi Omotoye, "The Growth and Expansion of Pentecostal Churches in Ilorin", in Y.A. Quadri,R.W. Omotoye, and R.I.Adebayo (eds) *Religion in Contemporary Nigeria*, (London: Adonis and Abbey Publishers Limited,2016), 177-178
6. A.G.A.S. Oladosu (eds) etal. *Ilorin: History, Culture and Lessons of Peaceful Co-Existence*,(Ilorin: Centre for Ilorin Studies)2013. See also, Z.I. Oseni (eds) etal *Ilorin As a Beacon of Learning and Culture in West Africa*,(Ilorin: Centre For Ilorin Studies), 2015
7. Rotimi Omotoye, "Christianity and Educational Development in Ilorin Metropolis (1855-1995) *Journal of Religious Studies*, Department of Religious Studies, University of Uyo, Uyo, 1(1), 1998,106
8. Rotimi Omotoye, "The Creativity and Identity of Ijesa "Osomalo" in the Socio-economic and Christianization of Yoruba land, South-western, Nigeria" *KWASU Journal of Religious Studies*, Volume 1,No 1,2017,4
9. Rotimi Omotoye, "Christianity and Educational development in Ilorin Metropolis (1855-1995)", 107
10. Rotimi Omotoye, "Historical Perspective of the Decolonization of the Church in Yoruba land (1842-1960) in S.O. Abogunrin (eds) etal. *Decolonization of Biblical Interpretation in Africa*,(Ibadan: Nigerian Association For Biblical Studies, 2005), 394-408
11. Rotimi Omotoye, "Christianity and Educational Development in Ilorin Metropolis (1855-1995), 107

12. E.T. Odunoye, *The Advent and Growth of the Diocese of Kwara*, (Anglican Communion 1974-2016), 19
13. E.T. Odunoye, *The Advent and Growth of the Diocese of Kwara*, 20
14. C.O. Amusan, *St Barnabas Cathedral Church 1910-2012*, (Ilorin: Samadex Printers, 2012), 21
15. C.O. Amusan, *St Barnabas Cathedral Church 1910-2012*, 46-51.
16. J.F. Ade Ajayi, *Christian Mission in Nigeria 1841-1891: The Making of a New Elite*, (London: Longman, 1977), 218.
17. S.A. Balogun, "Historical Significance of Ilorin: A Preliminary Survey" Published in Confluence: An Academic Journal of Kwara Council for Arts and Culture, 1, (1978), 17-18.
18. S.O. Ajayi and A.O. Akande, Headmaster and Headmistress of St Barnabas Primary school A and B at Sabo Oke, Ilorin
19. Bishop Smith Memorial College Old Students Association (BSMCOSA), Ilorin, Kwara State, Nigeria Celebrated her 60th year Anniversary between 22nd-26th November, 2017
20. Rotimi Omotoye, "Christianity and Educational Development in Ilorin Metropolis"111-112, E.T.Odunoye,69-70 and interviews of Anglican School Principals, Headmasters and Headmistresses held at Bishop Smith Senior Secondary School on 21st December,2017
21. E.T. Odunoye, *The Advent and Growth of the Diocese of Kwara*.
22. E.T. Odunoye, *The Advent and Growth of the Diocese of Kwara*.
23. J.F. Ade Ajayi, *Christian Mission in Nigeria 1841-1891*, 159
24. Rotimi Omotoye,"Christianity, and the Development of Science and Technology in Yoruba land", S.O. Oyewole (eds) etal. *Science in the perspective of African Religion (Afrel), Islam and Christianity* (Ilorin: Local Society Initiative (LSI) 2010), 265.
25. Rotimi Omotoye, "Use of African Traditional Medicine, Western Medicine, and Christian Faith Healing in Yoruba land, Southwestern Nigeria" in Ibigbolade S. Aderibigbe, Rotimi Williams Omotoye and Lydia Bosede Akande (eds) *Contextualizing Africans and Globalization Expressions in Socio-political and Religious Contents and Discontents* (London: Lexington Books, 2016), 127
26. Mount Olives Heights Quarterly Bulletin, December publication 2017, 1.

INDEX

A

AAA60, See American Arbitration Association
Abbas Shittu (Alhaji) 71, 72
Abbasid Caliphs Ventured 107
Abd Al-Salam Bagimbane 227
Abdul Azeez Ibiyemi (Alhaji) ...71
Abdul Ghaniy Abdul Hamid 72
Abdul-Azeez Ahmad Balogun (Alhaji) 99
Abdul-Fatah Kola Makinde 59
Abdullahi Dan Fodio 98
Abdulrasheed Alada Muhammad 29
Abdul-Rasheed Alawusa 70
Abdurrahman Oloyede (Prof) 109
Abesan Housing Estate 63
Abolarin, Isaac Adeshina 171
Abomination 99
Abortion 110, 195
Abortive 63, 83
Absence of Power And Energy 194
Abstinence 99
Abubakar Tafawa Balewa (Sir) 219, 224
Accommodation133, 135, 192, 198, 224, 226, 243
    Political 226
Accountability19, 20, 22, 23, 24, 52, 54, 223
    Issue of 22
    Political 190
Accountability And Service Delivery 223
Accounts 200, 201, 205
Foreign 54
Historical 200
Accreditation
    Failed 130
Accumulation 223
Achieving Gender Equality ...193, 197
Acute Panereatitis 100
Adamu Orisa79, 80, 82, 83, 84, 85, 86, 87, 89, 90, 91, 92
    Origin of 86
    Protection For 85
    Types of 84
Adamu Orisa Festival
    Developmental Dynamics of 79
    Developmental Values of 92
    Importance of 85
    Tourist Potentials of 83
    Values of 80
Adamu Orisa Festival And Development In Lagos 90
Adamu Orisa Traditions 83
Adeboye (Pastor) 163
Ademola Ajayi 150
Adeniyi, J. K. 183
Aderogba, O.A. (Venerable)...243
Adeyemi (Bishop) 242
Adimu Cult 85
Adimu Orisa 84, 86, 87, 89
    Origin of 86, 88
Adimu Pantheon 89
Adjudicate 62, 63, 208
Adjudicating 69
Administration21, 24, 60, 68, 69, 73, 74, 75, 158, 161, 162, 165,

166, 205, 218, 222, 223, 224, 225, 227, 228, 244
    Civilian 18
    Colonial 150, 151
    Immediate Past 21
    Model of 223
    New 17, 21, 24
    Previous 21
    System of 59, 219, 220
Administration of Justice59, 60, 68, 69, 73, 74, 75, 223, 227
Administration of Northern Leaders 225
Administrative Convenience 238, 240
Adolescent 147, 192
Adolphous Nzurike (Rev) 244
ADR60, 61, 62, 68, 70, 75, *See* Alternative Dispute Resolution
    Concept of 61
    Definition 61
    Mechanism of 75
    Objective of 69
Adr Mechanism 75
Adr Programmes 61, 70
Advent of James Welch .. 153, 155
Advent of Missionaries 148
Affiliation 84
    Religious 29
Afolabi, A. S. 119
Africa Church Grammar School 156
African Culture 44
African Traditional Religions 32
Agencies13, 14, 38, 44, 150, 205, 208
    Voluntary 143
Agencies Empowering Groups 13
Aghalino, S.O. 143
Agreement 17, 18, 66, 172
    Contractual 70
    Mutual 201

Agricultural Activities 229
Agricultural Practices 153, 192
Agricultural Research 228
Agunji Districts 173
Ahmadiyya Muslim Hospital 96
Ahmadu Bello (Sir) . 219, 224, 229
Ahmed Sani Yerima 19
Ailment Bedevilling 106
Ailments96, 99, 102, 103, 105, 106, 112, 120, 121, 123, 181
    Causes of 121, 123
    Form of 106
    Minor 122
    Physical 120
    Psychotic 121
    Spiritual 121
Aitken, J. D. 153, 155, 157
Ajani-Muritala 205
Ajase-Ipo 172, 173
Ajayi, Deborah (Mrs) 128
Ajayi, J. K. 238
Akeem A. Akanni 189
Akinlagun Tradition 88, 89
Akinlagun, A.B. (Chief) 87
Akinsemoyin (Oba) 88
Akinsiku of Lagos 83
Alakete Pupa 85
Albert Taylor 176
Alcoholic Beverages 91
Alex W. Banfield 176
Alexander Obuseri 152
Al-Huda Nasara Islamic Herbal Center 97
Ali Modu Sheriff 18
Allah (Almighty)46, 47, 66, 70, 100, 101, 105, 111, 196, 202
    Law of 66
    Way of 47
Allegiance 49, 50
    Oath of 44
    Statements of 44
Allergic Reactions 111

Alligator Pepper 84, 110
Alternative Dispute Resolution
.... 60, 68
Ambition 52
   Political 19
American Arbitration Association ...60
American Maize....................... 182
Aminu Kano (Mallam)219, 220, 223, 228
Amodu (Mrs) 134
Amputations 107
Amy Cutter 191
Ancestor 52, 89, 173, 217
   Maternal...................................88
Ancestral Precedents 147
Anglican Cathedral Nursery And Primary School 241
Anglican Cathedral Secondary School 241
Anglican Church In Ilorin..... 233, 237
Anglican Churches236, 238, 242, 245, 246
   Composition of 236
Anglican Denomination 237
Anglican Girls Grammar School 156
Anglican Grammar School ... 157, 240
Anglican Mission...................... 162
Animashaun Group 71
Annual Education Rate 159
Ansar-Ud-Deen Society 96
Antagonism........ 33, 154, 156, 159
Antagonistic 14
Anthony, E. (Rev) 176
Anthropologists..........................80
Antibiotics 100
Anti-Corruption War..................24
Anti-Development 29, 32
Antidote 99

Anti-Islam 111
Anti-Islamic System 220
Antimony 100
Antiretroviral Therapy............129
Apena Ajasa 83, 86
Apparatuses 154
Apprenticeship 147
Aquinas Work.............................82
Arabic 65, 66, 95, 174, 209
Arch-Bishop's Palace...............243
Archdeaconry 236, 237
   Adewole...................................236
   Eyenkorin...............................236
   Ilorin East 236
   Ilorin West 236
   Kulende 236
   Lokoja.......................... 236, 237
   Mount Olives........................236
   Offa/Ilorin.................. 236, 237
Armed Robbers.........................22
Aropale 84
Asabiyyah 15
Asibito Iye................................133
Aso-Oke.....................................90
Assassins 51
Assertion 16, 18, 29, 70
Assessment 242
   Critical 61
Assets Acquisition...................205
Assistance 134, 135, 158, 159, 235
   Financial 143, 159
   Foreign 135
   Spiritual......................... 96, 102
ATR32, 33, *See* African Traditional Religions
Attainment of the Sustainable Development Goals189, 190, 194, 207, 210
Audible to the Deaf..................48
Augustine Delise (Dr) 132
Auxiliary Nurses.............. 134, 135

Awo Opa 83, 86
Awo Opa Fraternity 86
Awofeko Emmanuel Olusegun 43
Ayandele, E. A. 120, 177, 178
Ayisat Afinni (Madam) 73
Ayo Fagbemi (Dr) 129
Ayo Oritsejafor (Pastor) 163

B

Bakassi Boys 35
Bante Sheda 89
Baptist Convention 162
Baptist High School 157
Barbaric Act 180
Barnabas Isa (Dr) 134
Basic Amenities 21
BBB60, *See* Better Business Bureau
Belief Systems 146
Beliefs ... 10, 12, 32, 145, 146, 179
    Erroneous 9
    Indigenous 179
    Religious 12, 31, 224
    Superstitious 105
    Traditional 164
Benin City 97, 149
Better Business Bureau 60
Biafran Agitators 160
Bida 175, 229
Bills 108, 243
    Customary Court Law 64
    Draft 63
    Medical 98
    Private 62, 63
Birth Attendant 124
Birth to Erelu Kuti 87
Bishop Smith Water Business 244
Bitter Experience 108
Black Seeds 101
Blasphemous 36
Blood Donors 129
Blood Pressure 101, 111

Body Odour 111
Boko Haram 17, 19, 20, 21
Boko Haram Insurgency 21
Bola Tinubu (Former Governor) 63
Bondage of Colonialism 218
Bookshelves 155
Born Again Christian 16
Bowen, T. J. (Rev) 234
Breadwinner 197
Breed Cotton 182
Bribery 48, 223
British Colonial Educational Policies 150
British Colonial Government . 235
British Colonialists 33, 151
British Rule 151
Buddhism 10
Building Blocks 171
Bumper Harvest 201
Burning Sensation 111

C

C & S234, *See* Cherubim And Seraphim
CA 33, *See* Constituent Assembly
CAC 234, *See* Christ Apostolic Church
Caliphate 107, 217, 218, 219, 220, 221, 222, 223, 224, 226, 227, 228, 229
    Division of 217, 218
    Establishment of 218
    Influence of 220
    Leadership of 218
Caliphate of Bello 228
Caliphate's Religious Policies .. 222
Camphor Tree 101
CAN38, 234, *See* Christian Association of Nigeria, *See* Christian Association of Nigeria

Capacity 32, 34, 62, 81, 91, 128, 145, 192
Capital 60, 205, 237
  Human 37
  Social And Economic 83
  Spiritual 81, 92
Cardinal Objectives 62
Care 45, 46, 62, 81, 96, 98, 101, 106, 119, 120, 122, 124, 125, 126, 127, 128, 129, 131, 132, 133, 136, 161, 196, 205, 220, 240
  Post-Natal 126
Catastrophic Occurrences 33
Catholic Caritas of the Federation of Nigeria 135
Catholic Dispensary 135
Catholic Missions 173
Catholic Superintendent 154
CCC 234, *See* Celestial Church of Christ
CCFN 135, *See* Catholic Caritas of the Federation of Nigeria
CCMP 183, *See* Church And Community Mobilisation Process
CEDR 60, *See* Centre For Effective Dispute Resolution
Celestial Church of Christ 234
Central Bank 21, 235
Centre For Effective Dispute Resolution 60
Centre of Cervical Cancer Screening 129
Cervical Cancer 129
Challenges Facing Muslim Practitioners In the Health Sector 110
Challenges In the Church 242, 245
Challenges of the Hospital 136
Character Formation 149

Character of Religious Conflicts In Nigeria 30, 34, 35
Character Training 147
Charity 195, 196, 202, 204, 205, 208
  Voluntary 195
Charles Robinson 176
Chemotherapy 106
Cherubim And Seraphim 234
Chieftaincy 88
  Honourary 71
  Traditional 71
Child Healthcare 128
Child Mortality 190
Chloraphinicol 132
Cholesterol 101, 111
Chris Ngige 50
Chris Uba 50
Christ Apostolic Church 156, 234, 235
Christ the King Anglican Church 236
Christian Association of Nigeria 38, 234
Christian Missionaries
  Activities of 136
  Early 148
  Era of 148
  Impact of 177
Christian Missionary Agencies 172
Christian Missions And Health Care In Okunland 124
Christian Nurses 130
Christian Rules 243
Christianity 9, 10, 17, 19, 30, 32, 33, 35, 39, 46, 80, 81, 88, 119, 132, 143, 144, 146, 148, 149, 151, 152, 164, 171, 176, 177, 180, 182, 183, 184, 233, 234, 235, 237, 243
  Expansion of 233, 238
  Influence of 180

Propagation of............ 235, 243
Spread of...................... 151, 152
Christianity And Educational Development In Delta State.. 143
Christianity And the Development of Health Care Services....................................... 119
Christianity And the Development of Healthcare Services In Okunland 119
Church And Community Mobilisation Process................ 183
Church And Socio-Economic Development of Ilorin Metropolis................................ 233
Church Mission Boards.......... 173
Church Missionary Society ... 173, 177, 234, 242
Church of the Lord................. 234
City of Qur'ān.......................... 234
Civil Law 64
Civil Rule......................................62
Clean Print Industry....................70
Climate Change191, 192, 194, 201
CMS 108, 149, 152, 153, 154, 155, 156, 177, 234, 242, *See* Church Missionary Society
Code of the Constitution 54
Collaborations.......................... 208
Colonial Administrators.......... 149
Colonial Authority 60
Colonial Experience...................30
Colonial Government124, 150, 159
British................................. 235
Effort of 136
Colonial Masters..........................96
Colonial Mission Schools........ 163
Colonial Overlords......................32
Colonial Period........................ 124
Colonial Rule 59

Colonialism.................................30
Bondage of.................. 218, 222
Community Affairs.................. 147
Community Health 129, 135
Composition of Anglican Churches In Ilorin Metropolis236
Concept of Adr..........................61
Concept of Religion And the Various Evolutionary Stages 31
Conflict Prevention 68
Conflicts30, 33, 34, 35, 36, 37, 38, 39, 79
Civic...81
Miss World Beauty Pageant. 35
Political..................................86
Potential 194
Resolution of 68
Conformity 105, 147
Constituent Assembly 33
Contemporary Abuse 144
Contributions of Ecwa Hospital 128
Contributions of Isp to Judicial Development In Nigeria...........68
Contributions of the Anglican Church to Ilorin Metropolis In the Field of Education 237
Controversies About Shari'ah ..18
Conventional Tax.....................208
Conviction 152, 178
Cooperative Society........ 244, 245
Corruption22, 24, 47, 48, 52, 203, 223
Attitude of.............................18
High Profile 48
Court Litigation..........................61
Court of Law 44
Court Settlements 68
Court System 59, 68
Courts44, 45, 59, 60, 61, 62, 63, 64, 66, 68, 69, 71, 72, 73, 74, 148, 152, 154, 198, 206, 208, 246

Civil 61
Conventional 60, 68, 69, 71
Customary 60, 64, 73
Federal High 60
Supreme 60
Criminal Acts 109
Cross-Examinations 65
Cross-Fertilisation 95
Cultural Associations 39
Cultural Imperialism 181
Cultural Symbolism 53
Current Trend In St. John Hospital 134
Custodianship 87
Custody of Children ... 67, 68, 206
Customary Court 60, 64, 73
Customary Court of Appeal 60
Customary Law Systems 60
Cyclical Process 15
Cyclical Theory of Civilisation . 15

D

Daniel Adeniyi 125
Daniel, Mary Taiye 171
Danoye Oguntola-Laguda 79
David G. Benner 12
David Olaniyi Oyedepo (Bishop) 163
David Smock 34
Decongestion 68
Defendants .. 45, 65, 70, 71, 72, 73
Deforestation 194
Deity Dances 85
Delta Province 144
Demobilisation 38
Derek Osborn 191
Descendant 53, 179
Development And Advancement 16, 23
Development Ethics 80

Development of Mission Schools In the Isoko/Urhobo Areas of the Delta Region 151
Developmental Dynamics of Adamu Orisa Festival 79
Developmental Efforts 143
Dexamethasone 132
Diabetes 107, 135
Diabolical 121, 122
Dialectic Variations 173
Diocese 132, 133, 236, 237, 238, 241, 242, 243, 244, 245
Diocese of Kwara 236, 237, 238, 241, 243, 244, 245
Dioko Joseph Igboro 155
Diplomacy 227, 228
Dirty Game 48
Discrimination 108, 136, 200
Diseases 99, 100, 101, 103, 106, 107, 112, 121, 123, 124, 135, 136, 181, 190
  Etiology of 123
  Infectious 135
  Non-Supernatural 121
  Sexually Transmitted 99
Dispensation 68
  Political 16
  Secular 18
Dispensation of Justice 68
Disposition 66
Dispute Resolution 59, 60
  Methods of 59, 60
Dispute Resolution Services 60
Disputes 30, 60, 61, 62, 63, 67, 68, 69, 70, 74, 75
  Commercial 68
  Family 62, 67, 68
  Imamship 67
  Labour 61
  Marital 62, 69, 70
  Monetary 62, 67

Mosque 62, 67
Trade 62
Disruptions 39
Divorce Actions 61
Dowry 197
Draft Bill 63
Drug Abuse 99
Drugs 100, 109, 126, 127, 131, 132, 135, 136
  Distribution of 98
  Expired 110
  Prescribe 111
  Retroviral 82
Du'ah Al-Ghayat Al-Maqsudat Al-Kubrah 99

E

Eagle Height International Montessori 163
Eagle Height University 163
Eckankar Movement 33
Economic And Financial Crime Commission 21
Economic And Political Development 79
Economic Behaviour 195
Economic Development 82, 92, 182, 183, 228
  Political And 39, 79, 81
  Religion And 82
  Social And 80
  Socio- 29, 233
Economic Development And Empowerment 82
Economic Empowerment Programme 82
Economic Impact 177, 182
Economic Policy 228
Economic Problem 24
Economic Recession 21, 109, 242
Economic Situations 48
Economic Stability 36, 245

Ecosystems 191, 192
Ecwa 128, 129, 130, 131, 132, 171, 174, 176, 177, 178, 179, 180, 181, 182, 183, 184
Ecwa Central Pharmacy Ltd ... 132
Ecwa Health Centre 131
Ecwa Health Centres In Isanlu, Mopa, Koro And Ponyan 131
Ecwa Medical Institutions 130
Ecwa Mission on Igbomina Land 177
Ecwa Nursing School 180
Ecwa Rural Development 183
Ecwa School of Midwifery 130, 131
Ecwa Staff Nursery And Primary Schools 183
Ecwa Theological Seminary ... 171, 179, 183
  Provost of 179
Educational Impact 177
Educational Sector 161
Educational Systems 143
EFCC 19, 21, 22, *See* Economic And Financial Crime Commission
Effect of Religiosity on Development In Nigeria 19
Efficacious 101, 106, 111
Efficacy 96, 101, 105
Egbe Maternity 128
Egbesu Boys 35
Ehalaiye (Dr.(Mrs)) 129
EHU 163, *See* Eagle Height University
Ejilu 87, 88, 89
  Children of 87
  Demise of 87
Elections 16, 18, 62
  Gubernatorial 18
  Rigging of 50
Elections Petitions 62

Electrification 18
Electrocardiogram....................128
Elimination 200
Elisha Renne 98
Emancipation......................80, 223
Embarrassment 108
Embezzlement..........20, 21, 22, 24
Emir of Kano 21
Emmanuel Ibuot 55
Emmanuel Uduaghan's Administration..........................162
Employment22, 83, 90, 123, 163, 165, 183, 191, 192, 199, 243, 244
Empowerment82, 86, 183, 197, 198, 245
Empowerment Loan Scheme 245
Enforcement Machineries..........74
English Canadian 174
Epileptic Power Supply 52
Era of Emergence of African Independent Churches 234
Era of the Missionaries............146
ERD183, *See* Ecwa Rural Development
Erelu................................84, 87, 88
Erelu of Lagos
    First 88
Erelu Square................................84
Erroneous Misconception 38
Etetie Daniel 155
Ethnic And Tribal Entities 224
Ethnic Groups 32, 226
Ethnic Issues...............................35
Ethnic Militias............................35
Ethnic Outbursts........................34
Etiological Categorisation 121
Evangelical Church of West Africa 130, 174
Evangelical Church Winning All 131, 174
Evil Spirit 102

Evolutionary Stages 31
Exploitation of Traders...........127
Extreme Interest And Belief In Religion 11
Eyo Adimu.................................85
Eyo Agere 85
Eyo Festival 85, 90, 91, 92
Eyo Groups 85, 86, 90, 91, 92
Eyo Masquerade.................. 88, 89
Eyo Okanlaba.............................85
Eyo Ologede...............................85
Eyo Oniko 85

F

Fafunwa's Observation 146
Fafunwa's Seven Cardinal Goals 147
Faith Based Organisations81, 82, 92
Fake..110
Falola, J. O. (Justice)..................72
Falola, S. O. (Justice) 71
Falumgun 33
Family Matters................. 197, 208
Farooq Ullah.............................191
FBOs82, 92, *See* Faith Based Organisations
Federal Capital Territory...........60
Festival80, 81, 83, 84, 85, 86, 88, 90, 91, 92, 179, 196, 204
    Adamu Orisa79, 80, 82, 83, 85, 90, 91, 92
    Osun Osogbo 82
    Socio-Cultural................. 84, 87
    Traditional....................... 82, 83
    Traditional Religious.............82
Festival of Animal Sacrifice ...196, 204
Festive Prayer 196
Fetish Oath 50
Field of Education 153, 237

Financial Aid 154
Financial Constraint 120
Food Insecurity 194
Food Security 191, 196, 201
Fornication 67
Fraud 20, 22
Fulani Settlements 135

G

Gabaro 88
Gantanmycin 132
General Medical Practice 129
Generation Imparts 143
Genetic Diversity 192
Geographical And Topographical Conditions 127
Geometrical Occurrence 34
George Adegboye (Pastor) 234
George Ohikeri 226
Geri Alimi 236
German Children's Ngo 135
God-Fatherism 54
God-Fearing 48
Goodluck E. Jonathan (Former President) 20, 21
Government Circles 159
Government Intervention 13, 150, 160
Government Takeover of Schools 159
Gynaecologists 98

H

Handicraft 153, 155
Hare Krishna 33
Harmonious Relationship 224
Hassan Usman Katsina 227
Hausa Community 37
Health Challenges 101, 102, 109, 125, 175
Health Education 98, 122, 182
Health Implication 111

Health Personnel 164
Health Problem 102
Health Service Delivery 92
Healthcare Institutions 98
Healthcare Service Delivery 95
Healthcare Services 81, 96, 120, 124, 125, 131, 132, 136
   Availability of 126
   Poor 52
Henry Venn 241, 242
Henry Venn's Policy of Self-Governing 241
Herbalists
   Traditional 126
Heritage Islamic Hospital 97
Heroes Academy 163
Hinduism 10, 81
   Influence of 9
Hirsu A-Rih Al-Ahmar Al-Kubrah 99
Historical Conjecture 172
Historical Role of Religion 144
Historical Survey 172
HIV/AIDS 82, 129, 135, 190, See Human Immunedeficiency Virus\Acquired Immune Deficiency Syndrome
HIV/AIDS Centre 129
Honourary Chieftaincy Titles ... 71
Hospital Administrator 135
House of Assembly 49, 63
   State 63, 64
Human Development 143
Human Immunedeficiency Virus\Acquired Immune Deficiency Syndrome 82, 135
Humanitarian Organisations .. 160
Humanitarian Services 245
Hypertension 101, 135

I

Ibefun 84, 87, 88, 89

Ibiye Oroye 87, 88
Ibn Khaldun................................15
Ibrahim (Prophet) 200
Ibrahim Imam (Alhaji)............ 220
Ibrahim Kefas......................... 161
Id Al-Adha 196, 204
Idahosa, B.A. (Arch-Bishop) . 163
Idea12, 13, 50, 63, 98, 222, 223, 224, 225, 226, 227, 237
    Caliphate's 222
    Impact of Political.............. 219
    Muhammad Bello's 221
    Political 218, 227
    Sardauna's........................... 221
    Sultan Bello's................221, 225
IDP 37, *See* Internally Displaced Persons
Idugaran.....................................85
Idumota Medicine Market 92
Ifa Oracle 123, 124, 136
Igbo People Congress.................35
Igbomina Land171, 172, 173, 174, 176, 177, 178, 179, 180, 181, 182, 183, 184
Igbomina Migrate..................... 172
Igbomina People172, 173, 176, 177, 180, 181, 182, 184
    Descendants of.................... 179
    Origin of.............................. 172
    Welfare of............................ 180
Igbomina Towns 180
Ihya'u Sunnah 97
Ijaw Youth Congress 35
Ijesa Osomalo Christian Traders 235
Ijesa Traders............................ 236
Ijomah, B. I. C. (Prof) 162
Ikirun Judicial Division 71
Ila Orangun............................. 172
Illegal Operations.................... 110

Ilorin29, 43, 95, 119, 128, 130, 143, 171, 176, 233, 234, 235, 236, 237, 238, 240, 241, 242, 243, 244, 245, 246
Ilorin Metropolis233, 234, 235, 236, 237, 238, 242, 243, 244, 245, 246
Imagination......................... 46, 122
Imam 65, 209
    Chief 70, 71, 72, 73, 109
    Deputy..................................72
    League of........................ 64, 71
Imamship 62, 67, 70, 71, 72
    Case of...................... 70, 71, 72
Imamship Disputes....................67
Imamship Position.....................72
Imamship Tussle 70, 71, 72
IMAN 98, *See* Islamic Medical Association of Nigeria
Impact of Christianity (Sudan Interior Mission) on Igbomina Land..171
Impact of Sokoto Caliphate on Post-Colonial Political Development In Nigeria 217
Impacts of Sim/Ecwa Mission on Igbomina Land 177
Implications For Political Stability And Development 36
Impression 17, 18
    False 107
Improvement13, 150, 180, 182, 223
Impunity......................... 15, 23, 51
Inadequate Finance..................130
Inauguration Speech..................54
Incessant Agitations.................162
Incubation Period 190
Independent Shari'ah Arbitration Panel 63

Independent Shari'ah Panels 59, 74
Indigenes 85, 91, 92, 176, 178, 182, 238
Indigeneship 89
Indigenisation 242
Indigenous Community 80
Indigenous Settlement 83
Indiscriminate Sexual Affairs 99
Indispensable Roles 49
Indoctrination 147
Industrial Developments 228
Industrialisation 200
    Poor 194
Influence 9, 10, 13, 31, 32, 33, 48, 54, 59, 60, 88, 121, 122, 154, 159, 219, 220, 221, 222, 224, 229
    External 33
    Negative 79
    Outstanding 180
    Political 222
    Religious 221
    Supernatural 124
Influence of Politics 33
Influence of Sokoto Caliphate on Northern Political Leaders 219
Informal Hearings 66
Infrastructural Development ... 21, 24
Infrastructure 23, 130, 161, 191, 199, 200
    Massive 200
    Social 20
Infringement 46
Initiative 129, 152, 153, 154, 156, 162
    Local African 151
Insecurity 37, 51, 100
Insinuation 30
Institutional Change 43

Institutions 31, 33, 37, 44, 59, 107, 130, 164, 179, 184, 191, 194, 208, 209, 245
    Medical 130
    Political 32, 173
    Self-Sustaining 136
    Societal 37
    Traditional 59, 223
Instrument of Peace 177
Insurgencies 51
Interaction 31, 68, 80, 95, 128, 194
Interest Groups 151
Internally Displaced Persons ... 37, 38
International Development 189
International Islamic Relief Organisation 97
Intervention 13, 71, 102, 160
Intoxicant Liquors 99
IPC 35, *See* Igbo People Congress
Isale Eko 80, 84, 85, 92
Isanlu 120, 126, 131, 132, 172
Ishaya Audu (Dr) 225
Islam 10, 17, 19, 30, 32, 33, 35, 39, 46, 47, 75, 81, 88, 95, 96, 98, 99, 100, 101, 102, 106, 111, 112, 164, 176, 189, 190, 195, 196, 197, 198, 200, 201, 202, 203, 204, 205, 206, 207, 208, 209, 210, 221, 222, 224, 225, 226, 230
    Acceptance of 105, 106
    Advent of 10
    Contributions of 205, 206
    Leaning of 35
    Oath In 47
    Propagate 98, 238
    Religion of 205, 221
    Spread of 95
    Teaching of 110, 112

Islam And Development In Nigeria Within the Framework of the Sustainable Development Goals 204
Islam And the Attainment of the Sustainable Development Goals 189
Islam As It Relates to the Sustainable Development Goals 195
Islamic 10, 17, 18, 30, 36, 59, 62, 63, 64, 65, 66, 68, 70, 73, 95, 97, 98, 102, 106, 107, 110, 111, 112, 195, 197, 198, 199, 200, 201, 202, 203, 205, 206, 207, 208, 209, 217, 218, 220, 225, 226, 229, 230, 238
Islamic Associations 62
Islamic Civilisation 10
Islamic Cooperative Societies 205
Islamic Education 206, 238
Islamic Etiquettes 112
Islamic Injunctions 70
Islamic Invocations 102
Islamic Jurisprudence 66, 197
Islamic Law And Procedure 66
Islamic Legal System 59
Islamic Medical Association of Nigeria 98
Islamic Mode of Healing 95
Islamic National Hospital 97
Islamic National Hospital For Women And Children 97
Islamic Principles 208
Islamic Religion 200, 207, 208
Islamic Scholar 65, 106, 198, 217, 218
Islamic State 201, 225
Islamic Tax 195, 208
Islamic Teachings 229
Islamic Tradition 36
Islamiyyah Schools 221

Isoko Language 153
Isokoland 151
ISP 60, 61, 62, 63, 64, 65, 66, 67, 68, 69, 70, 71, 72, 73, 74, 75, *See* Independent Shari'ah Panels
Contributions of 68, 74, 75
Establishment of 61, 62, 63, 75
Judgement of 73
Jurisdiction of 67
Lagos 66, 67, 68, 69, 73, 74
Modus Operandi of 64
Osun 66, 67, 69, 70, 71, 73
Sitting of 65
State of 69
Year of Establishment 69
IYC 35, *See* Ijaw Youth Congress

J

Jacques Le Goff 82
Jama'atu Nasril Islam 97
Jamat Ahmadiyyah 206
James Onanefe Ibori (Chief) .. 162
James Welch 151, 155, 156, 157, 158
James Welch Grammar School 156, 157
Jamiu Faleye (Alhaji) 70
Jeremiah Olagbamigbe Fabuluje (Rt. Rev.) 237
Jesus Christ 16, 234, 235
Jide Ige 119
Jihad 17, 217, 218, 222, 227
Jihadists 217, 220, 222, 223, 225, 227
Jimoh Adebisi Okunade Ii (Oba) 71
Jimoh Oyewole Erinkitola . 72, 73
JNI 97, *See* Jama'atu Nasril Islam
Joan Clathworth (Dr) 132, 133

Job Orientation 146
Joel Afolabi Ogundeji (Chief) 179
Jolly Tanko Yusuf (Ambassador) 225, 226
Joseph Baiyegunhi 133
Joseph Obada 133
Joseph Olorunshagba (Rev. Fr.) 135
Joseph Omoregbe 50
Joseph Schumpeter 82
Joseph Tolorunshagba (Rev. Fr) 134
Judaism 10
Judicial Development 68, 73
Judicial System 48, 59, 60, 61, 62, 68, 74, 75
Julie Duran (Rev. Sis) 133
Jumat Owolabi (Alhaji) 73
Justice And Accountability 222

K

Kabba 120, 124, 130, 132, 133, 134, 135, 136, 237
Kabba Deanery 133
Kabba General Hospital 136
Kabba Province 124
Karl Marx 79
Kazeem Abioye (Alhaji) 70
Kenya 178
King Ado
   Children of 88
   Reign of 87
Kings 10, 84, 87, 88, 91, 201, 236, 244
   Corrupt 217
   Deceased 86
   Incumbent 86
Kings Palace 91
Kola Nuts 90
Kubani Bridge 224
Kubwa Muslim Community Hospital 97

Kulugbe 87, 88
Kuti 88
Kwara State University 244

L

Laboratory Assistant 133
Laboratory Investigations 128
Lagos Administration 149
Lake Chad 175
Lakun Dinukun 99
Land Policy 228
Lauwali Gidan Jodi (Mallam) ... 97
Law 44, 45, 47, 51, 54, 59, 60, 62, 63, 64, 66, 72, 73, 74, 75, 88, 159, 161, 198, 201, 202, 217
   Civil 64
   Common 64
   Customary 60, 62, 73
   English 59, 60, 62
   Islamic Marital 208
Lawal, J. B. (Rev. Dr) 179
Lawan Dambazau 228
Lawlessness 23
Leadership Circle 223
Leadership Crisis 50
Leadership Decisions 53
Leadership Policies 220
Leadership Rivalry 173
Leadership Styles 219, 224
League of Imams And Alfas 64, 71
Learning Environment 161
Leather Materials 228
Legal Development 75
Legal Luminaries 64, 68, 75
Legal Scripts 44
Legal System 59, 60, 75, 206
Legitimate Successors 220
Lepers 107, 128, 180
   Rehabilitating 180
Leprosarium Centres 181
Leprosarium Hospital 182

Letham, M. C. (Rev) 155, 157
Lewu, M. A. Y. 119
Liberation Theology 80
Liver Cirrhosis 100
Loan Scheme 245
Local Chalk 84
Local Christian 160
Local Entrepreneurs 38
Local Food Vendors 91
Local Government Area 70, 131, 172, 182
    Egbedore 70
    Ejigbo 72
    Ifelodun 71, 180
    Ila 172
    Irepodun 173
    Isin 172
    Lagos Island 79
    Mopamuro 131
    Yagba East 131
    Yagba West 131
Local Market Women 90
Lokoja Catholic Diocese 134
Looting 20, 21, 23
Lord Lugard 235

M

Madaniyyah Women Muslim Hospital 96
Madinah 103, 200
Making Pregnancy Safe 129
Makkah 20, 200
Malaki 87, 88, 89
Malawi 178
Malevolence 124
Malik Bennabi 15
Malnutrition 192
Mamma Ile Ogun 128
Management 124, 129, 133, 134, 151, 157, 159, 182, 191, 198, 201, 204, 219

Management And Funding of the Mission Schools 157
Management Board 133
Marital Disappointment 109
Marital Disputes 62, 69, 70
Marital Infidelity 121
Marital Tension 100
Market
    Free 13
    International 18, 20
    Local 90
    Pharmaceutical 92
Marriage Dissolution 69
Marriage Proposal 197
Martin Olorunmolu (Bishop) . 134
Martins Marty 34
Marx Weber 82
Mary Slessor 180
Masquerade . 83, 84, 85, 86, 90, 92
Maternal Ancestor 88
Maternal Lineage 89
Maternity Clinic 126
Maternity Homes 181
Matters 60, 61, 62, 66, 67, 68, 69, 73, 75, 203
    Contentious 59
    Criminal 68
    Family 197, 208
    Judicial 73
    Legal 44
    Religious 68
MDGs 189, 190, 210, *See* Millennium Development Goals
Mediation 61, 69, 74
Medical Care 98, 120, 122, 132, 133, 136, 137, 206
    Modern 181
    Western 121
Medical Information 99
Medical Laboratory Scientists .. 98
Medical Malpractice 61

Medical Outreach 135
Medical Personnel 108, 109, 110, 112
Medicine 10, 92, 95, 100, 101, 106, 107, 108, 111, 112, 123, 127, 129, 164, 181
    Conventional 110
    Orthodox 103, 110, 112, 127
    Traditional. 110, 122, 124, 125, 181
Medieval Capitalist Development 82
Mediocrity 48
Men of Hidden Supernatural Power 123
Menstrual Cycles 198
Mental Disorder 121
Metaphysical Indices 120
Methods Adopted By Muslims In the Healthcare Delivery 99
Michael Audu Buba 225
Michael Obadofin (Dr) 129
Microfinance 192
Midwifery Training School 130
Midwives 98, 129, 131, 133
    Community 130
    Student 131
    Traditional 124
    Training of Basic 130
Millennium Development Goals 189, 190, 210
Misconceptions 38
Mismanagement 18
Mission Activity 181
Missionaries 130, 132, 143, 144, 148, 149, 150, 151, 156, 160, 162, 164, 175, 176, 177, 178, 179, 180, 181, 182, 183, 233, 237, 238, 246
    Early 131, 177
    Indigenous 128
    Portuguese 148, 233
Missionary Activity 149, 163

Missionary Impact on Modern Nigeria 177
Missionary Penetration 151
Missions And Education Before the Advent of Welch 153
Mobile Clinics 124, 132, 136
Modern Economic Analysis 82
Modern Farm 228
Modern Industrial Society 13
Modern Western World 10
Moline, A. J. 176
Mopa 120, 126, 128, 131
Moral Justification 44
Moral Sanctions 44
Moral Uprightness 146
Mosques 72, 107, 204, 207, 221, 222
Motivating Factors For the Muslims' Involvement In Healthcare Services 105
Mount Olives Anglican Church 236, 243, 244, 245
MTS 130, *See* Midwifery Training School
Mufassir 71
Muhammad Bello 98, 217, 219, 220, 221, 223, 224
Muhammad Bello S Ideas 221
Muhammad Buhari (President) 21
Muhammad Dahiru Shuni 217
Muhammad Jega 223
Muhammad Tukur 98
Muqaddimah 15
Musa Yusuf Owoyemi 9
Muslim Associations 64
Muslim Clerics .. 96, 101, 105, 111
Muslim Community 63, 64, 65, 70, 97
Muslim Community Central Mosque 63
Muslim Congress 97
Muslim Doctors 107

Muslim Exorcists 97, 102, 103
Muslim Hausa-Fulani.................21
Muslim Hospitals 96, 112, 206
Muslim Physicians................... 107
Muslim Politicians................... 230
Muslims
    Methods Adopted By .. 99, 106
    Role of.....................95, 96, 209
Muslims Achievements 106
Muslims In the Development of Healthcare Centres In Nigeria..96
Mustafa Ajisafe (Shaykh)...........71
Mustapha Alimi (Dr) 98
Mustapha Bajulu (Chief) 90
Myopia 150

N

NA124, 154, *See* Native Authority
NACOMYO70, *See* National Council of Muslim Youth Organisations
NAFDAC244, *See* National Agency For Food And Drug Administration And Control
NASFAT 81, 82, 97, *See* Nasrul Lahi-Il Fathi Societ
NASFAT Agency For Zakat And Sadaqat..97
Nasrul Lahi-Il Fathi Society......81
NATAIS209, *See* Nigeria Association of Teachers of Arabic And Islamic Studies
National Agency For Control of Aids 129
National Agency For Food And Drug Administration And Control 244
National Council of Muslim Youth Organisations...................70
National Development Issues ..32

National Postgraduate Medical College of Nigeria 129
National Treasury Looters........55
National Youth Service Corps239
Native Authority124, 154, 159, 228
NAZAS 97, *See* Nasfat Agency For Zakat And Sadaqat
Negative Values of Religion 79
New Testament Christian Mission 234
Nigeria Association of Teachers of Arabic And Islamic Studies209
Nigeria Union of Teachers 162
Nigerian National Petroleum Corporation 21
Nigerian Politics And Oath-Taking..47
Northern Civil Service.............226
Northern Leaders............ 224, 227
Northern Mentality..................219
Northern Political Leaders.....218, 219, 220, 221, 222, 223, 224, 225, 226, 227, 228, 229
Northern Politicians16, 17, 229, 230
Notre Dame College....... 156, 157
Npc Government......................220
Npc Prime Minister.................219
Npc's Invocation......................219
Nursing And Midwifery Council of Nigeria 130, 131
NUT 162, *See* Nigeria Union of Teachers
NYSC 239, 240, 241, *See* National Youth Service Corps

O

Oath 43, 44, 45, 46, 47, 48, 49, 50, 51, 52, 53, 54, 65
    Fetish 50

Hippocratic 48
Public Political 50
Oath of Allegiance 44, 47
Oath of Office 44, 45, 46, 47, 48, 49, 50, 51, 52, 53
Oath-Taker 49
Oath-Taking 43, 44, 45, 46, 47, 49, 51, 52, 54
   Effectiveness of 49
   Ethics of 47
   Tools of 52
   Traditional Aspect of 53
Obaagun Central Mosque 71
Odeigah (Dr) 129
O'dua People Congress 35
Oduduwa 173
   Son of 173
Oesophageal Varices 100
Offa 236, 237
Offences 68, 100
Office 16, 17, 43, 44, 45, 47, 48, 49, 50, 51, 53, 54, 65, 135, 154, 225, 237
   Political .. 16, 44, 47, 48, 49, 50, 52, 53, 54
   Public 49, 51, 53
Office Holder 43, 44, 47, 48, 49, 50, 51, 52, 53, 54
   Elected 47
   Political 49, 50
Officers 21, 45, 53
   Community Health 135
   Education 158
   Political 43, 227
Ogboni Iduntafa 87, 88, 89
   First 88
Ogun Oyinbo 181
Ogunmade Family 87, 88
Ogunmade Tradition 86, 87, 88, 89
Oil Boom 242
Oja-Oba Central Mosque ... 64, 67

Oju Olobun 89
Oke-Igbala Omuaran 182
Oke-Onigbin 172
Okun Belief 121
Okun Culture 120
Okun People's World 136
Okun World View of Medical Care 120
Olasoko of Isoko 73
Olasoro 87, 88
Old Oyo Empire 89
Olive Oil 103
Olives Heights 243
Olobaagun of Obaagun 71
Ologun Agan 84, 85, 86, 89
Ologun Agan Tradition 86
Ologun Atebo of Lagos 84, 86, 89
Olugbani Cult 85
Olugbani Family 87
Olusegun Obasanjo (Chief) 16
Onigemo Family 90
Onilegbale of Lagos 87, 88, 89
   First 87
Opanbata 84
OPC 35, *See* O'dua People Congress
Operational Difficulties 130
Operations .. 68, 75, 205, 206, 208
   Effective 133
   Illegal 110
   Modes of 64, 65, 66
Oppression 145, 230
   Tool of 79
Oracle Diviners 105
Oral Evidence 172
Oral Traditions 181
Orderliness 201, 202
Organisations 21, 38, 45, 60, 96, 112, 161, 178, 206, 208, 209, 243, 244
   Humanitarian 160
   International 189, 190

Orisa Adimu 85
Orisa Ologede................................85
Orisa Oniko 85
Orji Uzor Kalu 50
Oro-Ago Community 182
Orphanage........................... 128, 180
Orphans............................. 126, 196
Orthography 153
Osama Bin Laden................ 36, 39
Osomalo Textile Traders 234, 236
Osun State Muslim Community 64
Outbreaks................................... 136
Out-Patient Services 136
Out-Patients..................... 133, 135
Overview of Religion And Religious Conflicts In Nigeria ..32
Owhelogbo 152
Oyedeji Subair 70
Oyinbo Egbe 176
Oyinbo Oro 176
Oyo Ajaka 89
Ozoro............... 152, 153, 156, 157

P

P.O.D.. 183
Paediatricians 98
Pagan Practices 152
Pageant 35, 36
Palliative Measures 99
Palm-Tree Oil 110
Pantheon 86
   Lagos....................83, 86, 88, 89
Paradoxical 164
Paralysing Maladies 48
Paraphernalia 84
Parent Teacher Association ... 239
Patigi 176, 237
Patrilineal Home.........................87
Patronage.110, 136, 137, 182, 246
Paul Ojo................................... 134

PDP Candidate............................18
PDP Machinery...........................18
Peace 33, 35, 38, 51, 72, 79, 85, 86, 201, 226
Peace And Unity 72, 226
Peace-Making Components......38
Pentecostal Churches 144, 162, 246
Pentecostalism.........................162
People Oriented Development 183
Peptic Ulceration......................100
Perennial Issue 39
Peripheral Neuropathy............100
Perpetual Injunction..................71
Perspectives 31
   Functional 31
   Religious................................44
Pervasiveness..............................29
Peter Abejide Eyanro (Dr)......134
Peter Achimugu (Sir) 226
Peter Akinola Guest House...242, 243
Peter Ibiejemite 133, 134
Peter Jasper Akinola (Primate) 242
Petroleum Products..................18
Petty Trading............................245
Philosophers 10, 148
Philosopher-Scientists 10
Physical Development.. 14, 15, 22
Physiotherapists 98
Plant And Animal Products....106
Plural Society 32
PNO 135, *See* Principal Nursing Officer
POD *See* People Oriented Development
Polarisation 24
Police Barracks.........................150
Political Affairs........................221

Political Ambition 19
Political And Economic Development 39
Political Awareness 165
Political Campaign 16
Political Caucuses 54
Political Development 81
   Post-Colonial 217
Political Diplomacy 227
Political Force 33, 34, 38, 219
Political Freedom 227
Political Freedom And Right to Opposition 227
Political Inclination 230
Political Influence 222
Political Instabilities 51
Political Landscape 19
Political Manifestoes 51
Political Party Objectives 54
Political Revolution 43
Political Scene 226
Political Stability 29, 30, 31, 32, 36
Political Struggle 220
Political Support 48
Political System 32
Political Vocabulary 226
Politician Campaign 20
Politicians 16, 17, 22, 24, 33, 48, 49, 50
Politics 31, 32, 39, 43, 44, 47, 48, 49, 50, 52, 53, 54, 55, 83, 92, 147, 165, 218, 219, 228
   Domestic 33
   Post-Independence 219
   Traditional 83, 89
Polygamy 164, 198
Poor Sanitation 194
Portuguese 148, 149, 233
Post Development 13, 14
Post-Colonial 217

Poverty 19, 20, 23, 33, 38, 50, 80, 82, 99, 145, 190, 191, 192, 193, 194, 195, 196, 204, 205, 208
Poverty Alleviation 82, 99, 205
Power 14, 16, 18, 21, 22, 23, 47, 48, 50, 52, 53, 55, 65, 106, 194, 197, 199, 218, 221, 228, 240
   Curative 106
   Diabolical 122
   Evil 105
   Hidden Supernatural 123
   Mysterious 121
   Political 17, 50
Power Struggle 21
Precautionary Measures 111
Pre-Christian Okun Societies . 122
Predecessor 242
Pregnancy 129
Pre-Independence Period 33
Presbyterians 173
Prescriptions 102, 111
   Idolatrous 110
   Prophetic Medical 110
Preventive Measures 99, 100
Primary Education 159, 166, 178, 179, 190
Principal Nursing Officer 135
Principle of Takhayyur 66
Principles 54, 55, 60, 125, 201, 202, 208, 230
   Cardinal 222
   Ecological 201
   Islamic 201
   Islamic Economic 199
   Religious 44
Principles of Islam 201
Pro-Active Measure 189
Process 13, 14, 59, 80, 86, 101, 102, 103, 143, 145, 151, 161, 176
   Cyclical 15
   Historical 13
   Political 30

Societal 31
Projects 226, 246
  Community Development ... 92
  Developmental 38, 92
  Uncompleted 18
Proliferation 156, 163, 165
Promotion 68, 193, 199, 206, 218, 221, 237
Propagation 181, 235, 243
Propagation of Christianity 235
Prophet Muhammad 36, 39, 65, 196, 198, 199, 200, 201, 203, 207
Prophet Yusuf S Ministerial Activities 201
Prophetic Medical Prescriptions 110
Prophetic Medicine 101, 110, 111, 112
Prophetic Medicine Practitioners 110, 111
Prophets Ayyub 101
Prophylactic 123
Propitiation 87
Proprietorship 134
Prostitutes 51
Prostitution 37
Protectorate 149
  Amalgamated 235
  Northern 235
  Southern 235
Protestant Ethics 82
Provocation 197
Psychiatric Hospitals 97, 109
Psychological Cause of Psychotic 121
Psychological Make-Up 55
Psychotherapy 106, 124
PTA 239, *See* Parent Teacher Association
Public Funds Stolen 18
Punishment 46, 47, 54, 67, 68

Purification 86

Q

Qualification 153
  Medical 126
Quality Assurance 165
Query 10, 20, 21, 22
Qur'ān 46, 51, 52, 65, 66, 70, 95, 99, 100, 101, 102, 103, 105, 106, 109, 110, 111, 195, 196, 197, 198, 199, 200, 201, 202, 203, 204, 206, 207, 209, 210
Qur'anic Injunction 205

R

Radiotherapists 98
Rafiu Ibrahim Adebayo 95
Rahmaniyya Islamic Medical Center 97
Railway Corporation 235
Raimi Animashaun (Alhaji) 71
Ramadan 36, 99, 196, 204, 207
Ramifications 177
Rational Economic Response .. 82
Raymond Ogunade 43
RCCG 81, 82, *See* Redeemed Christian Church of God
RCCG's Economic Empowerment Programme For Widows 82
RCM 108, 120, 124, 132, 133, 156, *See* Roman Catholic Mission
Recession 242
  Challenge of 245
  Economic 21, 109, 242
Reciprocal Obligation 147
Reconciliation 70, 71, 81
Reconciliation Mechanism 70
Recruitment 239
Redeemed Christian Church of God 81

Referral Facility....................... 129
Region10, 35, 144, 151, 164, 219, 227, 230, 235
    Delta............ 146, 147, 149, 151
    Middle Belt.......................... 235
    Northern.... 220, 226, 227, 229, 230
    Old Western....................... 159
    South East Asia 10
    South Eastern 35
    Vegetation 174
Regionalism.............................. 226
Reincarnate.................................39
Relief Materials........................ 160
Religion
    Abusing............................... 109
    Adherents of................... 15, 24
    African 16
    Foreign Inspired....................32
    Issue of............. 16, 23, 39, 226
    Predominant 35
Religion And Development9, 11, 14, 79, 80, 82, 233
Religion And Development In Scholarship...................................80
Religion And Educational Development In Delta Region 146
Religion And Political Stability.31
Religion As An Instrument For the Attainment of the Sustainable Development Goals................ 194
Religiosity9, 11, 12, 13, 14, 15, 16, 17, 18, 19, 20, 22, 23, 24
    Concept of 18
    Dimensions of................. 11, 12
    Effect of 19
    Extrinsic 12, 23, 24
    Intrinsic.......................... 12, 23
    Issue of Political 23
Religiosity And Development .11, 12

Definition...............................11
Religiosity And Its Effect on Development In Nigeria.......9, 15
Religiosity In the Political Sphere 15, 16
Religious Activities.....................16
Religious And Tribal Sentiments 22
Religious Beliefs12, 32, 49, 52, 54, 81, 154
Religious Biddings....................207
Religious Conflict Prone Areas 37
Religious Conflicts29, 30, 32, 33, 34, 35, 36, 37, 38, 39, 171
    Cases of.................................33
    Character of........30, 34, 35, 36
    Effects of 39
    Ethno- 34
    Issue of..................................30
    Seed of..................................33
Religious Conflicts, Political Stability And Development In Nigeria 29
Religious Creeds.................. 12, 24
Religious Educators...................11
Religious Group.........................19
Religious Influence 221
Religious Intolerance 35, 171
Religious Leaders ..20, 38, 79, 195
Religious Plurality 33
Religious Tolerance172, 224, 225, 226
Religious-Based Dispute Resolution Mechanism of Independent Shari'ah Panels And Their Contributions to the Development of Judicial System 59
Relinquishment 236
Repercussions...........................46
Reprisal Effects 35
Resemblance.............................89

Resident Consultants 134
Resident Doctors 129, 134
Resources 19, 37, 38, 49, 51, 55, 74, 123, 158, 190, 192, 199, 222, 223
    Economic 192
    Government 223
    Human 132
    Marine 191
    Material 37, 74
    Natural 192
    Utilisation of Genetic 193
Revenue Generation 243, 244
Rhema Church 234
Rigging of Election Results 50
Risk 38, 52, 80, 100, 129, 175
Ritual And Religion 81
Ritual Killers 55
Ritual Sites 85
Ritualistic 11
Rituals 55, 81, 85, 90
    Demonic 109
    Religious 83, 99, 146
Role of Muslims In Healthcare Service Delivery 95
Roman Catholic Church 132
Roman Catholic Mission 120, 132, 137, 149, 152
Roman Catholics 156
Rotimi Williams Omotoye 233
Rowland Victor Bingham 174
Royal Cult 84
Rulers 237
    Local 227
    Traditional 126, 223
Ruling House 90
Ruqya 97, 102, 106, 109
    Forms of 97, 109
Ruqya Practitioners 97
Ruqyah 102
Rural Water Supply 224

S

Sacrificial Animals 204
Sadaqah 195, 208
Sahara Desert 174
Samuel Ajayi Crowther (Bishop) 234, 237, 238
Samuel Efeturi 155
Samuel Ogbemudia (Dr) 160
Sanitary Measures 198
Sanitation 100, 155, 191, 198, 204
Sanusi Lamido Sanusi (Emir) ... 21
Sardauna 219, 221, 222, 223, 224, 225, 226, 228
Sardauna of Sokoto 219
Sardauna's Attitude 225
Sardauna's Idea 221
School Curriculum 178
School Structures 158
Schools
    Early 153, 246
    Establishment of 120, 144, 149, 150, 151, 163, 177, 178
    Missionary 160, 164, 246
    Mushroom 160
    Muslim 112
    Private 160, 165
    Public 162
    Regular 153
    Vernacular 153
Schools of Health Technology 129
Scorpion Bites 102
Scriptures 46, 47, 51
SDGs 189, 190, 191, 194, 195, 197, 198, 201, 203, 204, 205, 206, 207, 208, 209, 210, *See* Sustainable Development Goals
    Attainment of 189, 190, 194, 195, 207, 208, 209, 210
    Goals of 207, 208

Realisation of 194, 204, 207, 209
Secret Society 83
Secretary to the Executive Council 226
Secrets 50, 123
Secular Dispensation 18
Security Risks 38
Selected List of Mission Schools In Delta State 156
Self Reliant 229
Self-Aggrandisements 48
Self-Centredness 47
Self-Discipline 145
Selflessness 147
Sentiment 20, 31
    Religious 17
    Tribal 22
Sentimental Attachment 39
Services 81, 96, 98, 105, 106, 109, 112, 127, 128, 129, 133, 134, 136, 164, 181, 182, 184, 192
    Healthcare 95
    Out-Patient 136
SEXCO 225, See Secretary to the Executive Council
Sexual Intimacy 112
Sexual Offences 100
Sharia Panel 72, 73
Shari'ah 17, 18, 19, 20, 33, 35, 59, 60, 61, 62, 63, 64, 67, 69, 71, 72, 73, 74, 75, 202, 206, 208
    Application of 64
    Implementation of 17
Shari'ah And Customary Law Systems 60
Shari'ah Court
    Establishment of 62
Shari'ah Court of Appeal 60, 62, 63
Shari'ah Courts 17, 60, 63, 64, 206, 208

Establishment of 62
Shari'ah Slogan 20
Shear Butter 110
Shehu (Mallam) 97
SIM 120, 124, 125, 126, 130, 136, 172, 173, 174, 175, 176, 177, 178, 179, 180, 181, 182, 183, 184, *See* Sudan Interior Mission
    Activities of 179, 180
    Impacts of 177, 184
Sim Health Care Services
    History of 125
Sim Heritages 184
Sim Hospital 120, 124, 125, 126, 136
Sim Mission 126, 176
Sim Motto 175
Skills .. 53, 145, 147, 155, 165, 222
    Functional 146
    Intellectual 147
Skills Acquisition 165
Smith Archdeaconry (Bishop) 236
Social Amenities 23
    Provision of 21, 22, 23
Social Infrastructure 20
Social Protection Systems 192
Social Revolution 178
Social Solidarity 15
Social Structure of Islam 208
Socio-Economic Activities 83
Socio-Economic And Political Values of Traditional Festivals . 82
Socio-Political Literature 81
Sodium Chromoglycate 132
Sokoto Caliphate 217, 218, 219, 220, 221, 222, 223, 224, 226, 227, 229, 230
    Idea of 223
    Ideology of 226
    Impact of 217
    Influence of 219, 220, 224
    Prominent 218

Tenets of 230
Sokoto Caliphate Heritage 223
Sokoto Caliphate Leaders 218, 223, 227
Sokoto Caliphate Literature ... 222
Sokoto Caliphate's Political And Administrative Practices 230
Sokoto Jihad Literature 222
Sokun Ologunkutere 88
South Africa 178
Southern Christians 16
Spiritual And Ethical Implications of Non-Adherence And Non-Compliance to Oath-Taking 49
Spiritual And Ethical Implications of Oath-Taking In Nigerian Politics 43
Spiritual Attacks 102
Spiritual Capital 81, 92
Spiritual Development 14
Spiritual Problems 120
St Barnabas Anglican Church 235, 237, 244
St Barnabas Anglican Primary School 238
St. Barnabas Cathedral 235
St. John Catholic Hospital 132
St. Peter Clavers College 157
Stella Obayotan (Mrs) 134
Strong Tower 234
Structure 52, 89
    Physical 242
    Political 86
    Social 208
Subordinate Positions 149
Succession 218, 237
Sudan Interior Mission 120, 125, 130, 137, 171, 172, 173
Sudan United Mission 173
Sulaiman Shittu 67
Sultan Bello Mosque Kaduna . 226
SUM 147, 159, 173, *See* Sudan United Mission
Summa Theologica 82
Sunday Awoniyi 222, 225, 226
Sunday School Teachers 133
Superiority 181, 200
Supernatural Influence 124
Supreme Court 60
Surgical Therapy 106
Sustainable Development Goals 189, 190, 191, 194, 195, 196, 197, 198, 199, 201, 203, 204, 205, 206, 209, 210
Swearing In 45
Symbolic Order 194
Sympathisers 152
Symptoms 100, 122, 124
Syncretic 110, 111
Syncretism 106, 164

T

Taboo 89, 179
Tadaa 103
Tafawa Balewa Complex 91
Tajudeen Akintayo (Mallam) 70
Talfiq 66
Taliat Akinlaja (Chief) .. 84, 86, 89
Tamar Ajwat 103
Taorid Ibikunle 83
Taxation 208
Tayo Ojo (Dr) 129
TB .... 135, *See* Tuberculosis
Teachers 149, 153, 155, 156, 157, 158, 179, 209, 238, 239, 241
    Certificated 155, 158
    Itinerant 153
    Probationary 155
    Qualified 153, 155, 156
    Sunday School 133
Teachers' Training Centre 156

Teaching Staff.................. 239, 240
    Non-................................ 240, 241
    Permanent........................... 240
Teething Problems.................. 144
Televangelism 163
Tenets
    Democratic.......................... 220
    Religious 38, 207
Territorial Boundaries............. 227
Terrorist Attack....................... 171
Testimony...................44, 225, 230
Textile Mills............................. 229
Theft 20, 22
Theologians...................... 105, 145
Theological Education............. 179
Theological Issues 35
Therapeutic 122, 123
Therapeutic Conditions........... 123
Thoedore Orji............................. 50
Thomas Aquinas 82
Thomas Kent............................ 174
Thuggery............................... 37, 52
Timothy Opoola (Evang. Prof) 234
Tirimisiyu Oladipo (Mallam) 70
Titcombes................. 125, 126, 127
Tolerance............................ 54, 147
Tools 17, 79, 133, 144, 181, 194, 195, 197
    Indispensable 143, 149
Tooth-Stick 198
Tourism Potentials..................... 92
Tourists................................ 91, 92
Tradition Legal Systems 59
Tradition Practitioners............. 119
Traditional African Herbal Practice 136
Traditional Chieftaincy Titles ...71
Traditional Education 146, 147, 148, 177
Traditional Health Practice 122

Traditional Herbal Preparations 126
Traditional Lawsuits Impractical 61
Traditional Medical Practitioners 122
Traditional Politics..................... 83
Traditional Society 146
Traditions And Culture 221
Traditions of Origin of Adamu Orisa 86
Training 90, 129, 130, 131, 136, 147, 149, 155, 156, 182, 238, 241
    Intellectual........................... 147
    Vocational 147
Transformation 13, 128, 145
    Social-Economic 172
Transformation of Egbe Maternity Into A Full-Fledged Ecwa Hospital 128
Transparency 47
Transportation Problem.......... 175
Transportation System 180
Treasury............................... 21, 23
    National................................. 55
    Public..................................... 20
Treasury Looters........................ 55
Treatment 95, 97, 98, 100, 101, 106, 107, 110, 122, 123, 125, 132, 181, 182, 224, 225
    Free Eye 96
    Inhuman................................ 96
    Medical 98
Treatment of Painful 100
Treatment of Painful Menstruation............................. 100
Treatment of Snake Bite 106
Trespassers............................... 242
Tribes.. 226
Trichina Worms 100
Tuberculosis 135
Twins 125, 126

Birth of 125
First 125
Killing of 180
Siamese 144

U

UAC151, *See* United African Company
Ughelli......151, 152, 156, 157, 163
UMS 178, *See* United Missionary Society
UN General Assembly 190
Undertone
    Political 34
    Religious 30
Unemployment 51, 194, 245
Unethical Practices 157
UNGA190, *See* Un General Assembly
Unification 90
Uninterrupted Academic Calendars 163
Un-Islamic Practices 111
United African Company 151
United Missionary Society 178
United States of America37, 171, 174
Unity And Solidarity 164
Universal Primary Education 159
Unpalatable Outcomes 51
Urhobo144, 146, 147, 150, 151, 153, 156, 159
Urinary Bladder Infections 100
Urine 110
USA37, 100, 127, 134, 136, *See* United States of America
Usman Danfodio (Shehu)
    Successors of 220
Usmaniyya 219, 220
Usmanu Danfodio (Shehu) 220
Uthman Ibn Fodio (Shaykh) . 111

Utilitarian Role 144

V

Valid Oath 47
Value-Addition 192
Values33, 38, 79, 80, 92, 145, 146, 147, 148, 159, 161, 164, 165
    Developmental 92
    Economic 80, 81
    Ethical 49, 50
    Negative 79
    Political 82
    Tourism And Cultural 91
Vernacular Literature
    First 153
Victims of Spiritual Attacks....102
Villagers 129, 131, 183
Villages125, 134, 135, 151, 153, 156, 158, 160, 178, 179, 180, 183
Violence.30, 36, 37, 38, 39, 81, 92
    Religious ... 19, 23, 37, 171, 172
Visible to the Blind 48
Vocational Centres 241
Voluntary Charity 195
Vulnerability 192
Vulnerable Situations 192

W

Wada Nas (Alhaji) 226
Wage 36, 199
Walter Gowan 174
Walter Rodney 145
War24, 36, 38, 39, 127, 156, 160, 171, 217, 228
    Civil 159, 160, 236
Ward Attendant 128
Wasiu Junaid 90
Water Production 244
Waters52, 84, 100, 103, 111, 128, 157, 191, 196, 198, 203, 204, 207, 224, 244, 246

Flowing 198
Mineral 229
Stagnant 100
Unclean 120
Wealth 18, 48, 50, 52, 163, 205
   Accumulation of 223
Wealth Creation 205
Wealthier Condition 164
Weather 175, 192
Welfare 95, 180, 195, 218, 223, 227
Wellbeing 95, 120
Well-Equipped Laboratory 128
West African Education 157
Western Civilisation 9, 10, 11, 177, 178, 180
Western Education 144, 149, 151, 157, 165, 177, 178, 183, 206, 238
   Agents of 177
   Development of 143, 177
   Inception of 160
   Origin of 148
   Perception of 159
   Pioneer of 151, 156
   Planting of 151
   Promotion of 237
   Spread of 150, 151
Western Sense 147
Whiteman's Medicines 181
WHO 129, *See* World Health Organisation
Witches 96, 105, 121
Witness Oil Spills 21
Witnesses 65, 66, 234
Wole Soyinka (Prof) 18
Women Disempowerment 194
Wool Material 84
Word of Life Bible Church 163
Work Ethics 74
Workers 54, 124, 135, 207, 235, 243
   Clerical 48

Community Health 135
Judicial 68
Railway 236
World 9, 10, 11, 14, 23, 29, 30, 31, 34, 35, 36, 39, 46, 47, 53, 60, 64, 75, 97, 107, 108, 120, 127, 129, 130, 143, 156, 163, 171, 172, 174, 189, 190, 191, 192, 193, 194, 195, 201, 208, 210, 221, 234, 242
   Contemporary 38
World Beauty Pageant 35
World Health Organisation 129
World Leaders 189, 190
World Market 242
World of Life Church 163
World Religions 46, 47
World War 127, 156
Worm
   Guinea 100
   Tiny Deadly 100
   Trichina 100
Worship 12, 84, 101, 146, 198, 204
   Deity 85
   Elements of 84
   Places of 225
   Traditions of 146
   Way of 210
Worship Centres 204
Worshippers 204, 236
   Muslim 204
   Traditional 176
Wrapper 84

Y

Yagbaland 125
Yahaya, Ibn Sina (Mallam) 97
Yinusa Oyebode Oyesala Ii (Oba) ... 73
Yoruba 35, 46, 52, 53, 59, 62, 65, 66, 81, 84, 90, 92, 96, 99, 103, 110, 119, 122, 123, 127, 136, 172, 173, 178, 179, 181, 233, 238

    Dialect of 119
    North-East of 119
Yoruba Alphabet 181
Yoruba Common Adage 46
Yoruba Communities 84
Yoruba Customary Law 62
Yoruba Kingdoms 173
Yoruba Mythology 172
Yoruba Proverb 233
Yoruba Traditional Cloths 90
Yoruba Traditional Religion 81
Youth Restiveness 194
Youths 22, 35, 51, 70, 90, 109, 146, 163, 194, 209, 239, 243, 244, 246
    Counselling of 129
YTR 81, *See* Yoruba Traditional Religion
Yusuf Turaki (Prof) 179

Z

Zakariyā (Prophet) 101
Zakat . 97, 195, 196, 200, 205, 208
    Administration of 205
    Collection of 208
    Impact of 205
    Operations of 205
    Proceeds of 199
    Role of 205
Zamfara State Initiative 63
Zamzam Water 103
Zaytun 103
Zink Suiphate 132
Zoroastrianism 10

www.ingramcontent.com/pod-product-compliance
Lightning Source LLC
Chambersburg PA
CBHW062006220426
43662CB00010B/1247